D1290322

Poetic Voices

FLORIDA STATE
UNIVERSITY LIBRARIES

MAR 6 1995

TALLAHASSEE, FLORIDA

Poetic *Voices*

Discourse Linguistics and the Poetic Text

Timothy R. Austin

THE UNIVERSITY OF ALABAMA PRESS

TUSCALOOSA AND LONDON

P
302.5
A93
1994

Copyright © 1994
The University of Alabama Press
Tuscaloosa, Alabama 35487-0380
All rights reserved
Manufactured in the United States of America

The paper on which this book is printed meets the minimum
requirements of American National Standard for Information
Science-Permanence of Paper for Printed Library Materials,
ANSI Z39.48-1984.

Library of Congress Cataloging-in-Publication Data

Austin, Timothy R., 1952–
    Poetic voices: discourse linguistics and the poetic text /
Timothy R. Austin.
        p.   cm.
    Includes bibliographical references and indexes.
    ISBN 0-8173-0726-5 (alk. paper)
    1. Discourse analysis, Literary.   2. Poetics.   I. Title.
P302.5.A93   1994
808.1′014—dc20   93-41329

British Library Cataloguing-in-Publication Data available

For David
and
for Catherine

But two are walking apart for ever,
And wave their hands for a mute farewell.
Jean Ingelow, "Divided"

Contents

Acknowledgments

This volume results from almost ten years of work. During that time, I have discussed its contents with many friends and colleagues, whose reactions helped to shape its final form. Each of them has my sincere thanks. I must single out a few individuals for special comment.

My interest in the stylistics of speech in poetry was sparked by courses I attended at the 1987 Summer Institute sponsored by the Linguistic Society of America at Stanford University. Debbie Schiffrin and Herb Clark, though they were at the time mercifully unaware of my intentions, taught their respective classes in ways that greatly facilitated my subsequent application of discourse theory to literary texts.

My participation at that 1987 institute was sponsored by Loyola University Chicago at a time when—on paper at least—my primary responsibilities were administrative. I am deeply grateful to Tom Bennett and to Ron Walker for the opportunity to attend and to Jim Wiser and the Committee on Faculty Appointments for a subsequent paid leave that enabled me to prepare the first draft of the text. As if these debts were not significant enough, the Center for Instructional Design and the Division of Research Services assisted in seeing the finished work through the press by preparing artwork and by contributing to the production costs.

Among my colleagues in the English Department at Loyola, Jack Nabholtz and Steve Jones have consistently offered the warmest encouragement even when they could not wholeheartedly endorse my conclusions. As successive department chairpersons, James Rocks and Suzanne Gossett never wavered in their support.

Mike Flynn, now on the faculty of Carleton College, has proven a tough-minded reader of my work ever since we were at graduate school together in the early 1970s. Sylvia Tomasch, his colleague at Carleton, alerted me to previous work by medievalists in the area of narrative framing and kindly mailed me an offprint of her own article on that topic.

An extended trip that I made to Carleton College in the fall of 1990 and an earlier visit to the University of Winnipeg gave me valuable opportunities to present portions of the material in this book in some detail. The energetic discussions that ensued on both occasions had considerable impact on the final form of my argument, most noticeably on sections of chapter 4. I was also able to present briefer synopses at a meeting of the Georgetown Round Table in Linguistics and at the International Congress of Linguists in Québec, Canada.

More formal versions of some of these ideas have appeared in written form in scholarly journals and in an essay anthology. I acknowledge with gratitude the assistance of the respective readers and editors whose thoughtful advice was instrumental in improving those earlier formulations.

Material now dispersed among chapters 2 through 5 was published in *Poetics Today* 10:4 (1989), Durham, North Carolina, Duke University Press, and is reprinted with permission of the publisher.

My own students played an important part in bringing this project into focus. Members of two graduate seminars in stylistics that I taught at Loyola in 1988 and 1991 read imperfect versions of the material, an ordeal that they suffered with equanimity while offering valuable suggestions and challenges, the most influential of which I acknowledge in the text itself.

My daughters, Jennie and Katie, were six and two, respectively, when I began work on this project; today Jennie is a high school sophomore and Katie is in fifth grade. My former wife, Shena, in contrast, has not aged and means as much to me as she did ten years ago. I have devoted many hours to my writing, and concrete results were painfully slow to appear, yet I heard not a word of complaint or of doubt. None of them will ever quite know, I think, how deeply I appreciate their kindness and their patience.

Permissions

An earlier version of the work on Shelley's "Ozymandias" appeared in Michael Macovski, ed., *Dialogue and Critical Discourse: Language, Culture, Critical Theory* (Oxford: Oxford University Press, 1994).

Lines from James Wright, "Autumn Begins in Martin's Ferry, Ohio," reprinted from *The Branch Will Not Break* (Middletown, Conn.: Wesleyan University Press, 1963), © 1963 by James Wright, Wesleyan University Press, are reprinted by permission of University Press of New England.

Lines from Robinson Jeffers, "To the Stone-Cutters," from *The Selected Poetry of Robinson Jeffers,* by Robinson Jeffers (New York: Random House, 1952), copyright 1924 and renewed 1952 by Robinson Jeffers, are reprinted by permission of Random House, Inc.

For permission to quote from "The Ruined Cottage" by William Wordsworth as edited in *The Music of Humanity* by Jonathan Wordsworth (London: Thomas Nelson and Sons, 1969), I thank Jonathan Wordsworth.

Portions of "The Death of the Hired Man" by Robert Frost are quoted from *The Poetry of Robert Frost,* edited by Edward Connery Lathem (New York: Henry Holt, 1969), copyright 1930, 1939, © 1969 by Henry Holt and Company, Inc., copyright © 1958 by Robert Frost, copyright © 1967 by Leslie Frost Ballantine, and are reprinted by permission of Henry Holt and Company, Inc., and Jonathan Cape Ltd.

Poetic Voices

Introduction:
Raising Expectations

*Above all, . . . linguistics can . . . prompt us to ask questions about
the language of the text that we might otherwise ignore.*
Elizabeth Closs Traugott and Mary Louise Pratt,
Linguistics for Students of Literature

Readers, it has been frequently observed, approach any literary text
armed with a formidable battery of cultural and linguistic means for
projecting, on the basis of its opening words, what is most likely to
follow in the remainder of that work. In the words of Nils Erik Enkvist
and Gun Leppiniemi: "As soon as [a reader] has started . . . reading the
text, he begins forming sets of anticipations as to what is to come next,
using all the means at his disposal" (1989:194).[1] For example, when they
encounter as the first two lines of a short Wordsworth poem

I wandered lonely as a cloud
That floats on high o'er vales and hills,
  ["I wandered lonely as a cloud," 1–2]

even readers with limited experience recognize the presence of lineation
and the simple metrical scheme as indications that they can probably
anticipate continued metrical regularity and perhaps some additional
phonological patterning such as end rhyme. In addition, the first two
words alone provide sufficient basis for categorizing this poem provi-
sionally as autobiographical and narrative; as with any narrative, there-
fore, readers will construct what Michael Toolan (1988:5) calls a
"narrative trajectory" for the text, based on the universal expectation
that narratives must "go somewhere." And they will certainly make
"conjectures about the . . . author or speaker" (Toolan 1990:77), their

initial supposition most probably being that the speaker who presents himself as "I" is the same individual whose name appears appended to the text as its author.

To the seasoned literary critic, such assumptions may seem naive; I discuss in later chapters ways in which several of them do indeed reveal a certain lack of sophistication. But the reactions of such a "general reader" deserve thorough examination, for however refined our training in literary studies, our own initial response to a poem, like our initial response to any discourse, will always owe much to linguistic skills over which we have little or no conscious control. What we may confidently— too confidently—dismiss as others' naïveté might be neither more nor less than the result of an instinct that we ourselves cannot wholly suppress.

In the case of Wordsworth's famous celebration of the daffodils, of course, the various elements that I have proposed as typical of readers' initial projections are for the most part fulfilled in what follows. Iambic tetrameter lines do continue to combine in six-line stanzas, rhyming a-b-a-b-c-c. The text, which is indeed predominantly narrative, turns out not only to be based on an autobiographical reminiscence but indeed to take as its principal theme the importance of one's capacity to reminisce in the absence of immediate pleasurable stimuli. And external evidence in the form of an entry in sister Dorothy Wordsworth's *Journals* (109) suggests that, in all major respects, the events narrated did actually occur as they are reported in the poem during a walk that she and the poet took around Grasmere in 1802.

It cannot be assumed, however, that matters will always run so smoothly. In this book, I shall examine a number of texts that do not conform to readers' expectations so comfortably, texts in which closing one's mind as soon as one's anticipations merely seem to have been satisfied may lead one to overlook other attractive and ultimately rewarding possibilities. I shall focus on first-person narrators and figures such as speakers in dramatic monologues who resemble them in some important respects (though differing from them in others; see Rader [1989]) and on the particular assumptions that readers make about the texts in which they appear. I shall also rely heavily on examples drawn from the heart of the traditional canon of romantic and Victorian British poetry. Such a doubly narrowed focus will make it easier to address certain more detailed aspects of my topic; nevertheless, in chapter 6, I shall take time to assess the implications of my proposals for a wider range of texts and to explore some specific ways in which the analyses presented in the earlier chapters may enrich appreciation of the genres and periods from which those works were taken.

First-person narrative poems constitute a particularly promising corpus for the study of texts' effects upon us as readers because they challenge us from the very start to commit ourselves to some clearly defined assumptions about the identity of their narrators, assumptions that then fundamentally affect the ways in which we interpret what follows. The very use of the first-person pronoun demands that we at least consider treating the poem as (or "as if it were") a private communication from some specific writer to us as individuals. If we read on, in fact, we tacitly agree to act as its audience in this way, since the option of merely "overhearing" what is said is not open to us as it might be with a text written in the third person.[2] For that very reason, linguistic intuition will lead us to make some effort to identify the person behind the words we read, since, as we shall see, contemporary language theorists are convinced that linguistic meaning cannot be divorced from a broadly defined discourse situation that includes contextual features provided by our awareness of the speaker's identity.

Consider for a moment a nonliterary analogy. Almost everyone has at one time or another picked up the telephone only to find him- or herself at an immediate disadvantage: the caller, assuming perhaps that one was expecting this call to come through at any moment or that one's receptionist already explained who is on the line, launches straight into the discourse without stating his or her name. Desperately, one tries to pick out from what is being said clues that will establish the appropriate context. Some clues may derive from the content of the message itself (names of other individuals evidently involved, the general topic under discussion, the type of discourse), while others may relate to aspects of linguistic form (the speaker's sex, approximate age or accent) or even to such wholly extrinsic factors as the quality of the phone line if it suggests an international connection. Until one does determine the relevant context, though, many aspects of what is said may be virtually meaningless: personal pronouns may lack suitable referents, *"that* memorandum" may bring to mind any of a couple of hundred items of office correspondence, and a challenge like "What are you going to do about it?" leaves one groping helplessly for an appropriate response.

First-person narrative poems pose a similar challenge to their readers, for they speak in a disembodied voice and the speaker's characteristics must be inferred from what is said. Our need to identify the speaker is of course less pressing in a literary context than in an everyday one but may be complicated by our extratextual awareness in such cases that the poem in question was authored by Wordsworth or by Shakespeare (or even that it was written by "Anon."), particularly if we rely on that knowledge and embark on our reading with a particular sense of the poet's historical persona or have his philosophical or political views in mind. And precisely as in our attempts to identify an unknown caller on the telephone, whatever we decide will determine many features of our overall interpretation of the rest of the discourse.

As we shall see in detail in chapter 3, linguists maintain that even spontaneous narratives never exist in a conversational vacuum; instead, they are told with some purpose relative to a specific discourse setting. While a third-person narrative poem may escape this constraint in some ways, being accepted conventionally as a self-justifying form of literary display or entertainment,[3] a first-person narrative demands a reading that respects its relation to just such a discourse frame (albeit perhaps a fictional one). Both the particulars of that frame and the function of the narrative within it must therefore be reconstructed by its readers. Even if they elect to adopt the most ostensibly straightforward course and assume that the poem is literally autobiographical, that determination itself will crucially affect how they evaluate the ensuing narrative;[4] and as we shall also see, it takes considerable effort to reverse such determinations once they have been made. Similar kinds of assumptions—most of them, I reemphasize, subconscious and intuitive—undoubtedly figure in our reading of any text. But in first-person narratives the choices are particularly vivid and may be easily discussed in terms of readily accessible, if oversimplified, questions such as: "Is the speaker in 'I wandered lonely as a cloud' really Wordsworth?"

In selecting for examination in this study first-person narratives presented in poetic form rather than in prose, I have complicated the picture somewhat. Elizabeth Traugott and Mary Louise Pratt (1980:21) allege that "[one] of the pragmatic conventions of fictional narrative is that the speaking *I* . . . is understood not to be the author of the work." This may hold true of much prose fiction. The author of a prose narrative can rely on a wide array of linguistic and literary cues to orient his or her readers to the identity of a first-person speaker. That speaker may employ an obviously regional or archaic form of speech; may claim knowledge or express opinions radically at odds with those that readers would naturally associate with the author in question or with any author; may, conversely, give evidence of being far *less* educated than the author would need to have been even to have been capable of writing the text itself; or may openly draw readers into active participation in interpreting the text, enforcing a reading that closely approximates interpersonal discourse.[5]

Now, in principle, all of these resources are also available to an author who elects to cast her or his narrative in poetic form; in poetry, however, other demands and expectations may prevent him or her from exploiting them in quite the same way. The comparative brevity of many narrative poems is one such factor (see Mermin 1983:10–11); another is that, for the vast majority of works in the traditional poetic canon, a sense of formality and decorum, more or less codified, has historically exerted strong pressure in disfavoring the use of colloquialisms, regionalisms, and the hesitations, false starts and repetitions that mark everyday talk. Of all the considerations that militate against our extending the openness with which we habitually approach the narrators of prose works to poetic texts, though, the most insidious may be the existence alongside first-person narrative poetry of a closely related and often overlapping genre: the lyric.

Lyric prose is a comparatively rare genre; consequently, most readers anticipate that all the prose works they encounter will be narrative, expository or argumentative. In any prose narrative (with the exception of such materials as personal correspondence and private journals never intended for public dissemination and, perhaps, with the exception also of the personal essay [see Heath 1994]), some distance can therefore be assumed between the author and the narrative voice even when that voice speaks in the first person. A very different set of assumptions obtains for poetry. It is widely held that lyric poetry functions by *eliminating* any gap that might otherwise separate the poet from the first-person voice speaking in the text. Matthew Arnold provided a representative articulation of this notion when he called lyric poetry "the *direct* expression of *personal feeling*" (Super 1960:I, 206, n., as cited in Mermin 1983:7; my italics). A more cautious contemporary formulation is given by Ralph W. Rader: "though the dramatic lyric speaker has no name or specified identity, . . . we are hesitantly prompted to call him by the name of the poet, because of our intuitive sense . . . that the poem reflects the poet's actual experience at a real point in space/time beyond the poem" (1989:341). Given the existence, therefore, of two poetic genres, one of which (the lyric) identifies the speaker "directly" with the poet and the other of which (the narrative) may not, readers who encounter poems that open "I wandered," "Much have I travelled," "I struck the board," or "In the Shreve High football stadium / I think of Polacks nursing long beers in Tiltonsville" immediately confront the issue of how to categorize them.[6]

Their preference for either the lyric or the narrative classification may itself depend to some extent on their knowledge of when and by whom the text at issue was composed. William Spanos (1968:14) points to a troublingly pervasive "conventional perception . . . that the Romantics, especially Shelley, were committed to the personal lyrical mode," a tendency aptly illustrated by Harriet Jump (1986) in her discussion of Wordsworth's early work *An Evening Walk*. In praising the young poet's efforts at polishing the text of that poem, Jump remarks: "In comparison with the conventional poeticisms and personifications of *1793*, the language of [the revised] text is simple and natural. It is easy to believe that Wordsworth is describing his own experiences and feelings" (158). It is alarming that Jump so uncritically equates "simpleness" and "naturalness" with *auto*biographical expression, but it is still more worrying that she later relies on this same assumption to motivate broader implicit claims about romanticism generally, alleging that "Wordsworth becomes a Romantic . . . when he gains the confidence to speak easily and freely about his own thoughts and feelings" (162). Karl Kroeber (1960:43) has argued persuasively that the early romantic poets often combined their enthusiasm for an older narrative genre—the ballad—with a desire to express "individual emotional memories and private moral imaginings," the results of that combination appearing in Wordsworth's composition of "lyric poetry with narrative organization" in works such as "We Are Seven" or "The Tables Turned." But one may be too easily trapped into assuming that all romantic poets invariably wrote in this mixed mode.

It will be a major theme of this essay to question any such "conventional perception" about romantic first-person speakers—or, by extension, about speakers in poems from other literary periods. Though highly influential, the lyric influence on romantic poets must not be allowed to ride roughshod over texts whose richest readings may stem instead from rejecting absolute identity between their first-person narrators and their respective authors.

Recent developments in theoretical linguistics (and collaterally in the applied field of linguistic stylistics) have both increased the variety and enhanced the precision of the tools available for examining literary texts (see Toolan 1990:273). In examining readers' initial expectations about first-person narrative poems and in exploring some of the shortcomings and limitations of the interpretations that they subsequently build on those foundations, I therefore propose to make extensive use of the methods of contemporary linguistic theory.

At this stage in its evolution as a discipline, linguistics is perhaps best regarded as an untidy cluster of subspecialties. Some, by all means, have traditionally occupied a more central position than others, with syntax, semantics, and phonology forming a conventional core triad. But even their privileged status would be accepted by fewer scholars today than was the case fifteen years ago, and the goal of establishing firm foundational links between the three seems even further from attainment now than it did then.

At various points during the past sixty or so years, key concepts emerged that seemed to show promise of transcending some of the major intradisciplinary divisions. In the 1940s, for instance, the contrast between minutely precise observations of individual phenomena and broader, more functional analyses of the same data, a contrast typically signaled by the use of the suffixes *-etic* and *-emic,* respectively, proved widely applicable not only in diverse branches of linguistics (as in *phonetic* versus *phonemic* transcription [see also Gumperz 1982:15]) but in other branches of anthropology as well. The *transformational cycle* became a similar focal point in the 1970s, as linguists found what appeared to be semantic, syntactic, *and* phonological variants of a single principle of ordered rule application. Most recently, though, linguistic theory has apparently reverted to an internally divided state, what Toolan (1990:2) calls a "new polyphony." While common sense dictates that some over-arching faculty must ultimately coordinate all human language process-ing, linguists remain far from discerning even the broad outlines of that comprehensive faculty either theoretically or experimentally.

Meanwhile, a wide spectrum of increasingly important subdisciplines crosscut and overlap the core triad: among others, psycho- and neu-rolinguistics; sociolinguistics and dialectology; pragmatics; and dia-chronic (historical) language analysis. Each offers valuable insights into the nature of language generally while simultaneously exploring the im-plications of those insights for some other, essentially nonlinguistic field of study. As a result of this dual focus, though, each typically develops its own array of fundamental assumptions and analytical methods, which complicates efforts to discern and assess exactly what that particular field has contributed to the discipline of linguistics as a whole or to compare the advances in that branch with recent discoveries in another. Mean-while, the spotlight of intellectual fashion shifts constantly from one subspecialty to the next, drawn by particular opportunities for making local headway, and stylists, seeking to appraise each breakthrough for its literary implications, find themselves tracking the spotlight's restless path.

In the early years of what Roger Fowler (1975:4) would later refer to as "the New Stylistics," Chomskian transformational generative grammar was in the ascendant. Paul Postal's analyses of "cross-over phenomena," Haj Ross's study of syntactic constraints, Joan Bresnan's overview of English complementation, and Ray Jackendoff's early championing of "X-bar syntax" all propelled linguistic theory forward in new and excit-ing ways (see Ross 1967; Postal 1971; Bresnan 1972; Jackendoff 1977). But all four of these studies, along with the great majority of the others published at that time, shared a fundamental assumption: that explicat-ing linguistic (and, still more narrowly, syntactic) "competence," the infinitely subtle and complex knowledge of a language that all its speak-ers hold in common (Chomsky 1965:3–15), represented the major agenda for linguistics. As early as 1966, William Labov's seminal studies on language variation had begun to cause a stir, but there was little sense either at conferences or in the pages of the leading journals that such work either could or should displace the drive to describe universal syn-tactic competence. In Labov's own words from his Introduction to *So-*

ciolinguistic Patterns (1972b:xiii), "[in] spite of a considerable amount of sociolinguistic activity, a socially realistic linguistics seemed a remote prospect in the 1960's."

Since that time, the balance has shifted. The unified forward momentum of research into syntactic competence has been deflected; a number of competing approaches now vie for attention, several of them questioning even concepts as basic to the generativist enterprise as the native speaker's capacity for genuine originality and inventiveness (see Tannen 1989:36–37). An alliance between theoretical linguistics, cognitive science and computer science has resulted in what Pratt (1987:58) rather polemically describes as a "retreat [by some linguists] . . . into neurobiologism and artificial intelligence" (see also Miller 1990). Simultaneously, studies of what were dismissed quite contemptuously by many in the 1970s as (mere) matters of linguistic "performance" (social register, gendered language, regional dialect, conversational style) have emerged as important foci in their own right (see Traugott 1989:51–52; Wilson 1989:11). It is by all means true, as Deborah Tannen (1989) points out, that the collective term *discourse analysis* nowadays embraces so many different approaches to language as to be almost useless scientifically. Nevertheless, its very emergence over the course of the past decade and a half[7] provides a valuable index of the fresh—or, as Tannen argues, reborn—interest in what she defines as "types of analysis of types of language that do not fit into the established subfields of linguistics, more narrowly focused, which had come to be regarded by many as synonymous with the name of the discipline" (6).

If the complexion of the field of linguistics has changed so significantly since the publication of Fowler's 1975 anthology, then scholars interested in applying linguistic techniques to literary texts should surely anticipate that a parallel shift might also have affected their own field. Such has indeed been the case, as Fowler himself has recognized in his more recent work (see Fowler 1984). On the one hand, a somewhat less self-confident tone that seems to reflect the less expansive claims of contemporary linguists has manifested itself in the literature of stylistics in the form of the appearance of fewer essays that take as their aim to provide all-encompassing definitions of *style,* of *poetic language,* or of *literariness.* Even those stylists who do still seek an "explanation of poetic distinctiveness" have become "less prone" to "assume from the beginning that a single explanation is necessary" (Attridge 1987:22–23; see also Fowler 1984 and Toolan 1990:2). On the other hand, certain of the more remarkable recent developments in the newly fashionable, non-traditional areas of linguistic theory—notably those in discourse analysis of various kinds—have stimulated considerable interest among stylistic scholars.

Two broad characteristics mark contemporary linguistic theories of discourse as departures from the sentence-based competence grammars of the 1960s and early 1970s. In the first place, they take as their domain language units that may be either smaller or (more probably) larger than the canonical sentence (Barthes 1977:83; Stubbs 1983:1). In the second, they analyze "language in use" in a particular setting (Brown and Yule 1983:1), seeking to explain its function as well as its form and, indeed, the crucial interconnectedness of those two aspects of language behavior. Brief consideration of these defining criteria (however much they over-simplify matters) surely suggests that literary scholars might be attracted to analytical methods of this general type. Literary texts almost invariably exceed the length of a single sentence, after all, and they certainly represent language in use, albeit in a specialized sense of that phrase.

It is hardly surprising, therefore, that specific linguistic theories of discourse should have been invoked in stylistic analyses of individual texts. Speech-act theory, one of the earliest such theories, informs Stanley Fish's treatment of *Coriolanus* (1980: chap. 9), Deirdre Burton's work on modern drama generally (1980), and an excellent paper on W. H. Auden's "Song V" by Ronald Carter (1983).[8] Toolan (1990) offers a detailed stylistic analysis of William Faulkner's *Go Down, Moses* that employs a wide variety of discourse-analysis methods. And in the allied field of narrative analysis, striking similarities link the theories of narratologists Wayne Booth, Seymour Chatman, and Gerald Prince on the one hand with those of discourse-theory psycholinguists Herbert Clark and Bertram Bruce and sociolinguists Labov and Erving Goffman on the other.[9]

Meanwhile, stylists have also begun to sound in their literary analyses a theme that reflects from language theory the establishment of that "socially realistic linguistics" whose impossibility during the 1960s Labov so feelingly deplored. Within a text, characters' use of language marked as belonging to a particular social register or regional dialect now merits close attention, the poet's or author's decision to assign them nonstandard dialogue being viewed as stylistically important. And in the broader context within which the very text itself constitutes an act of verbal communication, Fowler (1984:175) has proposed as part of his manifesto for stylistics that it should "show [how] a novel or a poem is [both] a complexly structured text" and, at the same time, "a communicative interaction between its producer and its consumers, within relevant social and institutional contexts."

One can scarcely deny that we have as yet barely scratched the surface in exploring the applicability of discourse theories to literary language. Nor, however, can one accept on its face Joyce Tolliver's allegation (which appeared as recently as 1990) that "[a] vast body of investigation into the linguistic structure of discourse, beyond the level of the sentence, has been almost totally ignored" (266). Indeed, it is as a result of the work that *has* already been done that we can assert with a certain degree of confidence that stylistics as a discipline can profit from paying close attention to the emergent field of discourse analysis within linguistics.

Interestingly, as is true of several of the analyses cited in the preceding paragraphs, some of the most interesting initiatives in this area have come from scholars whose intellectual roots do *not* lie in linguistic theory. As the recent appearance of essay collections such as Macovski (1994) demonstrates, work in this area commands a growing and increasingly interdisciplinary audience, and throughout the chapters that follow I use endnotes and citations within the text to reference the work of romanticists, Bakhtinians, and neohistoricists whose conclusions about individual poems approach my own, or even replicate them from other perspectives. My primary concern, nevertheless, remains that of demonstrating the significant potential for fruitful applications of linguistic approaches to discourse in literary settings, and in the interests of maintaining this focus, I base my exposition on explicitly linguistic theories of discourse (both literary and nonliterary), treating complementary or corroborative analyses by colleagues in other fields as a secondary, albeit often intriguing, topic for discussion.

In view of my enthusiastic endorsement in the preceding paragraphs of the application of certain kinds of linguistic methods to literary texts, it may be necessary now to enter an important caveat. That enthusiasm, after all, could appear foolish in light of Jacqueline Henkel's firm pronouncement in no less authoritative a forum than *PMLA* that "[we] have just witnessed the rise and fall of linguistic models in literary criticism. . . . For most critics, clearly, the project of a linguistic-literary theory has failed" (1990:448–449; see also Seamon 1989:303).

One must take care, however, to identify accurately the particular rise and fall that Henkel has in mind. In her article, she takes certain authors to task for having tried to fashion complete critical theories—lock, stock, and barrel—after the generative linguistic model. Most of those authors, she argues, misunderstood and therefore misappropriated the most fundamental concepts in linguistics, later professing surprise and disappointment when the attempted application to literature fell apart. "[When] critical discourse functions to reinvent, then reject, imported paradigms, as it does for generative grammar," Henkel observes, the outcome is doomed; yet, ironically, "as the projects of linguistics-based criticism fail, it is not the literary analogy but the linguistic model that increasingly takes the blame" (449, 460). In this essay, I advocate no such wholesale restructuring of critical theory along linguistic lines. What I have been discussing and what I shall be engaged in throughout the chapters that follow is an application of individual linguistic insights within a critical theory that is not itself "linguistics-based" in Henkel's sense.

To pursue for a moment another useful hint dropped by Henkel: "[since] works read as literature suggest no obvious, no natural, means of analysis, literary criticism must borrow its tools and models" from somewhere (449). The search for suitable sources from which to borrow may lead us far afield, many critical scholars even borrowing from a number of different sources in the formulation of a single argument. But Henkel's claim also entails, it seems to me, the conclusion that there is nothing illegitimate a priori about employing linguistic analysis in general, and discourse theories in particular, as one such potential "means of analysis."

Such an inclusive approach to the literary-critical endeavor has attracted distinguished advocates. In his 1989 presidential address to the Modern Language Association, Victor Brombert (1990:395) confessed: "My own preferences . . . go to critical methods that are flexible and eclectic . . . that seek to combine thematic, structural, deconstructive, historical, and even biographical approaches. Perhaps we need more

critical workshops that . . . explore the possibility not so much of recon-
ciling as of exploiting the combined resources of various methodologies."
In the final analysis, however, the inherent persuasiveness and the attrac-
tiveness of the readings that derive from such a method of analysis will,
in my opinion, demonstrate most dramatically the value of the approach
itself.

In this sense, my views as a stylist place me firmly within what Roger
Seamon terms the "hermeneutic" as opposed to the "scientific" camp.
Though the objective, systematic, and empirical study of language struc-
ture provides the point of departure for most of my work, I concede—
and even welcome—the primacy of interpretation as my final goal, and I
concentrate heavily on deriving explanatorily rich readings of individual
texts. Conversely, I remain relatively skeptical about the possibility of
defining "literariness" or of detecting principles that govern literature as
a field. In Seamon's words (1989:296), I situate my work " 'inside' the
literary system, as an extension of informal reading rather than as a
contribution to the establishment of a scientific discipline."

This theoretical (in some ways even pretheoretical) orientation emerges
throughout this essay in a number of ways. Thus, for example, I shall not
devote space initially to the task of defining rigorously the "reader"
whose "expectations" are to form the ostensible subject of my discus-
sion. The concept of the reader has been treated to extraordinarily
detailed analysis in the past decade. At one extreme, scholars such as
Jacques Derrida, E. D. Hirsch, Fish, Prince, and Wolfgang Iser have
fielded an army of abstract reader figures, each conceived on the basis of
some philosophical or literary theory about the nature of the critical
enterprise (for a review, see Wilson 1981). At the other extreme, radical
empiricists such as D. S. Miall (1990:323) have complained that "[the]
interests and experiences of *actual readers* have largely been overlooked"
(my italics); their response has thus been to develop experimental and
statistical techniques for measuring "actual readers' " responses to texts
presented to them for comment.

My own views in this regard have not changed materially since I wrote
in 1984 that "the generalizations one makes about 'the reader' in the
course of a stylistic analysis are . . . justified . . . by the critical insights
they promote" (134). Since the goal of each analysis is to illuminate some
literary text, its success or failure should be assessed primarily in those

terms and not as a function of the theoretical "correctness" of its premises. In their interpretations of various romantic and Victorian texts, the readers whose expectations I describe and whose reactions I characterize in the course of my discussions may indeed display personal biases and preferences suspiciously similar to my own. They may also lack substance in exactly the same way that linguists' "speaker/hearers" represent abstractions from the flesh-and-blood figures whom we all converse with daily. But neither of these limitations need constitute a significant obstacle to anyone who is reading the developing analyses *for the insights they offer into the literary texts.*

The local claims I make about how readers react to the language of a particular line or passage in a poem carry, I believe, a high degree of intuitive conviction; to the extent that they fail to do so, the interpretive conclusions that I base upon them will be deservedly weakened. But that risk is precisely the one—and the only one—that I am willing to accept.

It may also be symptomatic of my decidedly pragmatic approach to stylistic argument that this study is organized to achieve two essentially complementary but distinct goals. Chapters 2 through 5 address three distinct types of challenge posed to the analysis of literary texts (and in particular, of first-person narrative poems) by the recent discoveries of discourse theorists. Chapter 2 asks whether, and to what extent, speech in poems should be regarded as "natural." What evidence is there that readers "hear" it in the same way that they hear everyday conversation? And if indeed they do, do they use it in broadly the same ways, interpreting it, for example, as revelatory of the character of the person speaking? The third chapter studies narrative "framing," the technique by which one story may include within it a second, usually narrated by one of the characters in the framing discourse. What functions are played by the various narrative "levels" or "layers," and what expectations about them do readers bring to the text from their experience with nonliterary narratives? Chapters 4 and 5 merge the concerns of the two that precede them to examine in particular the speaking voice of the first-person narrator him- or herself. Who speaks as "I" in such texts, and how do readers go about discovering his or her identity from the limited information available on the printed page?

But a second organizational scheme also underlies the core chapters of this essay. For, at the beginning of chapter 2, I present what amounts to a literary puzzle, a somewhat surprising observation about a canonical text (Wordsworth's "Resolution and Independence"), a poem of which no commentator has provided an account that I find completely satisfying. From that point on, while discussion digresses frequently to examine topics germane to the broad theoretical issues under review in the respective chapters, it invariably reverts before long to the original puzzle, as I gradually work my way through to a thorough understanding of what is going on in that one Wordsworth poem. The final "solution" is both radical and somewhat counterintuitive;[10] therein, however, lies its greatest appeal. For if I have by that time clearly explained the discourse-based arguments that led me to reach the conclusion that I did, and if at the same time my reading of "Resolution and Independence" as a whole strikes those familiar with the text as plausible, or even as thought-provoking, in addition to being challenging in its unconventionality, then the worth of the technique itself (though not, of course, its objective validity) will have been established in the most effective way possible: by demonstration.

TWO

Conversations in Poems / Poems as Conversations

Why do you study the shell, except to represent to yourself the animal? So do you study the document only in order to know the man. The shell and the document are lifeless wrecks, valuable only as clues to the entire and living existence.

H. A. Taine, *History of English Literature*

William Wordsworth wrote the poem that we now know as "Resolution and Independence" in the late spring and early summer of 1802. (The full text of his poem is printed in the appendix.) In it, he told of a chance meeting between an anonymous first-person narrator and a leech gatherer (after whom, indeed, the poem was at first named).[1] As the poem's editors invariably note, Wordsworth based the poem on a real-life encounter about which we have independent information, since Dorothy was once again with him when the meeting took place and again recorded what happened in her *Journals* (42). But Dorothy's journal entry is dated "3rd. October" 1800; William was therefore recreating those events either from notes of his own or from memory when he wrote his poem, and a comparison of William's poetic version with Dorothy's meticulous prose description soon reveals that the two scarcely constitute parallel texts.

Both accounts do record the old man's "interesting" face, his bent figure, and, of course, his dreary occupation. But, in adapting the material, William altered many key details.[2] The individual in the poem stubbornly persists in harvesting leeches in the face of falling prices, for instance, whereas the man whom William and Dorothy had actually encountered in 1800 apparently confessed that he had given up the struggle and now "lived by begging." Nor does William's poem make any mention of the injuries sustained in a cart accident that had considerably aggravated the hardships confronting the Ambleside leech gatherer. Thus, even in the face of the poet's own testimony to Isabella Fenwick in 1843 ("the account of him [the Leech Gatherer] is taken from his own mouth"), we must read "Resolution and Independence" as at most an imaginative *re*-creation of historical events.

This evidence that the poem does not blandly versify Dorothy's journal account should in turn draw attention to a second assumption about the nature of this text, an assumption shared initially, I believe, by most readers of the poem but one on which its editors seldom comment. We take for granted, that is, that, as a report of an everyday occurrence (whether fictionalized or not), the narrative reproduces a typical episode of interpersonal social discourse. As a result, we assess the words that the two figures speak when they meet quite uncritically, just as we would any other detail. We may pay some slight attention to certain idiosyncrasies of each individual's manner of speaking that are drawn to our attention explicitly (I shall have more to say on that topic a little later) but only in the same almost casual way that we note what is said about their height and build. Instead, we concentrate our efforts primarily on establishing the significance of what each is saying, the *substance* of his contributions, virtually ignoring the interactive aspect of that exchange and the more complex question of whether that exchange remotely resembles a realistic instance of *conversation*.

In order to appreciate why this might be an important oversight, we must begin by examining closely the conversational section of this poem.[3] Initially, Wordsworth's rendition of the crucial dialogue proceeds by a series of familiar, even insipidly predictable steps. The first-person Narrator, out walking in a "lonely place" (52), meets and describes at length the figure of "a Man" (55).[4] In the Narrator's own words:

> a stranger's privilege I took;
> And, drawing to his side, to him did say,
> "This morning gives us promise of a glorious day."
>   [82–84]

As Herbert Clark and Catherine Marshall (1981:56) note, such remarks about the weather are indeed the "stranger's privilege," since the current state of the weather "is mutually identifiable by people in the same locale" and hence an impeccable source of that basis of "mutual knowl-edge" on which almost all conversations have to be constructed. This first utterance of the Narrator's is thus, as William Howard (1988:226) puts it, "an innocuous question designed solely to establish contact" with the stranger. The old man's response to this overture is, evidently, equally formulaic, since the Narrator fails to report it in detail: "A gentle answer did the old Man make" (85).

At this point, the Narrator hazards a second conversational "move"; once again, though, it is a thoroughly conventional one. Since he has as yet no clear sense of who the old man may be, no sense of "community membership" on which to base his selection of a suitable topic for talk with this particular interlocutor (Clark and Marshall 1981:35; Gumperz 1982:142), the Narrator selects one class of such communities (profes-sion or occupation) and seeks to discover which of its many members the old man belongs to: "What occupation do you there pursue?" (88).

Before we hear the old man's reply, Wordsworth's Narrator supplies us with an apparently extraneous but nevertheless useful item of non-linguistic detail:

> Ere he replied, a flash of mild surprise
> Broke from the sable orbs of his yet-vivid eyes.
> [90–91]

A number of discourse theorists have noted that everyday conversation involves contributions of both verbal and nonverbal kinds, the latter particularly evident in listeners' reactions to the ongoing talk (Merritt 1976:317; Clark and Schaefer 1987:19). Yet in practice, linguists have relatively few opportunities to explore the nonverbal dimension of dis-course because, as Susan Philips (1976:83) laments, tape-recordings, the most common source of analysts' data, "do not capture the listener's contribution to the regulation of interaction." Students of *literary* dis-course must of course struggle with a still more impoverished corpus; what one might call "standard" literary reports of spoken dialogue gen-erally lack even the limited information that tape recordings supply about pauses, most details of intonation, and speed of delivery.[5] Words-worth's Narrator, therefore, is unusually helpful when he alerts us to the fact that the old man shows heightened interest at this point where the banter of everyday pleasantries gives way to signs of an impending more sustained and (referentially as opposed to socially) meaningful conversation.

It should not surprise us, then, that the old man goes on to reply at some length to the Narrator's simple query. Instead of merely naming his occupation, he describes it in detail and to some extent even evaluates it:

> He told, that to these waters he had come
> To gather leeches, being old and poor:
> Employment hazardous and wearisome. . . .
> And in this way he gained an honest maintenance.
>   [99–101, 105]

Thus far, as I have suggested by my citation of discourse theorists whose work focuses on everyday conversation, Wordsworth's Narrator has reported a remarkably stock instance of what we might term a "meeting-between-strangers" scenario or "speech-event" (Merritt 1976:318). Only at line 106 of the text, in fact, do matters take a somewhat less standard turn, when the Narrator reports:

> The old Man still stood talking by my side;
> But now his voice to me was like a stream
> Scarce heard; nor word from word could I divide.
>   [106–108]

Many linguists have discussed conversation as a collaborative activity in which both speaker and listener are vital participants.[6] For conversations that involve narration, Barbara Herrnstein Smith (1981:228) insists "not only that every telling is produced and experienced under certain social conditions and constraints and . . . always involves two parties, an audience as well as a narrator, but also that, as in any social transaction, each party must be individually motivated to participate in it: in other words, that each party must have some *interest* in telling or listening to that narrative." But it is not even clear that a lack of interest alone will excuse a listener from his or her fundamental obligation to pay attention. As Harvey Sacks, Emanuel Schegloff, and Gail Jefferson (1974:727) note, a sophisticated "turn-taking system" underpins all conversational behavior and "builds in an intrinsic motivation for listening to all utterances in a conversation, independent of other possible motivations, such as interest and politeness." Listeners, that is, cannot afford to ignore the possibility that they may at any moment be called upon (or may themselves wish) to speak (see also Allan 1986:512). Naturally where, as in the case we are currently considering, there are only two parties to a dialogue, that possibility amounts to a near certainty (Sacks, Schegloff, and Jefferson 1974:712).

When Wordsworth's Narrator reports at this point his inability to separate "word from word," therefore, he implicitly confesses to having violated one of the more fundamental rules of conversational propriety: *Pay adequate attention to any conversation to which you are a party.* His failure to discern the old man's reply entails that he will not be able to glean the information that he originally requested by posing the question "What occupation do you there pursue?" and that he will therefore still lack common ground on which to pursue the dialogue further.

What immediately follows in the text confirms our worst misgivings:

My question eagerly did I renew,
"How is it that you live, and what is it you do?"
    [118–119]

Anyone reviewing this conversation thoughtfully, whatever his or her theoretical viewpoint (philosophical, sociological, anthropological, or linguistic), must surely suspect with this development that matters have gone seriously awry. Following the lead of John Searle, scholars like Marilyn Merritt (1976:347) have insisted that in an unmarked discourse context "a query is appropriate . . . only if the answer is not readily available" (see also Labov and Fanshel 1977:89). What we see here is a particularly egregious violation of that principle, since the Leech Gatherer was himself the source of the re-requested information, having just supplied it in the previous turn at talk. As a result, we would predict that this conversation is in danger of imminent collapse, since "if [the] constraints [that govern verbal activity of a particular type such as questioning and answering] are not met the activity breaks down" (Levinson 1979:370).

This is not to say that conversational improprieties can never be accommodated in everyday conversational contexts; languages characteristically provide subtle means for negotiating their "repair." Herbert Clark and Edward Schaefer (1987:26) list some examples from English of mitigatory utterances that inform the other participant in a conversation that the immediately preceding exchange of information was unsuccessful and forewarn her or him that some form of replay will thus be called for: "I'm so sorry; I didn't hear you"; "Pardon me?" Yet the Narrator in Wordsworth's poem offers the old man no such verbal flag of truce.[7] If we apply everyday conversational standards, therefore, we will surely anticipate that the discourse will at this point dissolve, the Leech Gatherer perhaps retiring in what Goffman (1967:23) charmingly calls "a visible huff."[8]

Returning to Wordsworth's text with this expectation in mind, we are struck by the observation that the Narrator's gauche repetition of his question does not earn him any rebuff at all. Quite to the contrary, the Narrator blandly reports of the old man: "He with a smile did then his words repeat" (120). And indeed the Narrator himself obligingly repeats them for us, indicating by his use of direct speech on this occasion his heightened alertness to what the Leech Gatherer is telling him.[9] Still more remarkable, perhaps, is the fact that, with the end of the old man's second reply (126), the Narrator abruptly loses all interest in reporting the rest of what was said, winding up his account of the conversation—and indeed the entire narrative—in the space of just fourteen lines. He summarizes what remains of the dialogue with the remark, "soon with this he other matter blended" (134), and slides quickly into the aphoristic close:

"God," said I, "be my help and stay secure;
I'll think of the Leech-gatherer on the lonely moor!"
    [139–140]

From the point of view of conversational analysis, then, this poem poses something of a challenge. Writing to Mary Hutchinson about a preliminary draft that he had sent to her in June 1802, Wordsworth insisted, "The poem is throughout written in the language of men" (304). But if this had indeed been his aim, why did he include in this (otherwise strikingly realistic) rendition of everyday discourse so complete an anomaly as an "echo" question-and-answer pair? We can examine this conundrum from the viewpoint of either of the two participants in the exchange. On the one hand, why does the inattentive Narrator not hedge (mitigate) his socially unacceptable reiteration of a simple, previously fulfilled request for information? On the other, though, why does the Leech Gatherer not take umbrage as we would expect him to? Why is he so compliant in the face of clearly inappropriate, even rude, conversational behavior?

I propose to offer answers to these questions over the course of this chapter and the three that follow. Before we embark on that process, though, it may be useful to adduce two items of more or less circumstantial evidence suggesting that the anomaly isolated here is of some literary, as well as linguistic, importance. In the course of an extremely stimulating discussion of "Resolution and Independence," Howard (1988:229) reports that the duplications of both the Narrator's question and the old man's answer seem to have been introduced by Wordsworth during the process of polishing his poem for publication (see also Ruoff 1989: chap. 4, esp. 136–137). Although he cautions that the "manuscript evidence [is] marred . . . by the absence of almost a whole leaf of the notebook" into which an outline of the original composition was transcribed, Howard himself is convinced that the unusual conversational structure at the narrative core of this poem was a comparatively late addition. Prima facie this suggests at the very least that we may rule out mere carelessness on Wordsworth's part as a cause of the conversational infelicity we have been discussing.

Less conventional—though more entertaining—testimony that the question I have raised carries substantial weight from a literary standpoint may be found in the work of Lewis Carroll, a reader whose ear for the linguistically offbeat seldom let him down. Carroll detected and exploited precisely the conversational disharmony that I have isolated in Wordsworth's text when he parodied "Resolution and Independence" in *Through the Looking-Glass.* The first-person narrator of "The White Knight's Song," Carroll's burlesque version of the poem we have been examining, resembles the Wordsworthian figure on whom he was modeled in his marked insensitivity to his "aged" interlocutor. In Carroll's poem, however, rudeness is allowed to run amok:

"Who are you, aged man?" I said.
  "And how is it you live?"
And his answer trickled through my head
  Like water through a sieve. . . .

So, having no reply to give
  To what the old man said,
I cried, "Come tell me how you live!"
  And thumped him on the head. . . .

I shook him well from side to side
  Until his face was blue;
"Come tell me how you live," I cried,
  "And what it is you do."
    [5–8, 21–24, 53–56]

To most of Carroll's readers, who are unaware of its parodic purpose, this conversation appears completely absurd and perhaps darkly humorous. This perception only emphasizes, however, how important it is that we should mount a strong case to demonstrate that, when Wordsworth employed these same unconventional conversational forms in "Resolution and Independence," he did so without anarchic or humorous ends in mind. For if no such case can be made, we shall be forced to question what separates the parody from its original; we shall find ourselves, in effect, unable to defend the Leech Gatherer against the complaint that Mark Foster (1987:21) lodges against Wordsworth's narrators as a class: that they are "fatuous or complacent." And once that concession has been made, it will be hard indeed to claim high seriousness for the poem as a whole.

As a first step in seeking an adequate explanation for the apparent conversational aberrations in this poem, we might ask whether discourse theorists, in the course of analyzing everyday conversations, have cataloged any naturally occurring, socially acceptable contexts for either (i) a request by a speaker for information already supposedly available to him or her or (ii), the still more marked case, a repetition by one speaker of the same request in two successive turns at talk.

Stephen Levinson (1979:367–368) observes that language use is invariably situated in specific contexts all of which are also "activity types, . . . goal-defined, socially constituted, bounded events with *constraints* on participants, setting, and so on." (See also Graesser et al. 1990:328 and sources cited there.) As "paradigm examples" Levinson offers "teaching, a job interview, a jural interrogation, a football game." Participants in each "activity type" fill roles that are broadly defined by the extralinguistic goals they are pursuing within that context, while each activity type also imposes "*constraints* . . . on the kinds of allowable contributions" that speakers can make to the ongoing dialogue. This theory of activity types (which has approximate analogues in Charles Ferguson's "genres" [1983] though not in Mikhail Bakhtin's; in Goffman's "frames" [1974]; and in Merritt's "speech-events" [1976]) allows Levinson to account for a number of everyday contexts in which speakers routinely request information they already possess without in the process endangering the talk in which they are engaged.

Legal counsel in a courtroom, he notes, is constrained by accepted definitions of what constitutes *a prosecution* (or, one might add, *a defense*) to ask questions that "request details that are already known to the questioner" (380). The act of posing these questions serves no purpose whatsoever if we assume that the only discourse function of a question is to make new information available to the questioner. But reference to counsel's goals in this particular activity type reveals that such seemingly anomalous utterances serve three contextually valuable ends. They furnish appropriate material to the judge and jury, who effectively "overhear" the ongoing dialogue; they serve to make public, to institutionalize, the information contained in the reply by inscribing it on the official record of the proceedings;[10] and, most important of all, they permit counsel to order the flow of information by juxtaposing individual replies in such a way as to invite the judge and jury to infer causal or logical connections.[11] In short, they enable counsel to "build a case" (381).

Other activity types also permit the posing of questions to which the speaker already knows the answer. Teachers commonly use this technique in their efforts to induce their pupils to display knowledge that they are supposed to have acquired (Labov and Fanshel 1977:89–90; Levinson 1979:384–390). Parents may sometimes offer young children an opportunity to confess voluntarily to some misdeed that they are in fact already known to have committed: "George, was it *you* who cut down the cherry tree in the yard?" And in so-called Socratic arguments, speakers may begin a complex series of interrelated questions with one or two whose answers they expect to be uncontroversial so as to establish a firm base for the increasingly disputable propositions that will follow (Labov and Fanshel 1977:102–103). Various activity types, then, may apparently suspend the broad general constraint that applies in neutral conversational contexts to prevent speakers from requesting information already known to them.

Unfortunately, this subtler understanding of how that constraint functions in specialized contexts will not help us to address the self-reported behavior of Wordsworth's Narrator in "Resolution and Independence." The almost obtrusively mundane chitchat with which the dialogue in this poem begins clearly characterizes this exchange as an unremarkable, casual encounter, an encounter designed to serve no extraordinary social purpose. It would be hard to imagine what Levinsonian activity-type label one could apply to these few turns of talk.

Paradoxically, we might move next to exploring the very banality of their encounter as potential grounds for explaining (or explaining away) the more remarkable features of the Leech Gatherer's and the Narrator's behavior. Deborah Schiffrin (1984b:315) notes an important distinction between the "referential" function of talk and its purely "sociable" use. In certain cases, Schiffrin suggests, even though all talk is inevitably used at some level "to convey referential information, . . . the meaning of that information [may become] subordinated by the meaning of the talk itself" (see also Klein-Andreu 1989:78). Suppose, then, that we view the scene that Wordsworth depicts in this text as lying at the extreme opposite end of the spectrum from Levinson's specialized activity types. Might not requesting known information, under the right circumstances, constitute a purely sociable use of language? When they first meet, as we have already seen, Wordsworth's Narrator and the old man do indulge in precisely the kind of referentially vacuous "small talk" (Goffman 1979:2) that Schiffrin is describing.

But brief reflection will lead us to reject this explanation too. Even at the most lackluster cocktail parties, explicit demonstrations of a failure to attend to one's collocutor (as evidenced by such faux pas as asking the same question twice) are not tolerated and appear either inexcusably inept or condescending.

Let me digress for a moment at this point to clarify an important premise for the argument I am developing: the assumption that we may legitimately analyze an early nineteenth-century discourse according to standards linguists have hypothesized in their efforts to account for conversational behavior in the 1980s. It might be argued, after all, that in Wordsworth's day "ineptness," "condescension," and even downright "rudeness" on the part of a gentleman when addressing a peasant by no means constituted a social failing.[12] Under this theory, the inherent imbalance of power between the two interlocutors emerges as broadly analogous to the more specialized twentieth-century contexts discussed earlier: the courtroom, the schoolroom, and the parental interrogation. In each instance, repeated questions are uttered felicitously by someone whose socially assured "face" effectively renders him or her immune to any charge of conversationally abusing the other party (in the poem, by a member of the upper classes; in the contemporary contexts, by an attorney, a teacher, and a parent, respectively).

I certainly respect the important contribution that a sense of the sociohistorical context in which any literary work was written can make to its full appreciation. But in almost all instances, readers who sit down with a text for the first or second time have no literary historian at hand to supply an extensive review of its cultural background. They thus read that text primarily with reference to their own, contemporary linguistic standards, whether syntactic, phonetic or conversational. While subsequent research may deepen and sophisticate their response in many invaluable respects, the initial impression, once registered, surely cannot be erased altogether. (Nor, incidentally, should Wordsworthians be too eager to embrace a reading based upon the class prejudices of the poet's own day. For such a reading only leaves one wondering what aesthetic purpose Wordsworth could possibly have had in mind when he allowed his Narrator's discourse to degenerate into an apparently gratuitous exhibition of social dominance over an elderly peasant.)

To return, then, to our discussion of the anomalous exchange at the heart of "Resolution and Independence," let us make one final attempt to resolve its deviant features, this time by briefly reexamining our (thus far unspoken) assumption that the Leech Gatherer ever answered the question posed to him by the Narrator in the first place. One legitimate reason, after all, for repeating one's utterance is because the first attempt failed to elicit the desired response (in the case of a question, because it failed to extract the information sought). Clark and Schaefer (1987:37) analyzed a highly specialized discourse genre: telephone calls made to directory assistance operators. These operators were trained to request information from callers in a specific, functionally determined order. If their standard opening question ("For which town, please?") was answered inappropriately ("Could you give me the number of Mr. E. Michaels?"), the operators simply repeated their first question without comment ("In which town?") (37). Less context-bound are cases discussed by Merritt under the heading of "calls for replay" (1976:330–333), where, in a tantalizing footnote, Merritt observes that "[a] questioner . . . may decide to replay a question . . . [because he or she feels] that *the focus of the question* was not properly interpreted" (332; my italics). For the conversation we have been considering, this would translate into suggesting that the old man's reply to the Narrator's first query, though lengthy, may not have addressed the substance of what was being sought; hence the need for a second attempt at isolating that crucial information.

Such an analysis in this particular instance actually gains in initial plausibility from the additional observation that the Narrator's question falls into a rather narrow class of "Who is X?" interrogatories. One can only ask who somebody *is* (or reply to such a question), it has been observed, relative to some specific discourse context. The question "Who is that woman in the red dress?" may be answered with any of the following sentences, even if, in practical terms, they all identify precisely the same individual:

That's Angelica Norburg.
That's Bill's wife.
That's the new vice-president for marketing.
That's our hostess.

In any particular conversational setting, however, only one or two of these replies may be perfectly apposite, while others may "miss the point," prompting the response: "Yes, yes. I know that, but who *is* she?" (Boer and Lycan 1975, cited in Clark and Marshall 1981:60). Perhaps, then, the Narrator's repetition of his question in the text before us should be viewed as his hint to the old man that the answer he has already given was inadequate, at least within the discourse context in which they both find themselves.

From a linguist's viewpoint, one of the distinct advantages of analyzing connected discourse (as opposed to isolated sentences) lies in the fact that the acceptability or unacceptability of its individual parts need not be asserted autocratically by the professional analyst (a phenomenon casti-gated by Toolan [1990:300] as "the tyranny of the asterisk"). For in conversational contexts, discourse-*internal* evidence may generally be adduced for the success or failure of each contribution; in the case of failure, in particular, "the parties themselves address the talk as revealing a misunderstanding in need of repair" (Schegloff 1987:204; see also Wilson 1989: chap. 4). Examined closely, each contribution to a dis-course can be shown to reveal (both to the interlocutors themselves and, derivatively, to the analyst) how prior contributions have been under-stood (see Clark and Schaefer 1987).

In the case we are currently considering, the availability of such rich evidence puts a quick stop to our nascent analysis of the Narrator's reiterated question as an effort to refocus his original query. Not only does the Narrator himself describe his second question as an unelabo-rated "renewal," but as we observed before, it prompts only a repetition of the old man's story, not an adaptation of it to some previously unap-preciated discourse context. Reluctantly, then, we must abandon this "replay-as-recontextualization" explanation of the dialogue.

Why else might a replay be requested by a participant in a conversation? Alas, we are now driven back to the simplest but least attractive of all explanations: the possibility that the Narrator's question simply re-veals that he has failed altogether to process the Leech Gatherer's first response. His repetition apparently constitutes the functional equivalent of the conversational "What?" or "What did you say?" (Merritt 1976:332, n. 29 and sources cited there). Like other readings that we have already rejected, this one fails to explain the old man's remarkable good humor in the face of the Narrator's rudeness and comes uncomfort-ably close to the interpretation that presumably gave birth to Lewis

Carroll's parody. All the same, it does seem to be the only explanation compatible with the findings of conversational analysts.

The general approach that I have adopted thus far in my discussion of "Resolution and Independence" may have occasioned in some readers an uneasiness far more broadly based than the neohistoricist objection outlined (and countered) above. To put it simply, skeptics may ask how I justify *at all* the analysis of sections of narrative poetry, albeit sections that are set out as what we loosely call "dialogue," using the methods of conversation analysis. Even purported "direct speech" in novels, after all, is demonstrably *not* transcribed conversation (see Clark and Gerrig 1990), and the far higher degree of linguistic formality in most poetry, certainly in poetry of the early romantic period, might be expected to place it at an even greater remove than novelistic prose from everyday speech.

This is clearly an issue to which we shall have to return later; some preliminary justification for the path I have chosen to follow is nevertheless in order. There is, for example, Wordsworth's own assertion, mentioned earlier, that "Resolution and Independence" was "throughout written in the language of men." While it can never be finally established exactly what Wordsworth intended by that remark, his claim surely invites us to explore at least the possibility of assessing the text from the standpoint of nonliterary usage.

And there is also the more theoretical argument well phrased by Toolan (1990:273–275):

> Traditionally, stylisticians have rarely addressed themselves to the logic, structure, or dynamics of *the talk in novels,* reflecting in this the tardiness in the parent discipline, linguistics, to take ordinary speech interaction as its subject matter. . . . Nevertheless it seems incontrovertible that many crucial structural and functional principles are at work just as much in fictional dialogue as in natural conversation. It is hard to see how we could recognize and respond to the former as a version of the latter if this were not so.[13] [My italics]

As the emphasized phrase makes clear, Toolan's own studies have concentrated on speech in novels, an area about which (in no small measure because of his work) we know far more now than we did a decade ago. It is hard, though, to see why the force of his argument should not apply with equal effectiveness to *the talk in verse*. As in prose texts, so also in poems, readers must interpret a single passage surrounded by quotation marks in some way that is linked, however distantly or tenuously, to actual speech.[14] And while they might just conceivably regard a sustained sequence of such passages as some random catalog of mutually independent transcribed remarks, readers are surely more likely to attempt first to interpret them as an approximation of what they experience every day as conversation.

A second aspect of my argument—my insistence on treating the speakers in "Resolution and Independence" as if they were "real people" by attributing motives to them, hypothesizing what their reactions should have been, blaming or approving their manners—may also have raised some eyebrows. Here too, however, my justification for having done so is based on common sense. As Geoffrey Leech (1987:83) notes, "there is no discontinuity, in functional terms, between everyday communication and literature. . . . In both literature and conversation, as readers or hearers, we have to engage our minds fully (in terms of background knowledge, intelligence, and imagination) to reconstruct the addresser's intention as well as we can." Once one accepts, that is, that literary dialogue approximates (even though it does not transcribe) everyday conversation, it follows naturally that its readers will deploy in their reading skills similar (though not identical) to those that they rely on as hearers and overhearers in day-to-day contexts (see Bernstein 1990). Those skills will be quite subtle; will be based on "pragmatic elements in [the readers'] own encounters, even if [they] cannot isolate or name them technically"; and will naturally involve more than mere semantic processing of the propositional content of the sentences: "If the novel [I would emend, "If literature"] is in any sense related to life, what the characters say must convey the implied as well as the overt content of their conversation" (Chapman 1989: 177, 159). And that implicit content must include as a crucial component some definition of the speaker who lies behind the words on the page.

One further and (for now) final extension of this line of thought leads me to assume more particularly that figures who feature as "I" in first-person narrative poems will similarly be examined by readers as if they were telling their stories face-to-face. With appropriate modifications, we hold those speakers to all of the standards of communicative competence that we elsewhere apply to a dinner table partner or a seldom seen

relative, standards that include coherence, "point," tact, and clarity.[15] At
the same time, we also make judgments about their characters and their
motivations on the basis of the specific ways in which they choose to
convey their stories.

To investigate the character and motivation of a first-person narrator
by means of close stylistic (that is, linguistic) observation of the text is,
then, a controversial move but one that common sense suggests we may
attempt. As we shall discover, it involves many complexities. It imme-
diately raises, for example, the question of which linguistic traits, which
motivations, which clues to the speaker's character are to be attributed to
the fictional narrator and which to the author her- or himself. It also flirts
with the kind of "pop-psychology" justly attacked by Fish, who accused
Richard Ohmann and other stylists during the 1950s and 1960s of mak-
ing the "highly suspect assumption" that linguistic style could be treated
as a mirror in which lay reflected an image of the "cognitive system" of
its user, the assumption "that one can *read directly* from the [stylistic]
description of a text . . . to the shape or quality of its author's mind"
(1980:72; my italics).[16]

Such problems may be held at bay, however, if we keep firmly in view
the principal goal of stylistic analysis: the provision of insight into a
particular literary work. If our purpose is to shed light on the text at
hand, and if, in a practical sense, linguistic analysis can shed such light by
means of the intermediate step of illuminating some aspect of the nar-
rator's character, then the literary insight gained will itself justify the
methods used.

As I conceded in chapter 1, this strategy is unabashedly pragmatic. But
let us recall, after all, where the present discussion began. Traditional
critical studies of "Resolution and Independence" fail, in my view, to
make adequate sense of the conversation that it not only contains but
indeed seems to take as its primary focus. If, by the end of my own
analysis, I can offer a more convincing, more comprehensive explanation
of that exchange—an explanation that originates in a detailed examina-
tion of the language attributed to the poem's Narrator and to its other
major character, the Leech Gatherer—then prima facie, the approach
itself merits serious consideration.

As an independent illustration of the explanatory potential of such a
methodology, and as a demonstration that stylistic analysis investigating

questions of speaker motivation in some detail may generate exciting, critically valuable leads without falling prey to Fish's attack on a mechanistically psychoanalytical stylistics, I propose at this point to turn away from "Resolution and Independence" for a while to consider the work of a poet from a different literary period.

Harold Bloom (1985:137) remarks of Alfred, Lord Tennyson's *Ulysses:* "however one wants to interpret the poem, it offers us a vehement and highly expressive selfhood." One could be more blunt: the voice we hear speaking in this poem repeatedly employs short, almost clipped declarative sentences whose subject is the pronoun *I*, sentences in which other first-person pronominal forms also abound:

> *I* cannot rest from travel: *I* will drink
> Life to the lees
>   [6–7]
> Much have *I* seen and known; . . .
> *Myself* not least
>   [13, 15]
> This is *my* son, *mine own* Telemachus,
> To whom *I* leave the sceptre and the isle— . . .
> When *I* am gone. He works his work, *I mine*
>   [33–34, 43; italics mine throughout]

to which catalog one should certainly add the following lines, in which a thoroughly disingenuous ambiguity surrounds the scope of the adverb *greatly:*

> all times *I* have enjoyed
> Greatly, have suffered greatly.
>   [7–8; italics mine]

Indeed, one is tempted to apply to *Ulysses* Christopher Ricks's (1972:132) comment about the poem *Tithonus,* an early version of which Tennyson composed in the same year: " 'I' and 'me' echo through the poem."

But the intuitive appropriateness of Bloom's characterization of the poem as a whole should not lead us to treat the work as stylistically monotonic. An attentive rereading of its brief opening paragraph, for example, may surprise even those who think that they know the poem well, for a number of factors combine there to transform what should be a straightforward enough assertion into a series of rhetorical misdirections and evasions:

> It little profits that an idle king,
> By this still hearth, among these barren crags,
> Matched with an aged wife, I mete and dole
> Unequal laws unto a savage race,
> That hoard, and sleep, and feed, and know not me.
>   [1–5]

The poem opens limply, a fact that can be traced to its first three words, which, albeit in different ways, figure as semantic lightweights: *it, little,* and *profits*. The opening pronoun, indeed, is all but semantically vacuous, as linguists will willingly explain. According to most pre–1975 versions of transformational syntax, that pronoun should be regarded as the stranded head of a noun phrase (or NP) from which the clause (or S-bar) that constitutes the underlying syntactic subject of *profits* has been removed by means of a transformation usually called extraposition (see figure 1). More recent accounts in the same general tradition might instead favor placing the subordinate clause in its final position from the start and treating the pronoun *it* as the overt realization of a special type of "semantically empty" proleptic subject (Van Riemsdijk and Williams 1986:114, 249). But whichever way we derive the sentence's overall structure syntactically, we cannot avoid the conclusion that its explicit surface subject *it* carries no semantic force of its own, representing little more than a metrically convenient stutter step.[17]

Consider next Tennyson's use of *profits* as the main verb of this clause. Modern dictionaries assign *profit* both an intransitive and a transitive usage, though I suspect that the latter is now at least obsolescent:

Intransitive
   The public profited (from the forced breakup of AT&T).
Transitive
   The forced breakup of AT&T profited the public.

Semantic (more precisely, thematic) analysis of these two usages reveals that the subject NP in intransitive sentences containing *profit* (*the public*

Figure 1

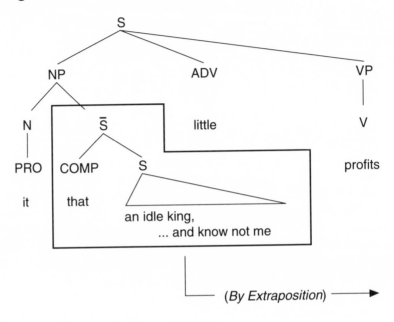

in my first example above) denotes the beneficiary (or *profit*-er) in the "transaction" described. In transitive sentences, the beneficiary appears as the (syntactically obligatory) direct object NP. We may thus generalize about both transitive and intransitive uses of *profit* in English that explicit mention is always made of the beneficiary, though the language does permit some flexibility with regard to the precise syntactic position in which that requirement may be met.

What we do not expect to encounter is a sentence such as the following in which no recipient whatsoever is specified:

* The forced breakup of AT&T profited.

Yet the most cursory examination of the opening lines of Tennyson's *Ulysses* reveals that the poet's sentence defies these expectations, enumerating no potential beneficiaries for the *profit* that it describes:

* It little profits ? that . . .

This discovery may lead our thinking in either of two directions. On the one hand we might query the assumptions lying behind the seductively familiar asterisk that precedes the two "unacceptable" sentences in the previous paragraph. In light of the attested use of *profit* without an explicit beneficiary in Tennyson's poem, should we perhaps revise our general standard for assessing its acceptability, admitting such constructions as "acceptable" and thus simply deleting the asterisk? Flora Klein-Andreu would presumably answer in the affirmative. Albeit in a different context, she insists with passion that "it is hard to imagine how we can ever hope to understand the characteristics of spoken language (or of any phenomenon, for that matter) if we start out by discarding examples of it, from the outset, as 'erroneous'" (1989:74). But I have argued elsewhere (1984:25–34) that the move to include in the corpus of acceptable utterances for a given language constructions found in literary works that would elsewhere be deemed unacceptable should be made only after the potential literary implications of continuing to exclude them have been thoroughly explored. One of the most significant metatheoretical breakthroughs of discourse analysis has, by all means, involved completely reshaping the very notions of acceptability and grammaticality to make them more inclusive. But in the world of stylistics, it has long been recognized that a major source of stylistic effect involves deviation from some linguistic standard or norm (see Freeman 1970: introduction and references cited there; and Hickey 1989a:5). From this perspective, whenever a seemingly anomalous sentence is assimilated to the standard grammar by amending some linguistic convention, we lose the chance to assess its potential stylistic importance as deviant language.

Let us therefore take the other path open to us and assume instead that, in the opening line of *Ulysses,* Tennyson employed the verb *profit* in a syntactic context that his readers instinctively register as inconsistent with the grammatical norms explained above. In particular, let us suppose that they perceive a syntactic and semantic lacuna in Tennyson's line:

It ([$_S$ that an idle king . . . know not me $_S$]) little profits $\boxed{\text{SOMEONE}}$

That perception in turn will invite speculation: who, readers will ask, might in fact "profit" from this king's choice of one role or another for what remains of his illustrious life? Or rather, who might be denied a profit they could otherwise have anticipated? For note that, sandwiched between the (vacuous) *it* and the (unfocused) *profits,* the adverb *little* virtually negates the entire, thoroughly complex proposition that the first and third words require one to (re-)construct!

We have drawn three conclusions from our examination of the opening words of *Ulysses:*

> i. The presence of *it* in
>
> > It   little profits [that . . .]
>
> forces the reader to await an extraposed clause before attempting overall semantic interpretation of the poem's first sentence.
> ii. Tennyson's idiosyncratic use of *profits* in the truncated construction
>
> > (It) [that . . .] little   **profits**   ?   ,
>
> leaves the reader wondering who might be the *profit*-er.
> iii. Finally, his introduction of the adverb *little* means that, even as the reader accepts the delay imposed by (i) and entertains the speculation invited by (ii), he or she must invert the semantic force of the hypothetical advantage accruing to the mysterious SOMEONE, by detracting from, rather than adding to, their "profit":
>
> > (It) [that . . .]   **little**   profits SOMEONE.

I shall return shortly to these points, and in particular to the challenging question of the identity of SOMEONE.

For a moment, though, let us turn our attention to the internal structure of the embedded clause, the clause in which Tennyson describes precisely what it is that "little profits" the enigmatic SOMEONE. Trimmed of its incidental details, Ulysses' major complaint is "that I mete and dole / Unequal laws unto a savage race." Were this indeed the final form of the clause, one would detect in it at best a jaundiced resignation to the status quo; at worst, an elitist snobbishness. But through his careful placement of the phrases that surround this clause's syntactic core—what James Richardson (1988:80) calls the passage's "accumulation of subordination and qualification"—Tennyson manages to obscure almost completely the first-person pronoun that constitutes its syntactic subject and thus mutes very effectively the speech's plaintively egotistical tone.

First he inserts a third-person NP immediately after the complementizer *that* (even omitting the parenthetical comma that might otherwise have forewarned the attentive reader of its true, appositive status):

[$_S$ that I mete and dole] →
[that , an idle king , I mete and dole] →
[that an idle king , I mete and dole]

Then he compounds this obfuscation by inserting three additional oblique phrases (two prepositional, one participial) between the initial appositive and the clause's true subject:

[that an idle king, I mete and dole] →
[$_S$ that an idle king, [$_{PP}$ by . . . hearth] [$_{PP}$ among . . . crags]
  [$_{VP}$ matched . . . wife] I mete and dole]

In the sentence that results from these syntactic sleights of hand, it is hard, particularly on a first reading, even to grasp that *I* is the subject at all.[18] Syntactically, in short, this portion of Ulysses' opening remarks, minimally assertive and only belatedly first person, strikes a tone *radically at odds* with what Bloom calls "vehement selfhood."

Much the same point could be made with equal force by turning from an examination of this passage's sentential syntax to an analysis of the discourse-related role of deixis in its discourse structure. Toolan deals extensively with deixis in chapters 5 and 7 of *The Stylistics of Fiction*, suggesting that in general "[every] deictic expression . . . may be viewed . . . as a marked choice, deliberately preferred in the narration to some other more neutral expression" (1990:178). He particularly stresses the relationship between deictic systems and narrative viewpoint: "Crucial to deixis is the notion of the egocentricity of the speaker in any language act: a speaker situates referents, both temporally and spatially, in relation to him- or herself, speaking 'here and now'" (127).[19] In everyday conversation, of course, hearers can often rely on the literal "here and now" of a discourse context in which they too are physically present. But when readers embark on the text of a literary narrative, they lack any such "anchor" (Halliday 1989:32). As a result, they must seek to establish inductively the appropriate narrative perspective (what Carter

[1983:382] calls "a coherent provisional universe for . . . the poem" and
Bernstein [1990:131] terms its "fictional world"), using as clues ex-
plicitly deictic terms (such as *this* versus *that,* or *now* versus *then*) and
other markers of temporal and spatial orientation such as verb tense.

The speaker in the opening passage of *Ulysses,* however, uses deictic
terms in a way calculated to confuse rather than to assist readers. Let us
again move slowly through those opening lines, considering this time the
assumptions about narrative viewpoint dictated by the deictic elements
that appear in them:

i. *It little profits that* . . . Syntactically, these words are virtually mean-
ingless, as we have already seen. But even without any further context,
the present-tense verb form might be taken to indicate that the speaker
is introducing some statement of generic truth on the order of "Rolling
stones *gather* no moss." (As we shall see later, it is not altogether
accidental that the text admits of misinterpretation in this particular
direction.) If, on the other hand, this is to be a straightforwardly nar-
rative poem—an option that the reader must, for now, also entertain—
then the choice of tense suggests a viewpoint contemporaneous with
the events to be narrated.

ii. . . . *an idle king,* . . . This too could be a generic reference, since the
indefinite article in conjunction with a present-tense verb permits such
an interpretation ("*A* rolling stone *gathers* no moss"). The narrative
reading, however, together with its concomitant assumptions about
temporal perspective, also remains perfectly plausible. In the latter
case, we cannot tell very much about the speaker's deictic orientation
with respect to the king except inasmuch as his introduction by title
alone and in an indefinite NP strongly suggests a referent nonidentical
with the speaker.

iii. . . . *By this still hearth, among these barren crags,* . . . The use of the
proximal deictics *this* and *these* all but excludes the generic reading and
suggests instead a narrator who is located spatially (as well as tem-
porally; see [i]) close to the scene of the events to be described.

iv. . . . *Matched with an aged wife,* . . . Though devoid of explicitly deic-
tic forms, this phrase, by introducing a delay, certainly allows the
assumptions already forming in readers' minds to solidify.

Furthermore, the decision *not* to use the alternative "*my* aged wife"
or even "*this* aged wife" seemingly confirms our decision to posit a
narrator who is commenting *ab extra* on the performance of a monarch

known to him. After all, as Dorothy Mermin (1983:30) observes, this reference contrasts vividly with Ulysses' subsequent allusion in line 33 to "*my* son, *mine* own Telemachus"; as a result, she points out, "Telemachus [is] real to us in a way that Penelope . . . is not." That the speaker should be so emotionally disengaged that he mentions his spouse in the same offhand way that a stranger might is, in short, hardly likely to be an option entertained initially even by open-minded readers.

By the time that they reach the middle of the fourth line of the poem, therefore, readers of *Ulysses* have encountered several temporally and spatially deictic clues. From those clues, they will probably have concluded that this is to be a third-person narrative, and they will have begun to formulate some preliminary hypotheses about the narrator's relationship to the spatio-temporal context that he describes. That hypothesized narrator will specifically *not* be the "idle king" himself (see points [ii] and [iv] above); he will however be that monarch's contemporary and perhaps even his fellow countryman "among *these* barren crags."

This high degree of (misleading) spatio-temporal specificity entails the conclusion that it will inevitably come as a major shock to most readers to encounter the long-deferred "true" subject, "I." "Here and now" must now be reinterpreted from the viewpoint of a first-person narrator who is himself the "idle king"—an option explicitly not entertained in their preliminary conjectures.

Two different types of linguistic analysis have led us, then, to the same general conclusion: both syntactic delay and deictic misdirection combine in the opening lines of *Ulysses* to suppress any straightforward recognition by the reader of the speaker's self-interested motivation.[20] But this discovery in turn exerts considerable pressure in determining how we should proceed when it comes to tackling the thorny interpretive problem noted in our earlier analysis of the *main* clause: the task of identifying the unspecified SOMEONE, the omitted object of *profits*.

An initially appealing option would of course be to interpret that hypothetical beneficiary generically. "Mankind," that is, might perhaps be judged the poorer if Ulysses' gifts for exploration and adventure were to "rust unburnished" (23) in the closing years of his life. This interpretation would jibe well with other evidence that favors a broadly "generic" tone in the first line (see points [i] and [ii] above) and remains a fairly attractive possibility even after the reader has reached the disruptive first-person pronoun in line 4 and has made the necessary adjustment in perspective. Reading the text in this way entails positing a speaker who blends a degree of kingly egotism with an approximately equal measure of philanthropic benevolence. While it certainly implies that the speaker considers himself influential enough for his decisions about his own life to affect significantly the lives of others, it also suggests that he recognizes a moral duty to devote his life to their general benefit (or "profit"). Let me stress that this generic interpretation of SOMEONE is at this point, *and always remains,* perfectly possible; it will, I suspect, play some part in every reader's understanding of these lines.

As a result of our analysis of the linguistic structure of the passage in question, however, a second option has now been introduced, an option far less flattering to Tennyson's narrator. To see why, one need only compare Tennyson's actual lines with the following adulterated paraphrase in which a first-person subject reading permeates the sentence with the fullest possible force:

It helps **me** little that **I**, an idle king,
Must dole unequal laws unto a race
That hoard and sleep.

Once the pronoun "I" has been discovered, skulking guiltily in the closing portion of the sentence, that is, it inevitably emerges as a viable candidate for the vacant thematic post of beneficiary-to-*profit,* the impact of its late emergence serving, if anything, to encourage that reading.

Such an interpretation, it should be reiterated, remains only one of at least two available to the reader. Its usefulness, as we shall see, derives from (though it can never be assured by) the fact that it accords well with the existence here and elsewhere in the text of a concerted stylistic strategy that repeatedly conceals first-person statements beneath a variety of ostensibly third-person (and, indeed, preferably generic) pronouncements. The lengths to which one must go as an analyst in order to bring that strategy to light and to evaluate its impact, however, offer a measure of just how effectively Tennyson executed his task, camouflaging the selfish bias of his speaker behind linguistic blinds that tumble down only when, at the very end of line 5, Ulysses finally concedes the importance of "knowing" (and, by implication, of understanding) *"me."*

Even at that critical juncture, incidentally, Tennyson's syntactic choices create a surface form that is characteristically ambivalent. Certainly, the poet maneuvers the all-important pronoun, *me,* into a position (line-final, clause-final, and even paragraph-final) where it will receive maximum emphasis; an earlier version of the text had reversed the order of the final two words of the (already extraposed) clause, reading "and know me not" (562n). At the same time, though, that climactic effect is achieved only as a consequence of exploiting nonstandard word order to withhold this first unabashedly unambiguous first-person reference in the poem for as long as syntactically possible. Even this line, then, sustains the strange mixture of apparent personal assertiveness and self-confidence on the one hand with syntactically oblique and obfuscatory expression on the other that I have proposed as a major feature of this poem's opening.

Before we proceed to trace this pattern through later sections of *Ulysses,* it may be helpful briefly to contrast both the style of the opening five lines of this poem and their tone with those of the lines at the start of two closely related works, *Tithon* (later rewritten as *Tithonus*) and *Tiresias.* Like *Ulysses,* each of these texts was composed by Tennyson late in 1833 and constitutes what we would usually describe as a dramatic monologue.[21] In those texts as in *Ulysses,* as Dwight Culler (1977:85) notes, the first-person speaker is an elderly figure, "an incongruous mixture of the human and the divine," plucked from classical mythology. Finally, both Tithon and Tiresias concentrate in their respective speeches on some less than entirely satisfactory aspect of their existence, Ulysses emerging in fact as markedly more optimistic than either of them.

Tithon begins as follows:

Ay me! ay me! the woods decay and fall,
The vapours weep their substance to the ground,
Man comes and tills the earth and lies beneath,
And after many summers dies the rose.
Me only fatal immortality
Consumes: I wither slowly in thine arms, . . .
    [1–6]

It may be too fanciful to allege that, phonologically at least, the poem's first four words could *all* be read as first-person pronouns *(I, me, I, me)*. But even without that license, the first two referential words in the poem *(me, me)* are still used by Tithon to denote himself; the generic statements in lines 3 and 4 are semantically "complete" and thus do not invite speculation of the kind that, I have argued, is possible with *Ulysses;* and the tortured word order of lines 5 and 6 *(fatal immortality consumes only me → Me only fatal immortality consumes)* seems designed to promote Tithon's importance as an individual, silhouetting him boldly against the generic figure of "Man" in line 4, rather than to obscure his function as narrator.[22]

Though less rhetorically emphatic, *Tiresias* also opens with a frankly first-person avowal and again employs two first-person pronouns in its first four words: "*I* wish *I* were as in the years of old" (1). In the wider context of these two parallel works, therefore, the extent to which *Ulysses* denies its readers that early clue to its genre that a more prominently placed first-person pronoun might have provided becomes all the more striking.

Let us now return to the text itself, whose "five-line proem" we have studied in such detail.[23] That opening section, with its ambivalence toward first-person expression, is followed by the passage whose bombastic, "I-am-become-a-name" tone presumably led Bloom to call the whole text vehemently self-expressive. In just thirteen lines, the subject pronoun *I* appears seven times and *me, my,* and *myself* are each used once. The result is a quickened pace that matches Ulysses' description of himself in line 12 as "a hungry heart." Yet in line 19, the tempo slows once more and linguistic analysis again reveals syntactic techniques of indirection and suppression at work, masking Ulysses' close personal investment in the apparently abstract philosophical claims he is making.

Again, too, the first telltale sign of the stylistic shift takes the form of the appearance of *it* as the surface subject of two sentences containing extraposed complement clauses: "How dull *it* is to" (22) and "and vile *it* were to" (28).[24] As was the case in line 1, these constructions exhibit in subject position the purely functional, nonreferential pronoun *it* where otherwise a personal subject NP, or at least an embedded clause containing such an NP, might have appeared:

Neither: How dull [$_{NP}$ *Bill*] is
Nor: How dull [$_S$ *Bill's* showing his vacation movies] is
But: How dull [$_{NP}$ *it*] is [$_S$ for Bill to show his vacation movies]

The now familiar depersonalizing effect of such a choice of syntactic form, furthermore, is considerably complicated in these cases by an additional feature that one notices only when one examines closely the deferred subject complements. In lines 1–4 of the poem, after all, at least the extraposed clause was finite; its subject, though heavily disguised, could ultimately be discovered, and, once "unearthed," proved to be the personal "I": "It little profits [$_S$ that . . . *I* mete and dole]." In lines 22–23, by contrast, the corresponding complement clauses contain nonfinite verb forms and no overt subjects at all:

How dull it is [$_S$ *to pause, to make* an end,
To rust unburnished, not *to shine* in use!]
    [my italics]

To appreciate the full significance of this syntactic observation, it will be necessary briefly to review how linguists treat the interpretation of clauses such as these. With relatively minor disagreements about the details, most schools of contemporary syntactic theory view truncated infinitival clauses as full sentences whose subject is a "phonetically null (i.e., 'inaudible') pronoun," called PRO (Van Riemsdijk and Williams 1986:132ff.; see also Bresnan 1972, 1982; and Culicover and Wilkins 1986). In some contexts, "control" of PRO's interpretation is obligatorily (that is, syntactically) determined:

Obligatory Control
    John wants to leave the party   =
        John wants PRO to leave the party
        [PRO = *John*]

Elsewhere, however, obligatory control does not apply and PRO may then be interpreted either contextually or generically:

Contextual Interpretation
It would have been wiser to have left the party   =
It would have been wiser (for) PRO to have left the party
[PRO = us? him/her? you?]

Generic Interpretation
It is never a good idea to hitch rides   =
It is never a good idea (for) PRO to hitch rides
[PRO = one, people]

At first blush, Ulysses' sweeping generalizations about life in the section of the poem that we are currently studying belong in the last-named category, paralleling the clichéd "all experience is an arch" theme of lines 19–21.[25] Out of context, I could not fault such an interpretation of lines 22 and 23:

How dull it is to pause   =
How dull it is (for) PRO to pause
[PRO = one, people]

A closer look at the second of these ostensibly very similar constructions (lines 28–30), however, reveals that, in keeping with the general practice of this poem, a bias toward first-person interpretation is never quite extinct even in a passage as devoid of explicit first-person subject pronouns as this one.

Here, as in "How dull it is to pause," the deferred infinitival complement must by all means contain PRO:

and vile it were
[s (for) PRO for some three suns to store and hoard . . .]

Here too, just as in the previous case, PRO appears in a structural context that would usually leave it free to refer to anyone or to everyone; notice the indeterminacy that immediately emerges when one adjusts slightly the content of the following VP:

and vile it were
For some three suns to store and hoard *the grain*   =

> Vile it were (for) PRO for some three suns to store and hoard
> the grain
>   [PRO = us? them? you?]

The key to our interpretation of the clause as Tennyson actually wrote it, however, lies in Tennyson's choice of a reflexive pronoun, *myself*, as the direct object of *store and hoard*. Since an independent syntactic constraint dictates that a reflexive pronoun may only be used when it refers back to the subject of the clause in which it appears, the appearance of *myself* deviously requires that PRO actually be interpreted, even in this otherwise open syntactic context, *as if it were under obligatory control* (see figure 2). Working, so to speak, through the syntactic back door, this apparently trivial pronoun effectively robs PRO of its initial freedom of reference.

Almost as soon as he has uttered "myself," we may note, Ulysses tries to override his dangerously self-revelatory gesture by referring to himself in the very next line (line 30) in the *third* person as "this gray spirit," an NP that functions as an appositive and can in turn control the PRO subject of "to follow knowledge." But the momentary intrusion of a first-person referent for PRO into this passage cannot by then be fully undone nor its implication for the tone of the poem altogether voided.

David Shaw (1976:283) astutely observes of Tennyson's syntactic style how often it "creates merely a temporary impression of being open. At first an 'underdetermined' grammar invites us to relate elements X and Y in more than one way. But then a third element, Z, forces us to reorder our thinking about the syntax." Our own discussion has certainly uncovered a perfect example of this process at work. It is important,

Figure 2

... and vile it were

(for) PRO... to store and hoard myself

Free   Controlled

though, to recognize that the effects that such a stylistic technique produces may extend far beyond the bounds of the sentences in which individual instances occur. As was the case in our discussion earlier of the syntactic form of the proem, so again here the discovery of a stylistic "cover-up" in progress may prompt us to review more carefully our readings of neighboring constructions that at first seemed quite innocuous. The earlier "How dull it is to pause" (22) now sounds suspiciously like yet another thinly veiled grumble rather than the energetic affirmation of vigorous old age that it first appeared to be.[26]

Consider too the clause that I cited above as a classic generic cliché:

> all experience is an arch wherethrough
> Gleams that untravelled world, whose margin fades
> For ever and for ever.
> [19–21]

Even here, as Ulysses attaches one sonorous subordinate clause after another to his relatively simple initial metaphor, he finally reaches a point where he cannot maintain the objective neutrality with which he started out. One would expect, after all, that this thought should conclude roughly as follows:

> all experience is an arch wherethrough
> Gleams that untravelled world, whose margin fades
> For ever and for ever as *one moves / we move.*

Ulysses' substitution of the first-person singular pronoun ("when *I* move") reveals yet again his uneasiness with truly disinterested generalization and his continuing insistence on the special value of his own personal perspective.

In the long run, repeated excursions down this speaker's rhetorical "garden paths" will tend to annoy the reader. Generic statements (even statements that merely appear generic at their outset) create certain expectations: "they purport to remind us . . . of that which we can take on trust, that which can be uncontroversially presupposed." As such they "are usually . . . a means of inserting general evaluative templates or standards of worldly wisdom against which the behaviour of characters . . . can be set . . . [and entail] a claim of a very much enhanced [narratorial] authority" (Toolan 1990:252, 268). Having been duped into conceding Ulysses this kind of authority, readers are unlikely to be amused to discover again and again that mere parochial "truths" are in fact being purveyed. Richardson (1988:80) discovers in Ulysses' rhetoric "gestures so large that they dissolve as much as they encompass." I respectfully disagree. For me, Ulysses' gestures fail not because of their size but because of his constant impulse to qualify and restrict them; rather than exploding toward the kind of fluid "vanishings" that Richardson claims to detect, they seem to me to implode, or to deflate, revealing the self-absorption of the mind that fathered them.

At this point, having learned a great deal about certain aspects of the linguistic form of *Ulysses,* we are in a position to review possible applications of that knowledge. What, that is, are we to make of a poem that lurches violently from a syntax that vigorously promotes first-person pronouns (in the style that Bloom describes so succinctly) to a syntax that represses that same feature (even though, as we have seen, it can never altogether suppress it)?

One such application, I suggest, begins with a reassessment of the conventional view that *Ulysses* is simply a poem about old age and about "the need of going forward."[27] William Fredeman's assertion (1981:182) that "the central fact about Ulysses is, of course, that he is old" should be weighed against another "central fact": that, regardless of his age, Ulysses is a character sadly uncertain of his role in life, of his situation within "his" country, and of his place in history. Richardson remarks that one can "detect something unconvinced in Ulysses' autobiography" (1988:80; see also Mermin 1983:7). That lack of conviction before others stems, it seems to me, from the confusion that clouds Ulysses' own self-knowledge. Although perfectly secure in his memory of what he *has been* and what he *has done* and blusteringly assertive when it comes to explaining what he *hopes yet to be* and *to do,* in the poem's present Ulysses sees his historically constituted self in danger of lapsing into mediocrity and his future self at risk of blending back into a "savage race" whom he knows he lacks the skill to instruct and yet against whose humdrum existence he passionately believes his own activities should continue to stand out in bold relief.

Viewed from this perspective, the syntax of this poem (particularly the dramatic contrast between, on the one hand, the style of the proem and of lines 19–32 and, on the other, the style of lines 6–18) matches a persistent tension in Ulysses' character between pride and insecurity, between assertive individuality and reluctant conformity. Of course it is only stylistically, rather than as part of its explicit thematic content, that the poem communicates this tension. But that very indirectness surely betrays the need that Ulysses feels (paraphrasing Fredeman [1981:185]) to convey his fragile emotional state cautiously, "without exposing the nerve-ends of his . . . subjectivity" (and thus also confirms Richardson's judgment [1988:90] that "Tennyson is a poet of deep inarticulateness, but . . . *emotional* intelligence of the highest order").

Thus far, I have relied on observations about the linguistic texture of Ulysses' discourse to isolate what I argue is a heretofore undervalued (if not unrecognized) undertone to the voice we hear speaking in Tennyson's poem, an undertone not at all easy to reconcile with the more conventional view of Ulysses as the John Wayne of antiquity, full of bluff optimism and gritty determination. Other critics to whom I referred in the preceding pages, notably Richardson, have expressed unfocused concern over the glibness of traditional readings of this work; stylistic analysis both validates that concern and suggests a possible source for it within the language of the text.

Such a function represents an entirely respectable goal for literary stylistics (though not, as we shall see, its highest). If the linguistic analysis of literary texts has the potential to prompt reevaluations, or to further refine current evaluations, of characters portrayed in those texts, this alone should establish its worth alongside other critical methodologies with comparable aims—at least in proportion as those evaluations and reevaluations themselves contribute to more comprehensive, more complexly satisfying accounts of the texts as wholes.

But I want to push this discussion just one stage further. One aspect of the historical context surrounding the composition of *Ulysses* poses a problem for students of literature. In early October 1833, Tennyson heard of the totally unexpected death of his closest friend, Arthur Henry Hallam, who had been traveling in Europe. In the decade or so that followed, his deep grief shaped a number of poems, many of which we now consider to be among his finest. *In Memoriam,* of course, remains the single work most readily linked with that tragic event, yet, as has been repeatedly noted, the poet himself insisted to Sir James Knowles: "There is more about myself in *Ulysses,* which was written *under the sense of loss.* . . . It was more written with the feeling of [Hallam's] loss upon me than many poems in *In Memoriam.*" Elsewhere he reiterated that claim, insisting that *Ulysses* "*gives the feeling*" of this period in his life.[28]

The histories of the texts in question tend to lend this assertion a certain a priori credibility. After all, Tennyson wrote many sections of *In Memoriam* years after his friend's death, and most had undergone some measure of revision in the seventeen years between 1833 and 1850 when the entire sequence was finally published. *Ulysses,* in contrast, he composed in its entirety on October 20, 1833, and altered relatively little before its appearance in print in 1842. It is certainly tempting, therefore, to accept the poet's hint and to look to *Ulysses* for a depiction of his initial anguished reaction to the shocking news from Vienna.

A preliminary examination of *Ulysses* from this standpoint, however, yields surprisingly unhelpful results. Nowhere in this poem is there any very explicit allusion to the death of a close friend. Ulysses does speak of "the great Achilles, whom we knew" but only in passing, at the very end of his monologue and with no very obvious display of distress. On balance, the poem's tone could scarcely be called elegiac. Tennyson's friends may certainly have feared that Hallam's death would drive the poet into what one of them termed "that bitterness of spirit" to which the Tennyson family's history of depression rendered him particularly vulnerable. And Tennyson himself may have spoken in a brief note during the winter of 1833 of his poor "state of health and spirits" due to "old remembrances" (Lang and Shannon, I:97, 105). But Ulysses expresses no sentiments of irremediable loss, no yearning for escape from life's toils, no black despair. On the contrary, he repeatedly characterizes his problems as both temporary and surmountable. What he finds lacking in his current lifestyle—even Achilles' companionship—may still be restored. Why, then, would it have been to this poem (rather than to *In Memoriam* or to "On a Mourner") that Tennyson repeatedly directed his acquaintances as the single work most reflective of his personal reaction to Hallam's death?

The responses to this challenge that have appeared in the literature strike me as less than satisfactory. Michael Mason (1981:157) confronts more honestly than most commentators what he describes as the "important complication" entailed by Tennyson's claims about *Ulysses*. He proposes a psychological explanation: the calm surface of this poem "reminds us," he suggests, "how artificial is the notion . . . of the poetic utterance of overwhelming grief. An overwhelming grief will overwhelm utterance along with everything else." But it is not difficult to spot the pitfall inherent in accepting this line of argument. It is one thing for Eric Griffiths (1989:46–47) to point to the *"not entirely articulable* grief" (my italics) of the final line of Wordsworth's "She dwelt among the untrodden ways," in which the speaker states his loss in the barest possible terms and then tellingly *under*states its emotional consequences:

> But she is in her grave, and, oh,
> The difference to me!
>   [11–12]

It is quite another for Mason to make the far more radical claim that, in *Ulysses*, Tennyson effectively "talks around" the issue that had suddenly come to dominate his life, too numbed to make explicit mention of Hallam's death even in an imaginative setting well suited to it. Not only does this scenario strike me as highly counterintuitive, but by finding evidence for the intensity of this poet's grief in the fact that he expresses none, it also implicitly licenses scholars to assert the tacit expression of almost any strong emotion in a literary work on the grounds of its absence from the text at hand. Rather than accept such an explanation uncritically, I suggest, we should at least begin by pursuing instead whatever positive leads we can identify toward corroborating Tennyson's (apparently sincere, apparently literal) claims for this poem's faithfulness in representing his emotions.

Adopting a different approach, Robert Martin (1980:186) asserts with striking confidence that "[if] one were in doubt about the connection of [*Ulysses*] with Hallam, it would be obvious from the linking of the pervading images of death with the vessel and the dark broad seas." I find this claim hard to follow. I am by no means convinced that "images of death" "pervade" this poem, while Tennyson also seems to me to have offset references to the sea as "dark" and "broad" (not to mention "vext," "dim," and "gloomy") with an equal number of far less dreary descriptions, depicting it as "the sounding furrows," "the baths / Of all the western stars," the route, indeed, to "a newer world" that is absolutely not the world of an afterlife, since it can be explored *"until* I die." One suspects that Martin, vividly aware of what he calls the biographical "connection" with Hallam, has allowed it to color his reading of the text. Despite the tantalizing extratextual relevance of the seashore setting, therefore, I do not accept that imagery alone can account for the extraordinary weight that the poet publicly attached to this work and to the circumstances of its composition.

Finally, one must consider the generally insightful discussion of all Tennyson's works from this period by Culler, an analysis to which I made brief reference earlier. Culler (1977:84–105) portrays each poem in turn as a "response to Hallam's death." Of *Tithon,* for example, he argues persuasively that it "is Tennyson's *Dejection: An Ode,"* his portrait of "a poet who feels his poetic powers failing." In *Tiresias,* he suggests, the blind seer bequeaths to Menoeceus the task of converting poetic good intentions into practical good deeds; he "passes the mantle," just as Tennyson himself felt that Hallam had left to him the responsibility for carrying forward the work they had planned together. The same parallel, in Culler's view, also informs *The Passing of Arthur,* though with greater emphasis this time on the viewpoint of the recipient (Sir Bedivere/Tennyson) than on that of the donor (Arthur/Hallam).

I happily grant Culler's interpretation of each of these texts individually; given his analyses, furthermore, it is clear that all three of these poems do relate quite transparently to the events of 1833. Culler sidesteps, however, the more challenging task of fitting *Ulysses* into his mold. Generically, *Ulysses* may by all means belong with *Tiresias* and with *Tithon* (see note 21). But the tasks Ulysses resigns to Telemachus are humdrum ones, mere "common duties"; he willingly passes on only his "sceptre" (the outward symbol of the conservatively "decent" monarchy he despises) and an "isle" whose "barren crags" he has roundly disparaged.[29] His dearest possessions (his "name," his "hungry heart," and his wide "experience") he firmly retains to himself, foreseeing ample opportunities to foster them in the course of continuing adventures. Most significantly of all, Ulysses' remarks on this topic conclude with an explicit refusal to concede that he shares any skills whatsoever with his son

("He works his work, I mine"). As a text, therefore, *Ulysses* refuses rather stubbornly to conform to the pattern discerned by Culler as characterizing the major compositions contemporary with it.

Previous scholarship, in short, has failed to establish any adequate explanation for Tennyson's vehement and repeated assertions that *Ulysses,* above all his other works, expressed his grief over Hallam's death. Neither psychoanalytical speculation, nor close study of the poem's imagery, nor even the tracing of simple narrative parallels provides convincing grounds for accepting the relationship that the poet himself clearly believed to exist between this text and that historical event.

In *Tennyson: The Unquiet Heart,* Martin discusses with great sensitivity the impact of Hallam's passing on his Cambridge friends: "After the initial period of disbelief the friends began looking to the others who remained. . . . The letters of the circle at the time are full of affectionate condolences to each other, . . . and reassurances of Hallam's greatness, as if their own being were dependent upon his having been a man of transcendent promise" (1980:183). If Tennyson's companions, all of whom could fall back on wider circles of acquaintance and on far more supportive families than his, reported such feelings of personal insecurity that autumn, we might surely expect the same symptoms to show up still more vividly in the case of the poet. Tennyson's close friend James Spedding, after all, had earlier noted in general of the poet that "he seeks for strength not within but without, . . . looking to outward circumstances for more than a great man ought to want of them" (quoted in Martin 1980:203). And that contemporary impression is confirmed by Shaw (1976:295) operating with the advantage of historical hindsight: "[Tennyson] is always afraid his identities are a fiction, a mask, that he is nothing in himself."

It should particularly be remembered that Hallam's death followed closely on the heels of several extremely severe reviews of Tennyson's *Poems,* which had been published late in 1832—reviews that the poet was relying on the influential and popular Hallam to rebut (see Martin 1980:168–173 for a detailed critique of the reviews themselves). Newly arrived on the literary scene, in fact, and personally happier of late than at almost any time in his young life, Tennyson must have felt doubly threatened by Hallam's death. The recent upward momentum in his career could so easily have dissipated without the enthusiastic encouragement, the critical support, and the business acumen that Hallam had been able to offer. Symptomatic of this state of uncertain apprehension is the letter that Tennyson ("normally a man of intense pride") wrote during this period to John Wilson, his most vicious detractor, in an attempt to resolve their differences. As Martin (1980:190–191) notes, the letter comes perilously "close to cringing to a reviewer," an act that the poet was certainly never to repeat.[30]

Biographical evidence, therefore, supports a profile of Tennyson in late 1833 that combines with the stoicism that critics have conventionally recognized an equally important vulnerability in the face of Hallam's death. And in that complexity, I suggest, we may finally detect one possible cause of the poet's repeated insistence in his later years on the emotional truth to life of *Ulysses*. Just as Ulysses mourns his lost youth, so too Tennyson sought through this poem to come to terms with the loss of something dear to him. But more to the point, both men interpret their respective losses as involving far more than mere bereavement, however painful bereavement alone might have been. For each sees in the ensuing situation a threat to his entire being: the respect he has earned in his field, his standing especially among his comrades, and his plans for a future in his chosen profession.

Ulysses, in short, confuses its more attentive readers by appearing to be both an elegy and an "exhortation against . . . elegiac tendencies" (Richardson 1988:4) at the same time. Both Tennyson and the character he creates within the text struggle painfully to respond to their new circumstances, fluctuating erratically from a bombastic to an almost apologetic tone, "[holding] both the regressive impulse and heroic yearning in balance" in their attempts from moment to moment "to stabilize [their respective] worlds" (Shaw 1976:85, 292).

In a section of his book aptly entitled "Tennyson's Two Voices," Griffiths discusses with admirable clarity passages from *In Memoriam* in which Tennyson's syntax and lexis balance certainty with doubt as the poet ponders the possibility of immortality for Hallam and the likelihood of their meeting again in an afterlife. He notes Tennyson's own admission that "assurance and doubt must alternate in the moral world in which we at present live," adding that in the poet's greatest work those two possibilities "do not alternate, they co-exist" (1989:117). What is most fascinating and unusual about this uneasy coexistence in *Ulysses* is the way in which it focuses our attention not on Hallam, not on the deceased as in a standard elegy, but on the effects of loss on the individual left behind. Both Ulysses and Tennyson consider with mounting apprehension not the transience of what has passed but their own insubstantiality in the present. *Ulysses* is, in a sense, not an elegy for Hallam or for Ulysses' lost youth but for Tennyson himself and for the middle-aged Ulysses in the throes of a major midlife crisis. In picking out *Ulysses* as the poem that best represented the emotional turmoil of this time in his life, then, Tennyson may have displayed both acute personal insight and considerable candor.

Ultimately, Tennyson was to regain his own "stability" through hard work and the society of his Cambridge friends. Toward the end of the poem we have been studying, Ulysses too turns with renewed energy to "my mariners, . . . my friends," and it is interesting to observe how, as he does so, the syntactic features that we noted before as sources of complexity and ambivalence in his discourse melt away. Extraposed sentential complements, for example, do recur but they contain finite verbs whose subjects are not only overt but concrete and in some cases even agentive:

> It may be that *the gulfs* will wash us down:
> It may be *we* shall touch the Happy Isles;
>   [62–63; my italics]

And while the string of four infinitival clauses that close the poem do each contain a PRO subject, figure 3 illustrates the way in which the referent of each pronoun is *syntactically* controlled and thus not open to the kinds of loose construal that caused problems in the earlier passages.

In this extended discussion of Tennyson's *Ulysses,* I first employed generalizations about certain syntactic and deictic forms in that work as the basis for inferences about the individual who, we assume, utters them within the "storyworld" of the poem.[31] I assessed, for instance, the impact that apparently insignificant linguistic anomalies, such as the semantic deficiency of the verb *profit* as it appears in the first line of the poem, would probably have on readers. Assuming that those readers will instinctively rely even on such comparatively minor aspects of what they

Figure 3

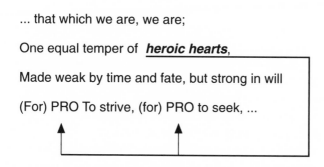

... that which we are, we are;

One equal temper of **_heroic hearts_**,

Made weak by time and fate, but strong in will

(For) PRO To strive, (for) PRO to seek, ...

encounter as "spoken" language (whether in a literary text or in everyday life) in their attempts to paint a portrait of its speaker, I sought to retrace their steps, inferring what the formal idiosyncrasies of Ulysses' speech might lead readers to hypothesize about Ulysses himself.[32] The resulting characterization of the language placed by Tennyson at Ulysses' disposal revealed it as a likely origin of the incertitude recognized by readers like Richardson who report having "detected something unconvinced" about the speaker's tone.

I then suggested, as an extension of that initial argument, that we might set our findings about the speaker *within* the text beside a partial psychological profile of its *author,* the juxtaposition casting interesting new light on the relationship between the two. By studying the discourse structure of Ulysses' speech, I proposed, we had enhanced our appreciation of his complex character; by examining the resemblance between that fictional character's circumstances and Tennyson's own, we might understand more clearly the importance the poet ascribed to the poetic persona he had created.

In fairness, I should note that the admissibility of any such reliance on extratextual material has not gone uncontested among stylistic theorists. Among those who object to any such strategy on principle, Leech (1987:68) alleges that "when we appraise a discourse as a piece of literature, we discount the reality of its interactants. . . . The implied author and implied reader are more relevant to our understanding of a narrative than the real author or reader." In a similar vein, Michael Rifaterre (1966:202) at first adopts the position that "the poetic phenomenon, being linguistic, is not simply the message, the poem, but the whole act of communication" but shortly thereafter emasculates that perspective by insisting: "This is a very special act, however, for the speaker—the poet—is not present; any attempt to bring him back only produces interference, because what we know of him we know from history, it is knowledge external to the message, or else we have found it out by rationalizing and distorting the message." If one accepts this argument, then "biographical curiosity about artists" will indeed be regarded as "irrelevant to the judgement of artistic work" (Griffiths 1989:94).

Other scholars have argued, however, that literary language resembles everyday speech in retaining an inalienable connection with some context of utterance. Thus, for instance, Diane Blakemore (1989:29) claims of language in general that "the truth conditions of an utterance can [not] be predicted simply on the basis of its lexical and syntactic properties." Even a sophisticated "semantic representation" is not sufficient, since pragmatic factors such as deixis, pronominal reference, and conversational context must be taken into account if that semantic representation is to be "developed and enriched into a complete thought" (36; see also Griffiths 1989:59).

Naturally, one task that confronts theoretical linguists and literary stylists as they examine discourses of any kind is to decide which contextual factors in particular they should permit their analysis to take into account. But while the *"actual* circumstances" may, as Griffiths asserts, be "innumerable, the number of *relevant* circumstances [is] usually finite, and, with patience, they may be stated" (50; my italics). Griffiths strongly believes that "the criteria for distinguishing the relevant from the actual must include reference to what the agent can plausibly be described as having thought himself to be up to," and this judgment in turn cannot be divorced from what we know of that agent outside, as well as within, the text: "our conception of him cannot, except in unusual circumstances, be entirely unimpressed by what we know of his conception of himself." [33] In my own analysis of *Ulysses,* I have adopted exactly this point of view—with what seem to me to have been critically constructive results.

Let me stress immediately that throughout my discussion of *Ulysses* I was at some pains not to hazard psychoanalytical inferences for which I had no independent (that is, *non*stylistic) evidence. "Psychoanalysis by linguistic analysis" (what Fish, as I noted earlier, terms "reading directly from the description of a text to the quality of its author's mind") can never work, since the subtleties and complexities of both thought and language defy simplistic one-to-one correlation. Instead, because I lay no claim to independent expertise in psychology, I leaned heavily on observations about Tennyson's state of mind recorded either by his contemporaries or by modern biographers and critics.

But my primary goal was, in any case, not to characterize the psyche of the poet. Rather, I sought to demonstrate a critical value in positing a link between assessments of Ulysses' character (itself possibly a reflection of Tennyson's own state of mind at the time of composition) and the striking syntactic and discourse structures that find their way into the text. That value, I suggest, is most clearly revealed when one considers the absence in the literature of convincing solutions from more traditional critical perspectives for the very real interpretive problems that my discussion addresses: the elusive tone of the speaker in the poem and the poet's own frequent characterizations of this ostensibly unelegiac text as an elegy. Any new proposal that offers coherent responses to either or both of these challenges surely merits consideration prima facie.

In what ways, finally, does this analysis of *Ulysses* inform our search for a similarly enhanced appreciation of Wordsworth's "Resolution and Independence"? Both poems rely on first-person speakers, but here the resemblances—at least, the obvious resemblances—end. Tennyson's narrator comes endowed not only with a name but with a well-established history and a character already fleshed out by classical mythology; Wordsworth's "I" carries no such extratextual luggage. In *Ulysses,* although other individuals are addressed, they do not speak, nor do we need to assume (as in a Browning monologue) that they respond, "outside the text," to what Ulysses says; if anything, in fact, Ulysses' tone verges on the declamatory rather than the conversational. Wordsworth's poem, in contrast, crucially involves a speech exchange between two parties both of whose contributions we read. Nor do the linguistic analyses that have supported my accounts of these two poems correspond at all closely. In examining "Resolution and Independence," I brought *conversation analysis* to bear on what I perceive to be a problem of *interper-*

sonal politeness in that text. My examination of *Ulysses,* on the other hand, explored subtleties of *sentential syntax and semantics* (extraposition; controlled versus free anaphora) backed up by consideration of *pronominal deixis.*

Despite the many profound differences between the two cases, however, we may still view them as mutually supportive in two important respects. For our primary interest lies in neither of the two quite distinct fields of linguistic theory or textual exegesis in their own right but rather in the ways in which the results of the former may be correlated with the insights of the latter; and in that respect there are useful lessons to be learned from these studies.

Our analysis of Wordsworth's "Resolution and Independence" is as yet at a comparatively early stage. Certain unexpected features of linguistic form have surfaced, but we have gone no further than to consider and dismiss some ways in which readers might parlay them into (ultimately, we concluded, unsatisfactory) readings of the poem as a whole. At the very least, our study of *Ulysses* suggests that it is not altogether unreasonable to continue the search for some more comprehensive and insightful account of Wordsworth's poem. More specifically, the example of *Ulysses* confirms that analysts can arrive at exciting critical insights by assuming that the speech of characters in literary texts is indeed some version of what we understand by "speech," so that my initial attempt to explain the behavior of Wordsworth's Narrator in terms of everyday conversational conventions was not unrealistic. That we have so far been frustrated in that attempt should not dissuade us from further exploration.

Second, the interesting way in which the language of *Ulysses* may usefully be viewed as having been "uttered" *both* by Ulysses *and* by Tennyson raises an issue that I shall not address in detail until chapter 4 but still deserves brief mention here. For it will always be possible to treat the text of any poem written in the first-person as having been spoken twice—once by the named or unnamed narrator and again by the poet himself. The productiveness of pursuing the implications of such a hypothesis in the case of Tennyson's poem should embolden us to follow up such leads aggressively.

Unfortunately, and despite its general value as a demonstration of the potential of conversational analysis as a basis for literary interpretation, the preceding discussion of *Ulysses* has failed to furnish any more precise clues to assist us in responding to the conversational chaos at the core of "Resolution and Independence." And indeed, finding the next clue to that conundrum will take us far off our present track—even, temporarily, in a totally different direction.

THREE

Framing Poetic Narratives

Good my lord, put your discourse into some frame.
Shakespeare, *Hamlet,* act 3, scene 2

British "B" films of the postwar decades, most often black and white, introduced countless moviegoers to the stock Old Bailey courtroom scene. A police constable stands in the witness box, delivering testimony for the Crown against a sullen prisoner (let us call him Harry), who glowers morosely from the dock. Reading from a well-worn pocket notebook with all the world-weary assurance of the professional bobby, the officer presents his report as follows:

> At 11.57 on the evenin' of Monday, July the 18th., M' Lud, I was walkin' my beat. I 'ad just arrived at Mr. Billings' Radio and Television Emporium at 127, Duffer's Lane when I observed the prisoner emergin' from a side alley carryin' a large cardboard box. When I appre'ended 'im, the prisoner said [here the constable consults his notebook with particular care]: "It weren't my fault, copper, 'onest. This fella met me in the pub last night and told me I could earn a couple a' quid if I'd do 'im a favour by pickin' up this box and takin' it round to 'is place."

Relaxing again, the officer concludes: "I questioned the prisoner further about 'is alleged 'friend' but 'e could not provide any further information. When I then charged the prisoner with theft of a television set, M' Lud, 'e shook 'is fist in my face and shouted, 'I tell you, I been framed!' " We need not decide whether Harry was guilty of the theft or whether he had indeed been set up as he claimed, because I do not intend to pursue this little drama to its conclusion. But I do want to focus on one respect in which his cry of protest, "I been framed," was both fair and accurate.

The police constable's plodding narrative testimony includes within it a discrete and completely self-contained segment of narration in the form of the unfortunate Harry's self-exculpatory story. That account of the "fella" in the pub and of the alleged arrangement to deliver the box is repeated by the officer—with especial care, in fact—because, after all, this was one of the events about which he has solemnly sworn to tell "the whole truth." As a faithful member of the local constabulary, he could no more omit reproducing it word for word than he could choose not to mention the date of the arrest or the address of the burgled premises. But the mere fact that he presents that narrative in court does not put the various events that it comprises on a par with other incidents described in the balance of his evidence, a point that becomes immediately apparent when one considers that the court will certainly not hold him responsible for their truth. (That is just as well, of course, since Harry's subsequent arrest makes it abundantly clear that the policeman himself never believed that line of defense in the first place.) The prisoner's narrative is, then, "framed by" or "embedded in" the constable's in a way that significantly affects the narrative status of the incidents it describes.

We may capture th.᾿ relationship schematically in figure 4, the precise format for which I have borrowed from the work of Bruce (1981:287) though both Chatman (1978:256) and Wallace Chafe (1980:36) employ essentially parallel formulations.[1] Briefly, a horizontal line connects the primary participants at each narrative "level" (indexed for convenient reference by the number in the top right-hand corner of the relevant box). The arrow at one end of the line indicates the "direction" of the narration at that level, pointing from the principal narrator to his or her intended audience. The substance of that act of narration then appears in the box with the next highest integer.

Such a method of representing narrative frames has both benefits and drawbacks, several of which will emerge as topics for more extended discussion elsewhere in this chapter and the next.[2] One major advantage lies in the fact that it provides on the page an image strikingly similar to that of the frame or mat that surrounds a painting or a photograph, an image easily and intuitively apprehended. As works' narrative structures grow more complex, such visual clarity pays steadily greater dividends.

Figure 4

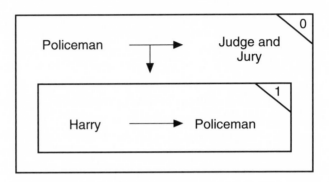

It is important, however, that we resist the attendant temptation to see the most deeply embedded story—which might, under that superficially appealing analogy, parallel the painting or photograph itself—as necessarily containing the most salient material. Nobody walks around an art gallery commenting on the beauty of the picture frames, so it is easy to assume with John Matthews (1985:25) that "in painting, sculpture, architecture, *or narrative art,* framing devices give themselves to setting off central artifacts" (my italics). But as Matthews himself finds out in pursuing his examination of a novel in which framing has long been recognized as a major strength, that interdisciplinary generalization does not hold, for *"Wuthering Heights* would be unimaginable without its framing" (56).

Then, too, this particular formalism draws unyielding black lines around each narrative level, representing each as discrete, while many examples of literary narration can be found that defy such absolute delineation of the boundaries between levels.[3] And while the bands of colored card, wood, or metal that surround a picture almost invariably produce symmetrical borders, of equal width on the left and the right, the amount of framing material at the beginning and end of a spoken or written narrative may vary considerably; and nothing at all, of course, corresponds in narration to the material at the top and bottom of a picture frame.

Diagrams along the lines of figure 4 run the additional risk that they may induce us to treat both the framing discourses (see Fajardo 1984:18) and the most deeply embedded narrative itself as static and inert. But the impact of this liability may be softened if one temporarily reconceives framing in the context of a third artistic medium to which it is at least equally well suited: film.

Discussing Jean Renoir's 1936 film version of Guy de Maupassant's short story *Une partie de campagne,* Chatman (1981:129, fig. 3) reproduces a single frame from that movie to illustrate how, cinematically, the director establishes narrative point of view. Renoir filmed the scene from inside a "gloomy dining room," Chatman explains, recording the activities of a group of characters gathered on the lawn outside from behind the shoulder of an observer, Rodolphe: "Rodolphe . . . opens the window, . . . making a little stage in the deep background against which Henriette and her mother move like cute white puppets." The visual parallelism between diagrams such as my figure 4 and the movie still that Chatman reproduces in his text is striking. But Renoir himself was not, of course, in the business of taking still photographs; instead, the narrative technique that Chatman describes actually characterizes a whole sequence of images that, when projected on the screen, reveal the dynamic nature both of the events taking place in the garden and of the foreground (or framing) scene in which Rodolphe reacts to and comments on what he sees outside. This cinematic example suggests the potential for analogous dynamism in both the framed and the framing narratives of a literary text, a dynamism that line drawings on the printed page would otherwise threaten to mask.

We need, then, to exercise due caution when summarizing the complex and constantly evolving form of some narrative in a diagram such as figure 4. Nevertheless, the abstraction and the precision that this method introduces can yield significant advantages, as we shall see.

In everyday conversation one discourse frequently frames a second. Speakers often use this technique, for example, to introduce, and to claim authority for reporting, events that they did not themselves witness: "I ran into Betty at the doctor's office yesterday afternoon and she told me all about her awful interview for that job at Fin and Feather last week. Apparently, she left her house in plenty of time, but the bus came late as usual, and . . . " Since this speaker was not with Betty on the day of her interview, she needs to account for the assurance with which she will assert the details of the narrative she is about to tell at second hand.

Such nonliterary cases of narrative framing, whether in the context of spontaneous everyday talk or in more specialized settings like the courtroom scene described at the beginning of this chapter, raise many intriguing questions. To what degree *do* listeners hold speakers accountable for the truth (either in spirit or in detail) of embedded material they include in their talk? In what ways can speakers signal that they are embarking on a framed narrative or have just concluded one? And in what circumstances *must* they do so? How complex can multiply embedded conversational narratives become before they begin to cause problems for those trying to keep track of them? (One recalls, from the television series *All in the Family,* Edith Bunker's endlessly rambling accounts of what one member of her family told a second about events that a third had alleged to have happened to a fourth—and Archie's frustration in trying to get her to come to the point.) And how do narrators manipulate direct and indirect speech in ways that indicate differing degrees of reliance on the word-for-word accuracy of the talk that they report?

As a feature of literary discourse, framing has been investigated at some length although usually from either historically or generically limited perspectives. Medievalists, for instance, have addressed the function of narrative framing in such canonical texts as Chaucer's *Canterbury Tales* and *The Book of the Duchess,*[4] and narrative theorists have commented extensively on its role in various works of prose fiction.[5] The play within a play in *Hamlet* that immediately (and ironically) precedes Guildenstern's line that appears as the epigraph to this chapter exemplifies a third type of literary framing that has been thoroughly studied.

Comparatively little, however, has been written about framing in narrative poetry from the romantic and Victorian periods, this despite a great deal of evidence that those works frequently exploit framing techniques in important ways. The little that has been done, furthermore, has generally been undertaken with regard to individual texts (notably Samuel Taylor Coleridge's *The Rime of the Ancient Mariner* and Wordsworth's "The Thorn" and "The Brothers") and without much attention to the general theoretical conclusions that may be drawn from such analyses.

In this chapter, I shall not attempt a comprehensive review of such studies. Instead, I shall concentrate on extending what has already been accomplished with the specific aim of closing the gap between how discourse analysts view everyday narrative framing from a linguistic perspective and how critics treat it when it appears in a literary text. Combining the methods of the two disciplines in this area, as I shall show, permits new insights both into individual texts that involve narrative embedding (including, crucially, "Resolution and Independence") and into the relationship between informal and formal, spoken and written discourse.

From the perspective of narrative structure, Wordsworth's early poem "The Ruined Cottage" is quite complex. It tells the story of a farmhand, Robert, his wife Margaret, and their two children, tracking the family's fortunes through several years of slow but inexorable decline. At first content and economically independent, Robert and Margaret lose their principal means of support when illness, bad harvests, and the economic impact of the war in America strike in rapid succession. Robert joins the army in a futile attempt to remedy matters, never to return, and Margaret tries desperately to keep the family intact but fails, her descent into destitution reflected in the dispersal of her children and in the gradual decay of her cottage and of the garden surrounding it.

This core story is quietly compelling, one of Wordsworth's best portrayals of the wretchedness of rural life in the second half of the eighteenth century.[6] But the poet does not simply offer it to us as a free-standing narrative. Rather, it is "told" by a peddler named Armytage, a man who knew Margaret and witnessed the effects of the successive disasters that struck her family. To complicate matters still further, the audience for Armytage's tale is not, at least in the first instance, the reader but still another intermediary, an unnamed Narrator. This individual introduces himself as "I" in the opening section of the poem, subsequently meets Armytage amid the ruins of Margaret's cottage, and then hears from him the story of her unhappy life. Actually, even this summary oversimplifies matters somewhat, for Armytage himself was not in all instances an eyewitness to crucial events and so has occasionally to rely on the reminiscences of local villagers and on Margaret's own

Figure 5

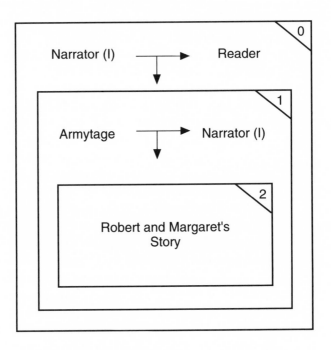

autobiographical accounts. Nevertheless, if we set such complications aside for the moment, we may use figure 5 to capture at least the broad outline of this text's narrative form.

Faced with the complexity of the narrative structure of this poem, its "multiplicity of human filters between the reader and narrated events" (Swann 1991:87), we may quite reasonably ask why that complexity exists. If Robert and Margaret's story packs a strong emotional and political punch in its own right, after all, why wrap around it so much narrative padding? Could Wordsworth not have told Margaret's story to the reader in his own words? "Why is it not sufficient," as Bertrice Bartlett (1987:47) asks in a different context, "merely to tell what there is to tell?" No external pressures will account for that decision, for, unlike our fictional British bobby, bound by his oath to tell "the whole truth," and unlike Betty's friend, whose auditors might demand that she account for her otherwise unexpected knowledge about Betty's affairs, Wordsworth could operate freely. None of his readers, one assumes, would set about checking up on the literal veracity of his literary tale. What, then, could his motive have been?

Merely by asking this question, I have already made one significant theoretical assumption about narrative framing. Among the commonest claims made about narratives in general (whether in everyday conversation, that is, or in literary contexts) is that they are felicitous if and only if they "make a point" (Polanyi 1985:187). As Bruce (1981:278) argues, even casual narrators and their audiences know instinctively that any story must be "told by someone to someone with some purpose."[7] It must be designed and delivered so as to meet that purpose and thus forestall the most damning of all criticisms of narrative technique: the hearer's "withering rejoinder, 'So what?'" (Labov 1972a:366; see also Labov and Fanshel 1977:105, 108; and Smith 1978:194–195).

Indeed, many analysts of spontaneous narrative have turned this observation to more theoretically constitutive ends, defining narrativity itself precisely in terms of its ordering of events so as to "make a point." Thus Livia Polanyi (1985:189) defines a well-formed story as "a recital of events and circumstances [that] must . . . be told *to communicate some message* about the world in which the speaker and hearer actually live" (my italics). A speaker who offers anything less than this, she argues, will be perceived as having "abused his access to the floor, . . . adding nothing substantive to what was being said." Polanyi's distinction here closely parallels that developed by Pratt (1977: chap. 4) between true "tellability" and mere "assertability." And both resemble in a general sense the contrast drawn by historiographer Hayden White (1981:5) between a "history proper" and mere "annals" or "chronicles" of events: "[In a history proper,] the events must be not only registered within the chronological framework of their original occurrence but narrated as well, that is to say, revealed as possessing a structure, an order of meaning, which they do *not* possess as mere sequence."[8] It is possible, of course, to set still higher standards for genuine narrativity (see Rigney 1992). William Brewer and Edward Lichtenstein (1981:367) reserve the term *story* for "narrative structures" that have been organized not just to some unspecified end but "so as to produce surprise and resolution." For our purposes, however, it will be sufficient to employ only the milder condition that *some* point emerge from all narratives, whatever the context in which they are told.

When we consider narrative felicity in literary texts, then, this condition will necessarily apply; but the stakes are raised, I suggest, in two important respects. In the first place, readers expect authors to make a point *at each level of narrative structure* rather than just with the narrative as a whole. During talk around the dinner table or in the hallway, speakers may frame a narrative by placing it in a context that is almost completely "transparent"; a narrator introduced as a part of that context may act as little more than "a neutral conduit" for the embedded material.[9] The same design in a literary text would, in contrast, be regarded as at least technically flawed, since the existence of the framing narrative would, in itself, serve no purpose and each literary act of retelling, we insist, should contribute materially to some narrative point, should add something to the sum total of the work's overall effect. Since "The Ruined Cottage" introduces an unnamed individual, therefore, who reports to us Armytage's reminiscences about events that happened to Margaret many years earlier, readers will adopt as one of their early assumptions that all of that narrative machinery—and specifically the very existence of the first-person narrator himself—is there for some purpose.

A second respect in which readers hold literary authors to higher standards than they typically apply to fellow conversationalists involves the salience, the quality, so to speak, of the point a literary narrative should make. Hearers and readers (even viewers) of any narrative constantly critique the appositeness and originality of the points that its teller is making (Polanyi 1985:197; Wilson 1989:44), but in conversational settings mere cohesion may be about as much as we demand. In literature, on the other hand, readers lay great stress not just on the effectiveness with which a work makes its point but also on the inherent importance of that point in the context in which the work is being read.[10] In the words of D. S. Miall (1990:324), summarizing the work of D. Vipond and R. A. Hunt (1984), among others, "[in] the type of reading most appropriate for literary texts, . . . the reader expects that the story will enable some value of cultural significance to be identified."[11]

At times, indeed, readers' anticipation of uncovering some striking

point in a literary narrative may even supersede their interest in its co-
herence as "a chronicle" (to adapt White's terminology). If they consider
only the events that the author records, as Toolan (1988:30) astutely
notes, readers who are asked "what happens" in certain kinds of "high
fiction" such as James Joyce's short story "Eveline" may quite possibly
respond "I'm not entirely sure." But those same readers will surely feel
slighted if such works do not furnish sufficient material for formulating
interesting conjectures as to the points their authors are making, con-
jectures sufficiently precise to be debated with other readers.

In the vast majority of cases, therefore, we may generalize that readers
expect literary narratives to make clearly defined, insightful points of
high cultural value and, in the case of embedded or framed narratives, to
do so at each level of their narrative structure. Examining "The Ruined
Cottage" with this in mind, it is easy to give Wordsworth high marks for
his creation of Robert and Margaret's story at Level 2 in figure 5.
Through that tragic tale, the young and politically radical Wordsworth
exposes the injustices of land reform and military conscription by pre-
senting in vivid detail their impact on an individual family (see Thomp-
son 1969:151–152). A suitably consequential narrative point at Levels 1
and 0 is, however, less easy to discern.

The first of two important steps in uncovering what is going on at
those higher narrative levels hinges on the observation that Armytage is
a peddler, a simple fact that has already drawn much comment from
scholars approaching the text from other perspectives. Marilyn Gaull
(1988:261), for example, concentrates on the historical and literary
heritage to which Armytage belongs (a heritage that she traces back at
least as far as the figure of the minstrel bard in Percy's *Reliques*), imply-
ing that Wordsworth included him in the poem on the grounds of a
nostalgic attachment to the type as a "living [heir] of the minstrel tradi-
tion." Jonathan Wordsworth (1969:92–93), in contrast, feels obliged to
defend the poet against allegations that the selection of a peddler as the
narrator of Margaret's story introduces into the text either sentimentality
(as Gaull intimates) or crudeness. Reviewing objections to the poem on
both of these grounds raised by the poem's early nineteenth-century
readers, he argues that Armytage's occupation is "rather beside the
point" and suggests that "[one] accepts that Armytage is a peddler for
convenience only." Neither of these suggestions, however, nor other ref-

erences to Armytage's trade such as that in Swann (1991), take into account the striking consequences of that feature of the poem for its shape *as a narrative,* consequences that I now propose to explore.[12]

Foster (1987:28) offers an interesting account of what it meant to be a peddler in England in the years between about 1770 and 1790.[13] As an itinerant merchant, Armytage would have traveled a long circuit through the countryside. Economic commonsense dictates that, equipped only with as much merchandise as he could carry on his back, he could not have afforded to stay long in, or to return too early to, a saturated market. His visits to Margaret's village, or to any of his regular stops, would thus have been occasional and largely unpredictable. He would have arrived, completed the round of his customers, and then passed on almost immediately. For his appearance to have coincided with particularly significant events in the lives of the individuals he met would therefore have been highly unlikely (hence, of course, his need sometimes to rely on others to fill in the details of Margaret's story). And his own firsthand testimony regarding events in any one place would necessarily have consisted for the most part of "snapshot" descriptions of scenes and characters linked only by the pseudonarrative technique of comparisons between each such description and the ones that preceded and followed it in chronological order.

This, of course, is precisely what we find in "The Ruined Cottage," and the result of viewing Margaret's story through the eyes of this individual whose perspective is conditioned by his trade in such a distinctive way is that, for us too, it becomes largely a narrative of compared states rather than of unfolding events.[14] Although Margaret's underlying life history (what Chatman [1978:19] would call the "story" of this poem) still consists of an orderly series of events, Armytage's telling of it (in Chatman's terms, the "discourse") distorts their even chronology by freezing a few scenes—and not even particularly crucial ones—for intense scrutiny while passing rapidly, usually at second or third hand, over the rest.

One reason for the existence of the Level 1 narration in this poem seems, then, to be that it allows Wordsworth to reveal the embedded story in a particular way. Ostensibly a matter of storyteller's craft rather than the source of some lofty philosophical or moral reflection, this hardly constitutes an impressive narrative "point"—until, that is, we integrate it with a second dynamic of the narrative structure of this text: the contrast between its Level 0 and Level 1 narrators.

At the heart of one's initial puzzlement over Wordsworth's decision to include not one but two narrative frames around Robert and Margaret's story in "The Ruined Cottage" is the fact that the two narrators involved (Armytage, of course, at Level 1 and "I" at Level 0) react in almost identical ways to the substance of the Level 2 narrative. Armytage begins telling his tale in the first place because, sitting beside the well in what remains of the cottage garden, he cannot restrain his grief and anger:

> When I stooped to drink
> A spider's web hung to the water's edge,
> And on the wet and slimy foot-stone lay
> The useless fragment of a wooden bowl. . . .
>
>   I loved her
> As my own child. Oh Sir, the good die first,
> And they whose hearts are dry as summer dust
> Burn to the socket.
>   [88–92; 95–98]

As the poem progresses, however, the natural surroundings exert an almost mystically curative effect, and by the end of the poem Armytage reports:

> I well remember that those very plumes,
> Those weeds, and the high spear-grass on the wall,
> By mist and silent rain-drops silvered o'er,
> As once I passed, did to my mind convey
> So still an image of tranquillity,
> So calm and still, and looked so beautiful
> Amid the uneasy thoughts which filled my mind,
> That what we feel of sorrow and despair . . .
> Appeared an idle dream that could not live
> Where meditation was.
>   [513–520, 523–524]

This is all very well—and of course thoroughly Wordsworthian. But to all appearances the first-person Narrator of the poem as a whole undergoes exactly the same process of spiritual edification. Arriving at the cottage "[with] thirsty heat oppressed" (48), he listens to Armytage's tale, which at first produces a "heartfelt chillness in my veins" (213). By its end he is so thoroughly moved that

> From that low bench rising instinctively,
> I turned aside in weakness, nor had power
> To thank him [Armytage] for the tale which he had told.
>   [494–496]

But not to be outdone, he too later reports that he has been reassured by

> The secret spirit of humanity
> Which, 'mid the calm oblivious tendencies
> Of nature, 'mid her plants, her weeds and flowers,
> And silent overgrowings, still survived,
>   [503–506]

expressing his newfound peace of mind in language so closely echoing Armytage's words that we are hard-pressed to remember afterward which words belonged to which speaker.

It might seem, therefore, that the almost perfect congruity—both in substance and in tone—of the reactions of these two narrative figures to the sad events of Margaret's life would make it doubly difficult to accept the redundancy that in any case characterizes the poem's tale-within-a-tale-within-a-tale narrative structure. A more detailed consideration of our schematization of the text in figure 5 allows us, however, to discriminate between these two men's superficially identical responses.

As figure 5 clearly indicates, the Narrator ("I" in the text), besides addressing the reader at Level 0, also appears as the audience, as a "character," in the storyworld he himself creates (that is, at Level 1). He drinks from the well; he wanders away to one side to meditate on what he has heard; and at the end of the poem he walks off into the sunset with Armytage to find their "evening resting-place" (538). What figure 5 does not reveal is that Armytage, too, functions on two narrative levels: both as the narrator of Level 1 and as a character at Level 2. By calling Level 2 "Robert and Margaret's Story," that is, I summarized its narrative content, but I obscured the way in which the story that Armytage narrates involves individuals whom he himself met, and with whom he discussed events as they occurred.

Once we recognize this oversight, our assessment of the way in which the Level 2 story affects Armytage and the Narrator inevitably changes. *Armytage*'s response to Margaret's tragedy remains a classic instance of what Geoffrey Hartman (1964:135) calls "the great Wordsworthian myth of Nature." Though intensely sympathetic toward Margaret's plight ("I loved her / As my own child"), Armytage receives mystical consolation when he places her death in the greater context of the cyclical processes of the natural world, processes that he finds very much in evidence now in the place where she passed her final days. The *Narrator,* on the other hand, never knew Margaret, never lived in the storyworld of Level 2, never had any reason to pay particular attention to the "ruined house . . . beneath a shade / Of clustering elms" (29–31). What he knows of her he learns only through Armytage's mediation at Level 1, his appreciation of Margaret and Robert's story thus being indirect, his emotional involvement in it vicarious.

The restorative power in Nature that occasions Armytage's pious remarks at the end of his act of narration cannot, then, apply in quite the same way in the case of the Narrator, whose sense of unease derives not from witnessing human suffering but from hearing someone else describe it. And what appeared at first to be a near-perfect parallelism between the two men's reactions to the events of the Level 2 narrative avoids redundancy precisely because their means of accessing the events that occasion those reactions are altogether different.[15]

We may summarize by suggesting that the "point" of the Level 2 narrative in "The Ruined Cottage" is indeed the social and political one well glossed by many commentators; Armytage's Level 1 response to it illustrates the equally well understood Wordsworthian thesis that Nature encompasses, and thus also resolves, human tragedy. But in addition to these two important "points" to the text, we may now also recognize a third.[16] For the Level 0 narrative functions as a vehicle by means of which the poet can illustrate the theory that was to reappear more explicitly in the *Lyrical Ballads* Preface a few years later: that poetry "takes its origin from emotion recollected in tranquillity"; that, while composing, the poet contemplates that emotion "till by a species of reaction, . . . an emotion, similar to that which was before the subject of contemplation . . . does itself actually exist in the mind"; and, crucially, that the rekindled emotion (now glossed as "passions") constitutes the heart of what the poet "communicates to his Reader" in such a way as to "produce excitement" of an essentially similar nature (148, 150).

At Level 0 in "The Ruined Cottage," we see how Armytage, reliving his own powerful emotions in the peaceful surroundings of the overgrown garden, succeeds in communicating them through narrative to the first-person Narrator so vividly that his audience is affected in precisely the same way he was, and we also see how the Narrator, empathizing with those emotions, subsequently succeeds in reconciling them with the peace of the cottage garden and the spear grass atop the wall. Wordsworth thus invites his readers to see in the Narrator an instantiation of the abstract "Reader" alluded to in the *Lyrical Ballads* Preface and, by extension, a model for their own actual performance as readers of this poem and of poetry generally.

Commentators have proven unable to agree about the extent to which the framing narratives in "The Ruined Cottage" (narratives that they typically and uncritically conflate as a single level) succeed in convincing us that Nature can exert the revitalizing influence that Wordsworth claims it can. Nor do they explain how, if the poet's aims in this general area are in fact achieved, narrative framing contributes to their achievement. Addressing the second of these questions, Evan Radcliffe (1984:115) suggests that whatever success the poem enjoys in this regard is due in part to the "dream-like" quality of Armytage's tale: "Since the dream-tale merges past and present, Margaret's trials . . . and the spear-grass vision . . . can exist together. . . . Involvement and detachment are simultaneous." Radcliffe's observation is certainly helpful. Crucial to the functioning of the double perspective that it supposes, though, is a feature of the narrative structure of this text that we discussed previously but left largely unmotivated: the technical device of introducing Armytage's unique point of view, that of the roving peddler.

For our ability to "merge" pivotal scenes of three chronologically and generically diverse kinds (the remembered experience of Margaret's story; those events as they are narrated to an audience that never knew her; and the description in the storyworld present of the physical surroundings of the cottage garden) depends crucially on the fact that those scenes are uniformly static, largely free from complications of movement and of character—in short, of events. The Narrator, and thus the modern reader too, can assimilate Margaret's wretched past with the calmness of the poem's present precisely because (and perhaps *only* because) Wordsworth has happily hit on a narrative means for robbing even the past-time narrative of its dynamism and thus blurring the boundary between past and present in the way that Radcliffe so persuasively describes. Treating the frozen instants that compose Armytage's story and the Narrator's own descriptions of the ruined cottage as if they were "before-and-after" pictures, we can place them side by side and draw consolation from their juxtaposition unhampered by the more harrowing details of what must have happened during the intervals between Armytage's visits.

Several aspects of the analysis I have presented in the preceding pages appear in various guises in the work of other commentators. Foster (1987:19) explicitly uses the word *frame,* for example, to describe the "introductory, digressive and concluding remarks" that surround "the tale of suffering Margaret," and he suggests, as I do, that "[the] overtaking of Margaret's tragic experience . . . by Pedlar's tale and Narrator's poem exhibits a distinctly literary process" (12). Stephen Gill (1985:538) points to the oblique, mediated nature of the Narrator's experience, commenting that "[it] is the Pedlar's eloquence that convinces the narrator." And Radcliffe (1984:113) stresses the absence of any direct contact between the Narrator and those whose story he hears: "Everything in the story *except the human characters* is actually present before the two men" (my italics).

Of these critics, Foster (1987:40) does perhaps the best job of integrating the various levels of narration within this text, arguing that they manifest a structural and thematic congruity. At each level, he proposes, we witness a pattern of "abandonment and return": "Robert abandons Margaret, the Pedlar leaves Margaret at their 'final parting,' . . . and at the end of the poem . . . he and the Narrator leave the ruin for a nearby inn; the Narrator circles back once more to tell the story; and finally, Wordsworth recurrently returns to recast the entire poem." This analysis certainly captures an important aspect of how Wordsworth's poem functions, and by citing as his fifth and final example of how this pattern is reiterated Wordsworth's own obsessive adaptation of this material to new contexts,[17] Foster raises a new concern that we should investigate briefly before we move on to discuss other texts: the question of how our conception of Wordsworth the poet relates to the various narrating figures within his text.

Implicitly, the logic of Foster's analysis posits parallel roles at different narrative levels for Wordsworth himself, for the Narrator, and for Armytage. Each functions as an individual who witnesses the events of Margaret's life, whether directly or indirectly; "abandons" her when her circumstances become too depressing to bear; and then returns to retell her story to others. This question of how to align Wordsworth with the other narrators in the text, however, has occasioned considerable debate in the literature.

Hartman (1964:139) adopts perhaps the least controversial position when he identifies "the poet" (one presumes that he means the historical William Wordsworth) with the Narrator. "Instead of centering transparently on Margaret," he alleges, "the tale reflects also the narrator, and tends to become a story about the relation of teller to tale. This reflexive (and modern) emphasis is achieved by *the introduction of the poet as a third person.*" And Jonathan Wordsworth (1980:17) seems to concur when he calls "The Ruined Cottage" "Wordsworth's first major *autobiographical* poetry" (the italics are my own in both cases). But Phillip Cohen (1978:188) disputes this position, arguing that the opening scene, in which the Narrator is seen struggling ill-temperedly across an arid landscape, is scarcely calculated to engage readers' sympathy. "Wordsworth," he suggests, "is talking through but around his narrator to his audience."

Radcliffe (1984:104) adopts a still less conventional line, arguing that in "The Ruined Cottage" "Wordsworth explores the concept of the poet as dreamer [employing] *the pedlar* as his ideal figure" (my italics once again), while both James Chandler (1986:206) and Foster (1987:26) favor a compromise position in which Wordsworth portrays certain aspects of his own perspective in the Narrator and others in Armytage. In Chandler's view, " 'The Ruined Cottage' presents" in the character of the Narrator "an enactment of its speaker's initial depravity of taste (one corresponding to Wordsworth's late picture of his own immature sensibility in 1793–94)" and then, in the person of Armytage, a depiction of a maturer self, one whose "soul [has been] humanized by the distress of Margaret."

The analysis that I have pursued in this chapter would, of course, lead me to side with Radcliffe in this debate. I see in Armytage's narrative role just those features that Wordsworth, in his early prose, associated with true poets, for it is Armytage who spontaneously allows his emotions to overflow (to paraphrase Wordsworth's characterization) and by so doing enlightens his audience, the Narrator. It is true that the Narrator essentially recapitulates this process in his Level 0 retelling of the whole story, "frames and all," to the poem's readers. But contextual factors explicitly present at Level 1 (spontaneity; the influence of a specific location for the narration; and the hearer's previously overwrought emotional state) are absent at Level 0, making it a less completely faithful vehicle for the Wordsworthian doctrine of redemption by composition.

Such a conclusion entails some rather significant consequences for a comprehensive theory of narrative framing. It implies in particular that, *just because a particular poem is narrated in the first person, one cannot assume that views expressed by its (Level 0) narrator approximate most closely those of its author.* Of course, critics and teachers of literature routinely attempt to inculcate in their readers and students some doctrine of skepticism along these general lines as a necessary premise for the careful reading of all literary texts (see Chatman 1978:147 and sources cited there). And in prose fiction, entirely fictive (frequently downright "unreliable") first-person narrators appear sufficiently often to keep every reader on her or his toes. As discussion moves from prose to poetry, however, as the focus shifts from either medieval or postmodern texts to those of the romantic era, and, indeed, as one tends to focus not on explicitly narrative texts like "The Ruined Cottage" but on works that are more lyrical in nature, I suspect that even experienced readers increasingly let down their critical guards. As I noted at the beginning of chapter 1, Wordsworth's "I wandered lonely as a cloud" quite blatantly invites autobiographical interpretation—an invitation that, in view of the poem's genre and period, most readers accept almost unthinkingly. Still shorter lyrical poems such as "A slumber did my spirit seal" are very seldom viewed as anything but expressions of personal emotion; critics speculate on the identity of "Lucy" in that work and in the other Lucy poems but not on that of "I."

Where if anywhere, then, should we draw a line? What features enable readers to identify first-person voices in poems as fictive or as autobiographical? And what options do poets have for voicing their own opinions through the speech of characters other than the Level 0 narrator? In chapters 4 and 5, we shall return to these important questions and apply them to other texts, texts for which the answers one proposes will have far more crucial interpretive impact than they do in the case of "The Ruined Cottage."

Before resuming my suspended analysis of "Resolution and Independence," I propose to turn briefly to a poem that exploits features of narrative framing markedly different from those that we noted in "The Ruined Cottage."

Robert Frost's "The Death of the Hired Man" takes the form of an extended dialogue between a husband and wife, Warren and Mary. (Only about twenty-five of the poem's 165 lines, in fact, do not appear inside quotation marks, and those lines simply describe the physical surroundings and a few of the speakers' gestures and actions during the course of their talk.) Earlier in the day, while Warren was out at the local market, a third individual whom Warren and Mary know well, a farm laborer named Silas, turned up at their farm looking for work. Warren resents the way in which, just as he has today, Silas routinely takes advantage of their generosity. At harvest time each year—when farmwork becomes harder and, since there is so much to be done, employment can easily be secured from the owners of larger farms who pay more than Warren can afford to pay—Silas leaves them; equally predictably, he reappears seeking shelter when the weather gets cold and no farm has enough jobs to keep him busy. Mary sees this pattern just as clearly as her husband; but today she has been shocked by Silas's exceptionally decrepit appearance and his erratic behavior. Now, sitting on their front doorstep so that Silas will not hear them talking, the two debate whether or not they should let him stay.

As discourse analysts tell us is common in such circumstances, Mary and Warren embed three short narratives within their conversation. First, Warren recalls a heated discussion he had with Silas the previous summer, a confrontation that resulted in his issuing an ultimatum: "If he left then, I said, that ended it" (14). Next, Mary describes Silas's arrival that morning and her dismay at his condition. Finally, they both recall at greater length a harvest scene from "four years since" (59), when Silas tried to teach Harold Wilson, a college-bound scholar, how to stack hay properly on a wagon (evidently without much success).

One important feature of the narrative structure of this poem that contrasts with what we have encountered so far is that Frost does not "nest" these three framed narratives one inside another as Wordsworth did in "The Ruined Cottage" (see figure 5) but presents them "in parallel" as I have indicated in figure 6.

Even such a simple structural difference invites speculation about the effects that different strategies of narrative embedding may produce: do readers find it easier to detect structural relationships between one level and another (parallelism, congruity, inversion) in one format or the other? can poets combine the parallel and nesting modes, or would such complexity tax readers' ability to keep track of the overall design? what

Figure 6

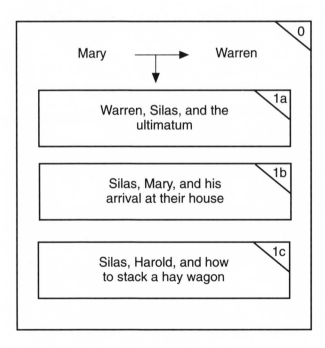

kinds of text, or what functions within texts, are best served by various configurations? For the moment, though, I am more interested in considering each of the embedded narratives within Frost's poem individually and more particularly in asking how "good" a story each of them really is.

None of the three in isolation, it quickly becomes clear, displays much by way of dramatic tension or, correspondingly, provides a very satisfying sense of resolution; none is, in Pratt's or Polanyi's terms, particularly "tellable"; none would rank highly on Brewer and Lichtenstein's scale of storytelling excellence. Even though Warren himself narrates the quarrel at the heart of Narrative 1a, for example, he and Silas emerge as little better than a pair of bickering preschoolers:

> "He thinks he ought to earn a little pay, . . .
> 'All right,' I say, 'I can't afford to pay
> Any fixed wages, though I wish I could.'
> 'Someone else can.' 'Then someone else will have to.'"
>   [18, 22–24]

And this narrative never resolves itself any more than the original argument did, at least from Warren's perspective; his stubborn insistence in the storyworld present that "I'll not have the fellow back" (12) apparently represents a halfhearted attempt to pick up the squabble again, despite the passage of several months.

Narrative 1b dangles still more awkwardly. In the first place, Mary has been unable to discover exactly where Silas has come from or what has caused his current state of dishevelment, so her account necessarily begins in midstream. She finds it almost impossible to put into words the most significant details of the day's events and repeatedly falls back on vague abstractions and on promises to Warren that he will shortly be able to "see for himself":

> "A miserable sight, and frightening, too—
> You needn't smile—I didn't recognize him—
> I wasn't looking for him—and he's changed.
> Wait till you see."
>   [36–39]

The climax toward which her particular story is presumably moving, furthermore, the point at which we will learn whether Silas is to be allowed to stay on or not, cannot by definition be reached until Warren and Mary have finished their conversation. Worst of all, perhaps, Frost has siphoned off whatever dramatic potential the story might otherwise have had for the reader by indicating in his title for the poem that the whole issue may in fact be moot.

Similar problems plague Narrative 1c. While Mary and Warren do develop that story in more detail than either of the others, it never reaches a decisive conclusion. Indeed, Mary embarks on it in the first place precisely because she has been struck by the incoherence of Silas's rambling reminiscences of the events in question. Like Warren, Silas is apparently reluctant to let bygones be bygones, refusing to concede, even after four years, that young Harold might have been right to choose a college career (studying Latin, "like the violin, / Because he liked it—that an argument!" [80–81]):

> "After so many years he still keeps finding
> Good arguments he sees he might have used."
>   [74–75]

This narrative too, then, fails to resolve what little tension it manages to generate, never even reaching an effective climax.

The three framed narratives in "The Death of the Hired Man," in short, hardly impress one as riveting stories in their own right; they certainly do not rank alongside the intensity of Margaret's story in "The Ruined Cottage." This is all the more remarkable when one considers that the Level 0 narrative in Frost's poem is equally devoid of the kind of dynamic action that might attract readers' interest. In the hushed discussion between Warren and Mary, to put it bluntly, very little "happens."

An approach to this poem that furnishes a means for resolving these apparent problems in its narrative structure derives from a second respect in which figure 6 (the diagrammatic outline of the narrative structure of Frost's poem) differs from figure 5 (which performs the same function for "The Ruined Cottage"): the use in figure 6 of a *double-headed* arrow connecting the principals at Level 0. This notation reflects the fact that the embedded narratives in Frost's poem are framed by a passage of dialogue and even dispute rather than by an act of (largely uninterrupted) narration. We might therefore investigate the possibility of exploiting this feature of the text, reinterpreting the Level 0 story as a narrative of purely conversational conflict, a story in which individual conversational turns—complete with the framed narratives that they contain—act as the "complicating action" (Labov 1972a:363). From this perspective, the seemingly inconsequential character of any embedded material would matter less than it would in a poem like "The Ruined Cottage," because the reader would focus not on those story fragments individually but on the Level 0 discourse that frames them. Their "point" would derive from their function within that conversation and not from their inherent (and, as we have seen, very marginal) tellability.

An analogy may help to make this distinction clear. Recall from the beginning of this chapter the British bobby testifying at the Old Bailey. In his court-appointed role as a witness, the officer included the prisoner's story about the man in the pub as part of his report not for its own sake (as a "good yarn") but because Harry's telling of it constituted an *event*, albeit a complex and entirely conversational one, in the story he himself was constructing. We can easily locate that event chronologically with reference to others in the series of incidents that compose his statement to the court: Harry's tall tale comes immediately *after* the constable catches him emerging from the alley and immediately *before* he is formally arrested. Within the policeman's testimony, it thus has effectively the same narrative status as those other, more physical events (see figure 7). The approach to "The Death of the Hired Man" that I am proposing here would treat the framed Narratives 1a, 1b, and 1c in exactly the same way, considering them as parts of the conversational events in the Level 0 story line that (together of course with the discovery at the very end of the poem that Silas has died by the fireside) make it in turn a worthwhile narrative.

Let us, then, review Frost's poem more thoroughly, this time focusing primarily on the dynamics of the conversation between Mary and Warren that it recounts at Level 0. As the poem opens, Warren is returning from his trip to market. Mary meets him at the door with just five words: "Silas is back . . . / Be kind" (5, 7). This seemingly innocuous greeting triggers a twenty-line speech by her husband. "When was I ever anything but kind to him?" Warren protests (11) and goes on to lay out the

Figure 7

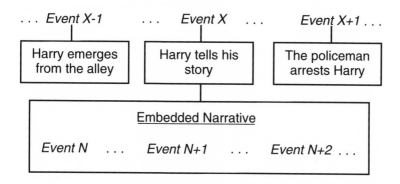

events of Narrative 1a, his lengthy outburst evidently serving as a conversational rejoinder to the rebuke he has inferred from Mary's instruction, "Be kind." His compassion, perhaps even his sense of fair play, has been called into question, and Warren is anxious to lay the groundwork to justify whatever annoyance he may later feel obliged to express toward Silas. Like most self-justifying speeches, this one ends up exactly where it began, with Warren insisting: "In winter he comes back to us. I'm done" (30).

As soon as she has the floor again, Mary launches abruptly into her own embedded story, Narrative 1b. On the face of it, this account of Silas's unexpected appearance in the farm yard bears no relation at all to Warren's Narrative 1a. By telling it, in fact, Mary seems to violate our expectation that participants in a conversation—even a vehement argument—will make their remarks relevant to what has gone before (see Grice 1975; Wilson 1989:42–45 and sources cited there). But let us consider where Mary and Warren find themselves at this point in their dialogue. Mary knows that she cannot dispute the historical facts that Warren has rehearsed so forcefully in his own narrative. She therefore decides instead to see if she can divert Warren's attention to Silas's current sad plight, apparently hoping that this may lead him to temper justice with a little mercy. Her Narrative 1b effectively reinforces her original request that he "be kind," just as his Narrative 1a enumerated the grounds for his possible refusal to accede to that request.

Mary's tactics meet with little success, for Warren stubbornly insists on maneuvering the conversation back around to Silas's attempt to secure work on the farm:

> "Mary, confess
> He said he'd come to ditch the meadow for me."
> [45–46]

In so doing, we may note, Warren does make a minor concession, re-orienting his discourse to the time frame of Mary's storyworld rather than that of the previous summer. But at the same time he refuses to confine himself to the events within that storyworld that she had selected to support her point of view. Instead, he uses his own previous experiences with Silas to surmise a detail that Mary had quietly elided: Silas's spurious offer of work that serves as his calling card. When his speculation pays off (Mary reluctantly agrees: "Of course he did. What would you have him say?" [48]), Warren has succeeded in tying this day's events back into the seemingly watertight logic of his own Narrative 1a: to allow Silas to "ditch the meadow" for them now would be tantamount to backing down from the terms that he set the previous summer, a major loss of face.

Aware that this first attempt to persuade her husband has failed, Mary initially flounders in search of a new tactic. She ventures a direct appeal:

> "Surely you wouldn't grudge the poor old man
> Some humble way to save his self-respect."
> [49–50]

She tries to square off with Warren on his own ground, intimating that Silas may have proposed more by way of work in return for his board than Warren guessed:

> "He added, if you really care to know,
> He meant to clear the upper pasture, too."
> [51–52]

And she briefly reprises her summary of Silas's sorry state:

"I wish you could have heard the way
He jumbled everything."
    [54–55]

But then, almost out of the blue, Mary embarks on Narrative 1c.
    As she reminds Warren of the impassioned dispute that Harold and Silas sustained throughout the "haying" season four years before, Mary's narration strikes us as purposeless, a haphazard accumulation of details:

"He thinks young Wilson a likely lad, though daft
On education. . . ."

"Harold's associated in his mind with Latin. . . ."

"He said he couldn't make the boy believe
He could find water with a hazel prong. . . ."
    [65–66, 78, 82–83]

For the two participants in the Level 0 discourse, however, for Warren and Mary themselves, these minutiae evidently conjure up a far richer and more inherently meaningful narrative than we can construct from them. We are at best overhearers of this conversation, after all, and must pick up as best we can on its many resonances.
    For example, we may infer that Mary's narrative has begun to have an impact on Warren when, after she has set the scene for Silas's and Harold's noisy altercations, he lets slip a stray remark confirming her memory of that summer: "Yes, I took care to keep well out of earshot" (70). Heartened by his concurrence, Mary continues to elaborate on her story,

    "But most of all
He thinks if he could have another chance
To teach him how to build a load of hay—"
    [85–87]

at which point Warren abruptly interrupts her in midsentence:

"I know, that's Silas' one accomplishment.
He bundles every forkful in its place. . . ."
    [88–89]

All of a sudden, we discover, Warren has assumed the role of story-teller—even though this was originally Mary's story—and from this moment on, Narrative 1c becomes a collaborative effort, Mary and Warren contributing in successive conversational turns the details that they remember best.

At this point too, I suggest, the reader senses that their initial disagreement has begun to dissolve and thus also that, for all practical purposes, we may assume that Silas *will* be offered the chance to stay on. Nothing has yet been said in so many words by either of the Level 0 speakers that could possibly be interpreted as signaling explicitly that a compromise has been struck. But then, in view of the way in which this poem works, that is hardly surprising. To appreciate the unfolding drama, readers must rely on their general understanding of how speakers use narratives to serve conversational (in this case, argumentative) ends; they must interpret each embedded narrative as a turn of talk that represents a step in the subtle (but perfectly customary) conversational dance that Mary and Warren execute on their front porch.[18]

Readers do not approach the framed narratives in "The Death of the Hired Man," therefore, in the same way that they do those in "The Ruined Cottage." In Wordsworth's poem, the most deeply embedded story, the tale of Margaret and Robert, was individually tellable; the Level 0 and Level 1 narratives were to that extent accretive, each designed to introduce some additional point into the work as a whole. In Frost's poem, in contrast, the embedded narratives come alive only if we recognize their function as moves in the framing drama of the disposal of Silas's fate. They would be flat, uninspiring, virtually point-less if read out of context. Our natural, and probably subconscious, reaction to their inadequacy is therefore to focus instead on what Mary and Warren are doing conversationally; on their constantly shifting goals; on the ways in which their narratives contrast with, respond to, or complement one another; and on the pivotal shift from single-voiced to collaborative narration.

I do not mean to suggest of either poem, of course, that any one level of narration ever completely excludes or eclipses another; as we read any poem, we assimilate all the concurrent levels of narrative structure and appreciate in addition the interplay between them (see note 16). But the discrepancy we have observed between the relative weights assigned to *framing* and *framed* narratives in the two poems we have studied closely in this chapter should surely alert us to the possibility that an even wider variety of relationships may exist between narrative levels and that embedded narratives may play many different roles within their framing contexts.

In light of this evidence of the potential importance of framing discourses in narrative poetry (including poetry of the romantic period), and furnished with some preliminary ideas of how framing may affect the ways in which readers interpret texts, we can now return to the discussion of Wordsworth's "Resolution and Independence" that we left unresolved at the end of chapter 2.

In that chapter, I argued that the conversation supposedly transcribed by Wordsworth in the closing stanzas of "Resolution and Independence" violates our expectations of how casual face-to-face discourse should proceed. By asking the same question twice (*and* in successive turns; *and* without in any way excusing his inattention to the Leech Gatherer's reply), Wordsworth's Narrator commits a major faux pas by normal standards of conversational good manners. Equally surprisingly, by calmly answering both the initial question and its subsequent repetition, the Leech Gatherer appears to condone this display of ineptitude. In the second half of the chapter, I explored in general terms the propriety of applying to conversation in poetic texts methods originally devised by linguists for analyzing everyday talk. I claimed not only that theoretical arguments strongly supported such an approach in principle but also that its adoption might in practice prompt insightful stylistic analyses of individual texts (such as Tennyson's *Ulysses*).

Unfortunately, those deliberations did little to resolve our difficulties in understanding the discourse dynamics of "Resolution and Independence." If anything, in fact, the findings of chapter 2 as a whole only confirmed that the problem in the linguistic form of that text that my initial analysis had brought to light was indeed a significant one and that appeals to the literary nature of the data would not enable us gracefully to sidestep the task of coming up with an adequate explanation for it.

In the remaining pages of this chapter, I want to lay the groundwork for a new analysis of "Resolution and Independence" that *will* adequately account for the conversational anomalies at its core, an analysis based in part on the observation that, like "The Ruined Cottage" and "The Death of the Hired Man," this poem too draws on the discourse technique of narrative framing. Figure 8, to be precise, illustrates how the Leech Gatherer in Wordsworth's later poem narrates his summary autobiography to the poem's first-person Narrator, who in turn relays it to the reader at a second level of narrative structure.

In discussing "The Ruined Cottage" earlier, I proposed that readers anticipate finding some "point" at each narrative level in a literary work that involves framing. In "Resolution and Independence," it is not difficult to establish a point for the Leech Gatherer's story (Level 1 in figure 8), in which he describes his uncomplaining pursuit of a difficult and depressing occupation in thoroughly unpleasant surroundings even as circumstances beyond his control make the profits to be expected from it less and less reliable:

> "Once I could meet with them [leeches] on every side;
> But they have dwindled long by slow decay.
> Yet still I persevere, and find them where I may."
>   [124–126]

Figure 8

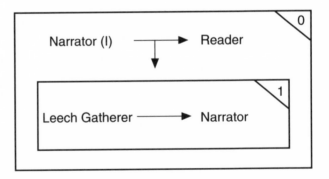

From the old man's point of view, of course, his story simply represents the appropriate response to the Narrator's inquiry; for him, its purpose is defined entirely by the immediate conversational context. Equally clearly, the announced intent of the Narrator in relaying the old man's abbreviated autobiography to us at Level 0 is to illustrate the importance of "perseverance" in the face of adversity, for that is the lesson that he claims to have grasped when he tacks on his own summation of the Level 1 story:

> I could have laughed myself to scorn to find
> In that decrepit Man so firm a mind.
> [137–138]

Polanyi (1985:193) suggests that a "story can be justified as worth telling . . . because of the significant alterations in the world [that result] from the events around which the story was built." If this is so, then these closing remarks by the Narrator, in which he draws attention to his reformed ethical perspective on life, would seem to have been custom designed to pick out this somewhat trite "moral" as the Level 1 "point" of Wordsworth's poem.

All of which brings us no closer to resolving our problems in understanding the text as a whole. For when asked about his gruesome trade for the second time, the Leech Gatherer repeats his answer virtually verbatim. (Figure 9 thus gives a more accurate picture than did figure 8 of what we actually witness in the text, the identical indexes affixed to the two embedded narratives reflecting the fact that the second is no more than an iteration of the first.) As a result, one might reasonably argue that the Level 1 point paraphrased in the preceding paragraph could have been just as effectively presented had Wordsworth included only one of the old man's two responses. From this perspective, in fact, the repetitiveness of the episode's dialogue represents a complication not only for the text's conversational realism but also for its narrative strength, since it serves only to prolong the distinctly self-righteous and clichéd moralizing of the old man.

Recalling our analysis of "The Death of the Hired Man," however, let us try a different approach, this time considering the text more carefully from the perspective of the Level 0 Narrator, and let us begin by attempt-

Figure 9

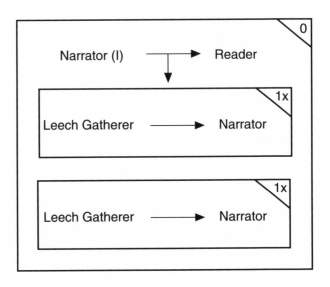

ing to infer the Narrator's justification for launching into the story of his encounter with the Leech Gatherer in the first place.

Wordsworth's Narrator lacks the supporting context of a dynamic conversation to justify the tellability of his story. (Compare his situation, if you like, with that of the Leech Gatherer, who, as we saw, introduces his snippets of autobiographical narrative in response to explicit discourse prompts in the form of the narrator's question, "What occupation do you there pursue?"). He thus resembles the more typical speaker characterized by Labov (1972a:366), who needs to indicate clearly *within* his or her narrative "its raison d'être: why it [will be] told, and what the narrator is getting at" (see also Chafe 1980:41–42).

Analysts have isolated various means by which storytellers accomplish this crucial task. Some narrators, for example, rely on an "abstract" to preview the gist of their story (or on a "coda" to recapitulate it) and to relate it to the evolving discourse context; others insert contextualizing material into the "orientation" section of their narratives (the section that characteristically precedes its first significant event) so as to establish characters or settings that will be inherently interesting to their auditors.[19] Given the potential importance of an abstract or orientation section in establishing a narrative's point, therefore, we might scrutinize the opening stanzas of "Resolution and Independence" with particular care.

As it happens, Wordsworth's Narrator offers no clear abstract for his narrative, but he does devote several stanzas to a general orientation before embarking on the story itself. In the opening stanzas of the poem, the Narrator initially describes a pleasant pastoral setting ("on the moors / The hare is running races in her mirth" [10–11]); he depicts his own mental state immediately before he first sees the old man ("fears and fancies thick upon me came; / Dim sadness—and blind thoughts, I knew not, nor could name" [27–28]), and he sketches the suddenly bleaker scenery amidst which he almost collides with the motionless figure of the Leech Gatherer standing "[beside] a pool bare to the eye of heaven" (54).[20] How might this extensive and detailed passage of orientation help us to discern the point of the narrative that follows it? To put it another way, what integrative purpose will account for both the Narrator's lengthy description of his moorland walk and his subsequent report of the meeting itself?

The crucial clue may lie in a surprisingly minor detail. In the course of describing his mood in Stanza 7, the Narrator makes a brief, apparently offhand reference to Thomas Chatterton, a promising young poet who had committed suicide at the age of seventeen "in . . . loneliness and dire poverty" (Abrams 1979:207n). Though this reference does serve generally to illustrate his morose state of mind, it is striking that the Narrator stresses three specific aspects of his thoughts about Chatterton: the poet's youth (he was a "marvellous Boy" [43]); his animated nature (he was also a "sleepless Soul" [44]); and his untimely death (he "perished in his pride" [44]). For, cursory as it may be, this portrait then furnishes a vivid contrast to the initial impression created several stanzas later by the figure of the Leech Gatherer. "The *oldest* man . . . that ever wore grey hairs" (56), the Leech Gatherer appears "not all alive nor dead, / Nor *all asleep*" (64–65; my italics), barely more animate than the drab surroundings in which he lives, "motionless as a cloud" (75).

The marked physical contrast between the young Chatterton and the old Leech Gatherer invites the speculation, I suggest, that the two men might also differ in other significant respects. Since Chatterton was a gifted poet, for example, and since he apparently represents for the Narrator living proof of the gloomy generalization that "We Poets in our youth begin in gladness; / But thereof come in the end despondency and madness" (48–49), it would follow with perfect logic that the old fellow by the pool, a man who is in other respects Chatterton's complete opposite, should turn out to be, if not despondent and mad, then at least virtually mute, as paralyzed verbally as he apparently is in all other physical respects.

The reader is surely as surprised as the Narrator, therefore, to find in the old man not just an individual of "firm . . . mind" but an enthusiastic and even eloquent speaker. The Narrator takes great pains not to allow us to miss this point. From the moment when the Leech Gatherer first responds to the Narrator's formulaic greeting, the old man's manner of speech is given particular emphasis:

A gentle answer did the old Man make,
In courteous speech which forth he slowly drew.
   [85–86]

His words came feebly, . . .
But each in solemn order followed each,
With something of a lofty utterance drest—
Choice word and measured phrase, above the reach
Of ordinary men; a stately speech; . . .
   [92–96]

Cheerfully uttered, with demeanour kind,
But stately in the main;
   [135–136]

And even after he has completed his description of their meeting, the same emphasis colors the Narrator's summary account of how the whole episode left him with three disquieting memories. That he should report having been impressed by "the lonely place" and by "[the] old Man's shape" is unremarkable; to these, however, the Narrator once again adds a special accent on the important contribution made not so much by the Leech Gatherer's story as by the manner of its delivery, by the old man's "speech" (127–128).

The Narrator repeatedly mentions the Leech Gatherer's eloquence in this way, I submit, because, coming when it does, that eloquence represents the best possible proof that it is not only those who die young, like the unfortunate Chatterton, who exercise lifelong power over language. The old man does demonstrate remarkable physical *perseverance* at his job; still more important, though, he manifests great *articulateness* in speaking of the need for such perseverance. His powers of speech have been affected only slightly—if at all—by age and by "the ways of men, so vain and melancholy" (21) that had earlier loomed as such daunting obstacles on the Narrator's own horizon.

And it is in this context that we can—finally—begin to account for one aspect of the markedly offbeat conversation between the Narrator and the Leech Gatherer that lies at the heart of this poem. For if one point of the Level 0 narrative in "Resolution and Independence" is to reveal how the old man, despite his advanced years, is capable of speaking with the verbal composure that he does, then his utterances will be remarkable on those grounds alone, regardless of the content that they express at Level 1. And so struck is the Narrator by the manner of the old man's speech (rather than by what he has to say) that, rather like a child with a talking teddy bear, he excitedly repeats his original discourse prompt so as to make the old man "perform" his utterance a second time. The fact that he has already heard (though not assimilated) the content of the answer that he then hears reiterated is fundamentally irrelevant, for, given his (admittedly unorthodox) interest in the old man's verbal performance, the standard emphasis in conversation on the exchange of information has been suspended in favor of a focus on the mode of its presentation.

J. Douglas Kneale (1986:356–359) offers a provocative examination of the "complex set of echoes" that connect the figure of the Leech Gatherer in "Resolution and Independence" with that of the Blind Beggar in Book 7 of *The Prelude*.[21] In that episode, Wordsworth describes how once, "far travelled in . . . a mood" of deep reflection (608), he was "[abruptly] . . . smitten with the view / Of a blind beggar" (611–612). When he learned "the story of the man, and who he was," he recalls,

My mind did at this spectacle turn round
As with the might of waters, . . .
And on the face of this unmoving man,
His fixèd face and sightless eyes, I looked,
As if admonished from another world.
     [616–617; 621–623]

The parallelisms between this story and the Leech Gatherer narrative leap from the page. Particularly interesting from the perspective of our analysis of the earlier poem, however, is the peculiar form taken by "the story of the man" in the episode from *The Prelude*. Speechless as well as blind, the London beggar tells his story by means of "a written paper" (614) or "label" (618) hung "upon his chest" (613).

On the one hand, Wordsworth is admittedly not concerned in this part of *The Prelude* as he is in "Resolution and Independence" with questions of fading poetic vision or failing poetic voice; neither Chatterton nor "We Poets" appear in the immediate context. On the other hand, though, it is certainly noteworthy that, in reporting here another instance of one individual's having been overwhelmed by his discovery of a complete stranger's life story, Wordsworth again treats that autobiography not as a sustained and internally complex narrative but as an unanalyzed whole, a "label" whose contents in this instance he does not even bother to repeat. While the Leech Gatherer's story, being spoken rather than written, cannot be so effectively conflated into a single physical object, it has been my contention in the preceding pages that the Narrator initially perceives it and responds to it in precisely that way, not so much listening to it as a *story* as marveling at the unexpected *label* that its style of delivery places on the teller.

Careful consideration of the nature of its narrative framing thus permits us to account for one of the two major problems that we encountered initially in our analysis of the discourse in "Resolution and Independence." For we may use the notion of narrative levels to tease apart two essentially complementary "points" to the story of the encounter with the Leech Gatherer. At Level 1 (see figure 9), the Leech Gatherer, reacting to the Narrator's inquiry, describes his life history in terms that the Narrator takes as an object lesson in the moral excellence of perseverance in the face of adversity. (I would certainly not wish to deny the importance of that relatively explicit theme in any reading of "Resolution and Independence.")[22] At the same time, though, by framing the Leech Gatherer's remarks within the broader context of a Level 0 narrative that also includes the prefatory material about Chatterton and the evanescence of poetic genius, the poem's Narrator employs them as a way to account for the newfound hope that displaces his initial despondency, since the mere fact of the old man's speech constitutes the strongest possible practical evidence that old age need not entail communicative paralysis. In the context of this, his second purpose, the Narrator's act of repeating his question becomes far less problematical, since it represents his attempt to verify the nature of that evidence, a "call for replay" directed not toward the content of the original but toward the mode of its verbal actualization.

We are not yet clear of the woods, however. For, though we now have an explanation for the Narrator's awkward repetition of his question about the old man's occupation, we have as yet found no way to rationalize the old man's good humor in the face of being treated like a clockwork toy by his nosy yet inattentive interlocutor. Conversational analysis, as we saw in chapter 2, would predict that this aberrant use of language should anger a participant like the Leech Gatherer who is not, after all, a party to the Narrator's unconventional agenda and should therefore be expecting that his contributions will be treated in the usual, "serious" way. The search for a solution to this second unorthodox aspect of the dialogue will take us off on another, altogether new tangent.

FOUR

"So whose story is this anyway?" The Elusive First-Person Narrator

In the tale, in the telling, we are all one blood.
Ursula Le Guin, "It Was a Dark and Stormy Night"

In the course of chapter 3, I pointed out one intriguing implication of my analysis of narrative framing in "The Ruined Cottage" to which it would have been inappropriate at that point to have devoted lengthy discussion: the relationship between the poet and his first-person Narrator. The Narrator in that poem, I noted, does not act in a way that, on the basis of other available evidence, we would regard as reflecting accurately Wordsworth's image of himself as a poet. Instead, it is Armytage who, despite the apparent discrepancy in their ages, fits the description of the young Wordsworth that appears, for example, in prose essays such as the Preface to *Lyrical Ballads*.

From a theoretical standpoint, this suggestion cannot be advanced lightly, for it assumes that readers may—and perhaps, for the richest possible reading, should—interpret a text in light of the historical and biographical context in which it was "uttered" (using that word in the legal sense, which does not restrict it to oral delivery alone). It implies that identifying the person who uttered the poem with a first-person narrator within the text, if one exists, is at most a preferred or default option, while other alignments are both possible and potentially detectable by its readers.

In order to explore in greater depth this implication of my earlier analysis (and indeed, others that flow from it), I need first to amend the simple formalism for narrative framing that I introduced in chapter 3 by adding two features that will enable it to reflect a higher degree of sophistication. In the first place, while I shall continue to designate as Level 0 the narrative level *within* any work for which no "higher," mediating narrative can be defined, I now propose to allow for the inclusion of additional frames, indexed with *negative* integers, to characterize broader discourse contexts within which the text as a whole is situated. In addition, I shall also attach alphabetic subscripts wherever they are appropriate to co-index narrators or auditors at one level with narrators, auditors or characters who appear at more deeply embedded levels of the narrative.[1] To illustrate how this augmented scheme works in practice, compare the representation of the narrative structure of "The Ruined Cottage" in figure 5 with the more informative figure 10.

It is immediately evident that this enhanced method of depicting narrative structure brings to the fore a number of formidable theoretical questions. What constraints govern the co-indexing of narrators or characters at various narrative levels? Are the negatively indexed (extra- or supratextual) levels inherently different in character from the positively indexed (intratextual) ones? Is there some limit, either pragmatically or theoretically determined, to the number of extratextual levels that a text may involve? I shall suggest partial answers to several of these questions later in this chapter and in chapter 5; let us, however, defer addressing them for the moment, so that we may first assess how useful the new apparatus proves in practice as a tool for analyzing a specific text.

H. M. Richmond's summary description of Shelley's "Ozymandias" (1962:65) as "a familiar and impressive poem" epitomizes the less than benign condescension bestowed upon it by many (perhaps even most) literary critics. Among the works of a poet most admired for his bold poetic experiments and red hot emotional fervor, the very strengths that make "Ozymandias" easily accessible to a broad readership have resulted in its having been virtually ignored in comprehensive critical studies of Shelley's poetry.[2]

Because it lacks the zealous indignation and ad hominem attacks of such political satires as "The Mask of Anarchy," for example, this text is often treated as their pale shadow, Shelley's fiery antiauthoritarian rhetoric muted either by the historical remoteness of his subject or by the restrictiveness of the sonnet form (see Janowitz 1984:488).[3] For other

Figure 10

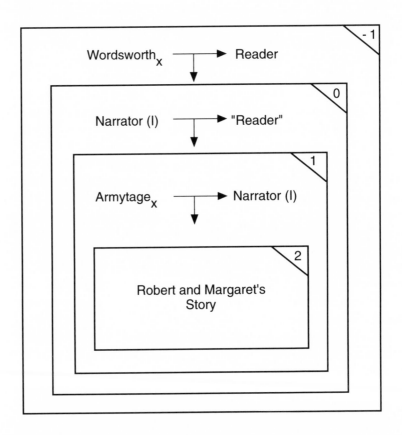

commentators, attracted to Shelley by the bold formal experimentation of "Lines Written among the Euganean Hills" or "Stanzas Written in Dejection," the only mildly unconventional rhyme scheme in "Ozymandias" appears a feeble gesture in the direction of aesthetic originality. Even the historical context in which the poem was written only contributes to its reputation for solid (even stolid) respectability. Composed as part of what seems to have been a poetic parlor game between Shelley and his good friend (but undistinguished poet) Horace Smith during the late autumn of 1817, "Ozymandias" belongs to that awkward period of personal insecurity—a period aptly characterized by Richard Holmes (1974:406) as one of "gloom and indecision" for Shelley—between the emotional drama of the court fight with Harriet for custody of their children and the equally traumatic decision to leave England for Italy in March 1818.

Even as a freestanding poetic composition, "Ozymandias" has played to very mixed reviews. Though Holmes (1974:410) calls it "the finest sonnet he ever wrote," W. Van Maanen (1949:123) places that plaudit in context by firmly reminding us that Shelley only wrote sixteen sonnets in his short lifetime. After all, Van Maanen continues, the poem contains many apparent flaws: "Its opening line is almost too prosaic; the eighth line is clumsy and obscure; some of the rhymes are false." Flanked in the corpus by *The Revolt of Islam* on the one hand and by "Julian and Maddalo" on the other, then, and apparently eclipsed by them both, "Ozymandias" has slipped virtually unchallenged into a quiet backwater of the poetic mainstream, constantly reanthologized by editors attracted to it precisely because it exemplifies Shelley's characteristic anti-monarchist views in a conveniently short work that also avoids the complexities of thought and style typical of many of the more critically acclaimed texts.[4]

For one persistent group of literary bloodhounds, it is true, "Ozymandias" has offered a continuing challenge. The scent they follow is laid in the very first line of the poem (the line that Van Maanen criticizes as "almost too prosaic"): "I met a traveller from an antique land." Led by J. Gwyn Griffiths in 1948, these literary historians have struggled in a series of notes, queries, remarks, and replies to pin down the identity of Shelley's unnamed "traveller."[5] Their discoveries, to which I shall return in greater detail later in this chapter, range from the intriguing and insightful to the wildly speculative. Without exception, though, their analyses remain coldly antiquarian, uninvolved with the passionate core of the sonnet as it is encountered by today's readers—readers who remain unaware, for the most part, of the intellectual and social history of early nineteenth-century England.

In the pages that follow, I shall draw on a few of the more valuable contributions to that debate about the identity of the Traveller, but I shall integrate those insights into an approach to the text that acknowledges and explores its complexity both as a narrative and as an alleged record of spoken discourse; and I shall motivate, through this analysis, a radical revision in our view of the overall thematic structure of "Ozymandias." That comprehensive reassessment will in turn, I believe, enable us to mitigate some of the harsher indictments of the text's apparent imperfections and to establish "Ozymandias" as a remarkably sophisticated and even daring poetic creation.

Let us first examine a passage that spans the poem's first and second quatrains, a passage often misinterpreted or misremembered even by those who, like Richmond, claim to have been "familiar" with it for many years:

> Near them, on the sand,
> Half sunk, a shattered visage lies, whose frown,
> And wrinkled lip, and sneer of cold command,
> Tell that its sculptor well those passions read
> Which yet survive, stamped on these lifeless things,
> The hand that mocked them, and the heart that fed.
> [3–8]

The verb *tell* that begins line 6 takes as its syntactic subject the several unattractive features of the "shattered visage" of Ozymandias's colossus: its "frown, / And wrinkled lip, and sneer of cold command." Since facial features (or *expressions*) such as these are normally taken to convey (or *express*) human emotions *(anger, sorrow, amusement)*, the reader might expect the direct object of *tell* in this context to enumerate some such emotions:

> These features *tell* (of) Ozymandias' disdain, contempt, pride. . . .

In fact, however, the syntactic direct object of *tell* consists of a clausal complement:

> These features "[tell] *that* its sculptor well those passions read
> Which yet survive. . . ."

Shelley focuses, that is, not on Ozymandias's emotions as such, but on their realization by an anonymous sculptor and, more particularly, on the striking effectiveness with which that rendition was accomplished.⁶ Not, of course, that Ozymandias's emotions are irrelevant, for they still appear syntactically as the preposed direct object of *read* in the clausal complement to *tell*. This leaves us, nevertheless, with a two-step rather than a one-step view of the statue's role in revealing Ozymandias's character (see figure 11).

Lest we miss this subtle shift in emphasis, Shelley manipulates the syntactic and semantic form of line 6 to foreground his concern with the pivotal position of the Sculptor. One formal linguistic array places the all-important, *semantically* complementary verbs of transmission (*tell* and *read*) at opposite ends of the line, bracketing the mention of the Sculptor himself (see figure 12), while, in a poem that makes heavy use of *rhyme*, both internally and line-finally (as for example with *land/stand/ sand/command/hand/Ozymandias/sands*), line 6 also divides neatly into five-syllable half lines, *tell* this time patterning with *well* to stress the excellence of the Sculptor's work (see figure 13). Yet another formal configuration depends on a balance which Shelley achieves by setting *metrically* congruent phrases denoting first the artist and then his subject on either side of the word that evaluates their successful collusion in the creative act (see figure 14). Close formal analysis of this crucial line reveals, in short, that it exhibits elaborate patterning at a variety of levels, all of which conspires to direct our attention as much to the active contribution of the artist in creating the statue as to the part played by Ozymandias in "sitting" for it.

We should also note in passing that, despite this passage's exclusive concern on its surface with the plastic art of monumental statuary, Shelley has chosen, in characterizing it, to employ vocabulary conventionally associated with verbal communication (*tell* and *read*) rather than either medium neutral terms such as *express, render,* or *convey* or

Figure 11

Figure 12

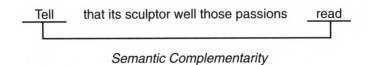

Semantic Complementarity

those specifically applied to the visual arts such as *depict, show,* or *portray.* We shall have reason to return to this observation a little later in our discussion.

A second striking feature of the long sentence that occupies lines 3–8 of this poem is the sharp contrast it sets up between two storyworlds. Shelley links line 6 with line 7, employing parallel metrical templates similar to those I isolated earlier within line 6 itself (see figure 14), this time with the purpose of inviting the reader to compare a chronologically distant but emotionally vibrant past with the more proximate but comparatively colorless present (see figure 15).[7]

Other linguistic features of the text again combine with the metrical congruence between these lines to highlight this important thematic distinction. On the one hand, Shelley's characteristic reliance on vivacity as a major evaluative criterion is reflected in crucial morphological choices; on the other, his emphatic use of deictic modifiers is evident not only in lines 6 and 7 but throughout the poem.

As an index of the importance of vivacity and lethargy as defining properties of the two contrasted eras, we may note that Shelley employs the suffix *-less* on just three occasions in this sonnet. In each instance, he

Figure 13

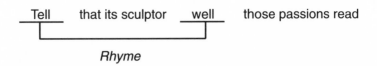

Rhyme

Figure 14

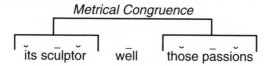

does so when describing the statue's ruined remnants (rather than its original magnificence), employing the morphologically marked form to stress the wreck's unlifelike, dismembered state and the aridity of its surroundings: "*trunkless* legs of stone" (2); "these *lifeless* things" (from the passage currently under consideration, line 6); and

> Round the decay
> Of that colossal wreck, *boundless* and bare
> The lone and level sands stretch far away.
>   [12–14]

This set of morphologically linked lexical items contrasts vividly with the language Shelley uses to describe the power and energy that he wants us to associate with the world of Ozymandias's empire, a world where individuals *frown, sneer,* and *mock;* where the *heart feeds* the *passions;*

Figure 15

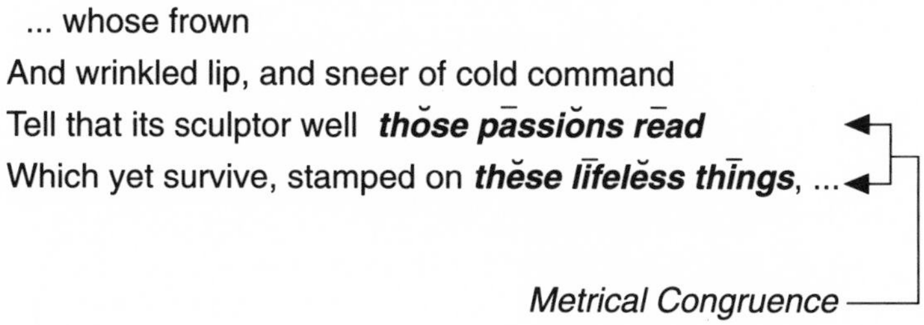

... whose frown
And wrinkled lip, and sneer of cold command
Tell that its sculptor well ***thŏse pāssiŏns rēad***
Which yet survive, stamped on ***thĕse līfelĕss thīngs***, ...

Metrical Congruence ————

and where, amidst all this activity, the most energetic deed of all is surely that of the Sculptor as he *stamps* his portrait of the dictator into heretofore "lifeless" stone.

Shelley also repeats the technique of using contrasting deictic demonstratives elsewhere in this sonnet after first introducing it in lines 6 and 7. He refers to the ruined statue as *"that* colossal wreck" (13) but to the inscription that "appears" on the pedestal as *"these* words" (9). In this particular instance, *these* may of course be read cataphorically, its referent then being the quoted material that immediately follows in lines 10 and 11:

<u>these</u>   words appear   "My name is Ozymandias. . . ."

That cataphoric reading must at least coexist, however, with a simpler deictic one *(these* words, *look, over here),* particularly in light of Shelley's far from obligatory use of the contrasting *that* (rather than *the*) to modify "colossal wreck" just four lines later. Even without this parallel emphasis on spatial deixis later in the text, though, the sheer weight of the poem's thematic emphasis on contrasting the glories of the past with the desolation of the present will inevitably predispose readers to associate the proximal deictic in line 5 temporally with the present storyworld, and the distal one in line 6 with the past.[8]

In lines 3 to 8 of "Ozymandias," to summarize, Shelley describes how the physical fragments of a time-ravaged statue can transmit, even in decay, the artistry of an earlier, more vital society to the denizens of a later, less spirited age. It is the artistic accomplishment of such "transmission," I stress again, at least as much as the spirit itself of that distant time, that the wreck conveys. While the passions have indeed "[survived] . . . / The hand that mocked them," that survival is expressed only as a rider to the testimony that provides the central focus for this sonnet: the speaker's recognition that the "sculptor well those passions read." The Sculptor's triumph results not from mere mechanical recreation, not from the journeyman fashioning of a waxworks dummy, but from an original act committed by an artist whose gift is to "read" and to "retell" rather than just to mimic his subject.[9] It is in this interplay between a text and an interpreter, implied by the reading metaphor, that what is most worth telling emerges; inevitably, too, it is the product of that same synthesis that alone survives to be read by those who later encounter the artifact outside the context of its original creation.

That Shelley should have advanced such a critique of the role of the artist will surprise nobody familiar with the views on poetic theory he expressed in his more famous theoretical works such as the *Defence of Poetry*. That the unnamed Sculptor should effectively usurp Ozymandias's place as the primary agent merely confirms, after all, the function of all artists as the true but "unacknowledged legislators" of worldly affairs. What I do wish to suggest by way of departure from such familiar ground is that it may be appropriate to reconsider from this perspective this particular text, a text whose very obvious political message has generally overshadowed its second (but hardly secondary) concern with the nature of artistic creativity.[10]

Despite Shelley's evident interest in both Ozymandias and the Sculptor, both of whom we identify with the storyworld of ancient Egypt, we cannot ignore the importance to this poem of a figure from a relatively later epoch, albeit not necessarily the poet's own: the nameless Traveller whose account of that "antique land" this poem purportedly reports. For, as a narrative work that involves framed discourse (see figure 16), "Ozymandias" resembles the poems I discussed in chapter 3 in that Shelley explicitly draws attention to the frame as well as to the "picture." My interpretation of the work as a whole will thus have to take into account this structural dimension and describe the contribution to its overall effect of each of its narrative levels.

As with "The Ruined Cottage," the presence of elaborate narrative machinery surrounding the core story of Ozymandias in this sonnet has not gone unnoticed by critics. In the words of Von Rainer Lengeler (1969:537), "Das Sonett baut sich im wesentlichen aus drei ineinandergeschachtelten Fiktionsebenen auf, die durch das Ich, den Reisenden und Ozymandias in der Rolle des Sprechenden bezeichnet werden." [The sonnet is constructed essentially out of three narrative layers boxed one within another, which are indicated by the I, the Traveller, and Ozymandias in the role of the speaker (my own translation).][11] In a similar vein, Spanos (1968:14) invites scholars to take up the challenge of establishing "why Shelley presents the tale . . . within the framework of a contemporary conversation and what artistic value is achieved by doing so," a

Figure 16

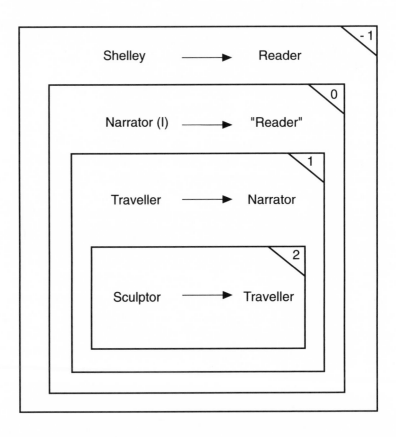

question that in his view represents a "very real interpretative and critical problem."

Most of those who have tackled this aspect of the text, however, have ignored Spanos's interest in *"artistic* value," concentrating instead on literary-historical detective work worthy of Hercule Poirot (see note 5). They have sought, that is, to discover the "true" identity of the shadowy Traveller mentioned in the first line of the poem, its Level 1 narrator. The full intricacies of their debate will rapidly tire those who attempt to follow its every twist and turn; nevertheless, the question at its center is, as we know from our own analyses of similar texts in chapter 3, far from trivial. Shelley's striking description of the statue of Ozymandias, after all, just like Wordsworth's account of Margaret's life and death, could easily have been written without any account of its origins in some chance meeting with its teller.[12] And to discern what part if any the Traveller plays in the way that the poem as a whole functions, it may be necessary to examine his background just as we did that of the peddler as the narrator of the core story in "The Ruined Cottage."

We may begin by noting that readers' views about the Traveller are inevitably affected by two other interpretive considerations: first, by whatever assumptions they make about the poem's Level 0 first-person Narrator; and, second, by the way in which they interpret that Narrator's assertion in line 1 that he "met" the Traveller. The influence of this network of interwoven conjectures is easily discernible behind the discussions that have appeared in the literature.

One major group of commentators who have attempted the task of identifying the Traveller, for example, take the Narrator to be Shelley himself and the verb *met* to have been intended literally. (Spanos's characterization of Ozymandias's story as occurring "within the framework of a *contemporary* conversation," cited earlier, places him for one among this group.) As a result of their presuppositions, these scholars have devoted their energies to associating the Traveller with some specific individual from late eighteenth- or early nineteenth-century Britain; nominees have included several members of Shelley's immediate circle and perhaps a half-dozen antiquarians and adventurers whose exploits the poet might plausibly have learned about from the press or by attending public lectures. Minutely examining the travelogues of their preferred candidates, adherents of this first school have championed the names of men such as Thomas Medwin (J. Gwyn Griffiths 1948:84) or Richard Pococke (Richmond 1962:68), the details of whose *prose* accounts might explain the precise combination of particulars that we find in Shelley's *poetic* rendition. Johnstone Parr (1957) even reproduces maps, line drawings and photographs of archaeological sites to amplify his discussion of their probable importance with regard to "Ozymandias."

A recurring problem for the members of this school is that the statue of Ramesses II, remnants of which lay scattered in the desert sand in

1817 and descriptions of which almost certainly provided the initial impetus for Shelley's poem, had been ill-treated by the elements. As Parr (1957:32) explains, "[in] Shelley's day the face . . . was so obliterated that no one could have discerned a 'frown,' a 'wrinkled lip,' or a 'sneer of cold command.'" No (literal) Traveller whom Shelley had (literally) met, that is, could (honestly) have included such details in his account of what he had (personally) seen.

A second group of scholars have successfully evaded this particular obstacle, arguing instead that the Traveller should in any case be seen as a figure whom the poet had "met" only in a literary sense. (We already noted, after all, that Shelley uses terms conventionally restricted to verbal communication [*tell* and *read*] later in the sonnet to describe processes that are in no sense linguistic; could we not see in his employment of *met* in line 1 the obverse case—a nonlinguistic term being used to describe what may in fact have been a literary rather than a face-to-face encounter?) Adopting this interpretation of *met* naturally enables these critics to enlarge very considerably the pool of candidates for the part of the Traveller.

One highly touted contender in this expanded field has been Diodorus Siculus ("Diodorus the Sicilian"), a Greek historian who lived during the first century B.C. and thus some twelve hundred years after the death of Ramesses.[13] In his world history, a work characterized by the *New Columbia Encyclopedia* as "uncritical and unreliable," Diodorus certainly describes the statue of Ozymandias in an unblemished, unweathered form—a form, that is, in which facial expression would have been easily discernible. He also mentions prominently a hubristic inscription on the pedestal, a feature that Shelley, of course, places at the climax of his sonnet. But significant problems also beset the theory that Diodorus "is" the Traveller. Most important, the disjoined legs and torso that Shelley's Narrator describes do not fit well with Diodorus's account of a "work of art" in which, "despite [its] great bulk, neither crack nor flaw can be seen" (Murphy 1964:63; see also J. Gwyn Griffiths 1948:84). Instead, the disposition of the "trunkless legs" and of the "shattered visage" partially buried in the sand stubbornly recalls those nineteenth-century travelers' reports of the "Ramesseum" adduced by Parr and his colleagues.

We appear, in short, to have reached an impasse. Neither Diodorus writing before Christ's birth nor some nineteenth-century European explorer can adequately fill the Traveller's shoes. The former, though in a position to report the presence of a "frown" or a "wrinkled lip," would have done so only in the context of a statue still intact (and, as a simple matter of historical fact, reported no such things). The latter would by all means have seen a wrecked statue eroded by the elements but would have found its half-buried head altogether devoid of identifying facial features.

This standoff would be troubling if we were committed to the view that "Ozymandias" simply represents a historical fragment addressed as a poetic cautionary tale to power-hungry European despots. "Lessons of history," after all, lose much of their impact when the reliability—indeed, the very existence—of the historian who supposedly recorded the original events is thrown into doubt. In the concise formulation of Ora Avni (1991:497), "firsthand accounts . . . owe their truth-value to the authors' direct knowledge of the facts . . . and [their] historiographical . . . force coincides . . . with their autobiographical force." As I suggested earlier, however, Shelley repeatedly invites his readers to detect a second thematic thread running through this poem in the form of his thoughtful probing of the complex role played by all "authors" (whether sculptors or, as we now see, historians) in relaying real-world events and characters. Reassessed in that context, our inability to locate the Traveller unambiguously in historical time need neither surprise nor frustrate us.

The Sculptor's acts of "reading" and of "retelling" the dictator's "passions," after all, have already distorted our view of the real Ozymandias. The Traveller, seeking to transform what he witnessed *visually* into words in order to (re-)transmit it *narratively,* faces a challenge of at least equal magnitude and cannot possibly avoid some measure of partiality and subjectivity in his own act of transmission. Even if as a specific individual he turns out to be historically elusive, therefore, we shall in fact be no worse off than we were before, for the representational accuracy of our picture of the historical truth was fatally compromised as soon as the Sculptor first placed his chisel against the block of stone.

The defiantly fictive character of the Level 1 narrator in this poem thus reemphasizes the equally inherent artificiality of its entire narrative superstructure. By drawing attention to that artificiality, Shelley enables his poem to achieve a double effect: we may—indeed, we should—both note and learn from the ironic contrast between Ozymandias's vainglorious boasting and the ignoble fate of the colossus he ordained, but in so doing, as Shelley also insists that we recognize, we will be uncritically assuming that all of the intervening artists who reported either the tyrant's deeds or his appearance (whether verbally or visually) "read" their respective subjects "well." Absent such faithfulness to their originals, the poem veers from historical *exemplum* to mere fable across a dividing line that is at best blurred and at worst completely nonexistent.

The argument just concluded may seem to some to depend too heavily on a literal-minded and picayune attempt to reconstruct the background of a figure, the Traveller, whom Shelley mentions only briefly, after all, and in an essentially prefatory sentence. I believe I already met this objection in part. Spanos's call for some rational, aesthetic explanation of why Shelley should have included that framing discourse in the sonnet at all coincides with my own more general hypothesis developed in chapter 3 that readers expect all frames in narrative poetry to serve some nontransparent function (see also note 12 in this chapter), but we could not hope to have arrived at such an explanation of the function of the poem's "framework of . . . conversation" without first establishing some apparently basic information about the identities of the participants.

Happily, our examination of that issue has now shown that the enigmatic presence of the Traveller as the Level 1 narrator in this sonnet foreshadows the more central (but no less confusing) role played by the Sculptor at Level 2. Each represents a link in the chain of transmission by virtue of which alone we have any glimpse of Ozymandias's character; each, furthermore, would most probably have been taken completely for granted, had not Shelley subtly thrown their trustworthiness into question. In this function as a virtual doppelgänger for the Sculptor, then, the Traveller fully deserves the space that we have devoted to his delineation.

This still leaves, however, the problem of accounting for the presence in the poem of the other participant at Level 1, the Level 0 first-person Narrator—and the related problem of determining *his* identity. These, again, are not minor considerations, since, as I remarked earlier, assumptions we make about the identity of the Level 0 Narrator themselves interact in important ways with our determination of who the Traveller may (or may not) be.

Thus far, although we have considered two conceivable interpretations of the verb *met* (the literal and the literary), we have left unquestioned the supposition that the "I" who speaks in line 1 is the historical Percy Bysshe Shelley. To put it more formally, everything we have said so far assumed that "Shelley" at Level -1 and "Narrator" at Level 0 in figure 16 should be co-indexed. This was scarcely a radical assumption to have made, given the history of the scholarship surrounding "Ozymandias." As Spanos (1968:15) notes, *all* the contributors to the debate about the identity of the Traveller outlined earlier in this chapter take as given "the conventional equation of author and speaker." In light of our experiences with "The Ruined Cottage," though, *we* might choose to be rather more skeptical, refusing to accept without closer study that this initially plausible and natural "equation" should necessarily hold sway throughout our reading (and subsequent rereadings) of this or any other poem. In company with Spanos, we should perhaps accept the challenge to adduce some "authentic artistic function" (14) for the first-person narrator in "Ozymandias," whether that function involves interpreting the narrator as Shelley himself or not.

Spanos's own approach relies upon the wide temporal and cultural gulf that separated an audience of Shelley's contemporaries from the historical figure of Ozymandias/Ramesses II. He proposes that the text's "I" is not Shelley *in propria persona* but a figure loosely representative of nineteenth-century European civilization. The Traveller, he argues, represents the very different culture of the ancient Middle East. By means of the account that he gives of Ozymandias, Spanos then suggests, the Traveller hopes to induce the Narrator to apply lessons learned from the collapse of another once dominant civilization to the similarly precarious plight of his (the Narrator's) own. This stimulating interpretation assumes, in short, that each narrative level in the poem is autonomous and that the Level 0 Narrator is not to be co-indexed with Shelley at Level -1 (or, for that matter, with any other speaker at any other level within the text).

I myself prefer a somewhat different approach that combines Spanos's useful skepticism regarding the transparency of Shelley's Narrator with some inferences from a striking feature of the original text of Diodorus's "uncritical and unreliable" tome—a feature that has, as far as I can tell, been passed over by all previous commentators. For a close examination of Diodorus's world history reveals that *even he* never saw with his own eyes the ruins of the Ramesseum that he so carefully described for posterity. *Even Diodorus* only repeated at second hand a description he had himself culled from the pages of a prior Greek chronicler, Hecataeus (or Hekataios) of Abdera, who had written two centuries before him: "And it is not only the priests of Egypt . . . who corroborate what we have said, but also many of the Greeks who traveled to Thebes in the days of Ptolemy . . . and who wrote books on Egyptian history: Hecataeus is one of these. Now Hecataeus tells us that ten stades from the oldest tombs . . . there stands a monument to the king named Osymandias [*sic*]" (Murphy 1964:62 and n.99). Earlier in this discussion, I pointed out that no contemporary of Shelley's could reliably have reported on the frown, lip, and sneer so central to our understanding of the importance of the statue that appears in his sonnet. Now, however (by his own confession, so to speak), even Diodorus forfeits his eligibility for that honor, leaving the shadowy Hecataeus as the only historically attested firsthand witness.[14]

But if Hecataeus is the Traveller (and setting on one side momentarily the previously outlined problem that, in Shelley's poem, the statue is described as a ruin), then might not the first-person Narrator ("I") be Diodorus, the whole poem representing, so to speak, a freewheeling versified paraphrase of Diodorus's own text? (I find it, at the very least, tantalizing that Diodorus's thumbnail sketch of Hecataeus should refer to him as one of the "Greeks who *traveled* to Thebes . . . and wrote books.") Or again, in the most radical interpretation yet, could we not posit as the poem's Narrator an unnamed contemporary of Hecataeus, a Greek citizen of the *third* century B.C., who could literally have "met" Hecataeus and heard what he "said" as *neither* Diodorus *nor* Shelley could?

It appears, in short, that we need to place alongside the complex *narrative* structure that we have already discerned within the text of this sonnet and formalized in figure 16 an account of the *historical* transmission of its raw material at least as complex as that shown in figure 17.[15]

What finally threatens to bog down even the most dogged investigator, however, is the extraordinary variety of ways in which the intratextual roles labeled *Shelley, Narrator,* and *Traveller* in figure 16 could potentially be aligned with any one of several workable combinations of *Shelley, Diodorus,* and *Hecataeus* in figure 17—with or without a supporting cast of unnamed extras from assorted historical eras:

Figure 17

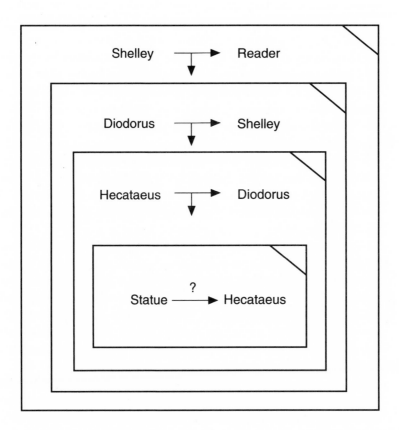

- The historical Shelley might, for example, be both the author of the whole text at Level −1 and the Narrator at Level 0 (the default assumption described earlier). If so, then candidates for the Traveller, as we have seen, include Diodorus, Hecataeus, or one of Shelley's contemporaries.
- If, however, Shelley's participation is restricted to Level −1 alone, and if Diodorus speaks as "I" at Level 0, then Hecataeus remains, on the grounds of Diodorus's reference to him in his historical study, a strong candidate for the Traveller's spot at Level 1.
- But if, to take just one more permutation, the Level 0 Narrator is some anonymous third-century Greek citizen to whom Hecataeus tells his story

(before subsequently setting it down in his own words in his prose history of the ancient world), then Diodorus is bypassed altogether in the chain of narrative transmission described in the poem (though not, of course, from the real-world sequence of narrators that lies behind the text).

Let me stress at this point that none of these speculations invalidates the conclusions that I already reached about the identity of the Traveller in this poem (or, more precisely, about his lack of a single, discrete identity). No proliferation of research into possible historical sources for the Narrator, however subtle, can overcome the fundamental obstacle to any unified historical account of the Traveller: that is, that, in order to have reported as he does, a historical Traveller would have to have lived at a time when the statue of Ramesses had disintegrated but was not yet featureless, whereas in actual fact no such time has been recorded.

But my intention in spelling out in such detail the constantly multiplying uncertainties that pervade every level of this text was never, in any case, to pursue some magical resolution of that paradox. Instead, I sought to highlight what Shelley himself must certainly have been aware of, whether he had read Diodorus's history in the original or in one of its translations (see note 13): namely, that his sonnet repeated yet again a story whose roots lay over two thousand years in the past and whose previous tellers had served at best as well-intentioned transmitters of what they might or might not have believed to represent some original "reality."

While Spanos uses the doubt that he casts on the traditional equation of Shelley with the Narrator to broaden the impact of this poem's *political* message, then, I am advocating that the lack of a well-focused "I" in this sonnet can also be seen as reinforcing Shelley's *literary* theme of the inevitability of slippage in renarrations of history and the importance of recognizing the creative dimension inherent in what too often and too easily passes for objective reportage.

This technique works as effectively as it does, of course, because, as in the opening lines of Tennyson's *Ulysses*, Shelley's use of the first-person perspective provokes readers to speculate about a speaker somewhere outside the text. In the words of M. A. K. Halliday and R. Hasan (1976:48, as cited in Toolan 1990:132), "a third person form typically refers anaphorically to a preceding item in the text. First and second person forms do not normally refer to the text at all; their referents are defined by the speech roles of speaker and hearer, and hence they are normally interpreted exophorically, by reference to the situation." But once readers have committed themselves, even provisionally, to a particular interpretation for the "I" whose voice they hear as the sonnet begins, they inevitably go on to define the Traveller within that context. When the Traveller then turns out to be contextless, the logic that defined him in the first place is similarly discredited and the "I" too becomes suspect.[16]

If one goal of the octave of this sonnet is to cast doubt, albeit indirectly and inexplicitly, on the whole concept of narrated or re-presented history, then that theme (just like the ironic political theme that parallels it) comes to a head in its sestet. In a poem in which time has begun to seem almost infinitely flexible and in which secondhand knowledge is apparently the best that one can hope for, the quotation marks that herald Ozymandias's boastful inscription, "My name is Ozymandias" seem to offer a welcome foothold. Direct quotation, after all, enjoys a very special status in narration. At least in contemporary anglophone North American culture (see Tannen 1989:106) and in the absence of any indications to the contrary, direct quotation is widely presumed to preserve perfectly the linguistic shape of its original—including even such inherently relative, and thus vulnerable, features as tense, modality, deixis, and pronominal reference. In Marianne Shapiro's words (1984:74), the primary aim of rendering material as direct speech is so that "the speech act [may be] faithfully recorded" (see also Chatman 1978:167). And as if to foster this particular prejudice in the context of this particular poem, Shelley surprisingly abandons his previously prominent vocabulary of verbal transmission; neither *told* nor *read,* the words of this inscription merely "appear."

Whoever "I" is in this text, therefore, and *whoever* the Traveller may be, are not the words on the pedestal, literally "carved in stone," immune to the weathering effects of both meteorological and narrative storms? As a relieved Lengeler (1969:536) suggests, "[wir hören] nun . . . Ozymandias selber sprechen" (we now hear Ozymandias himself speaking [my own translation]).[17] To put the same point schematically, we may now evidently replace figure 17 with figure 18, in which the dashed line up the right-hand side represents a narrative "escape hatch" that gives the

Figure 18

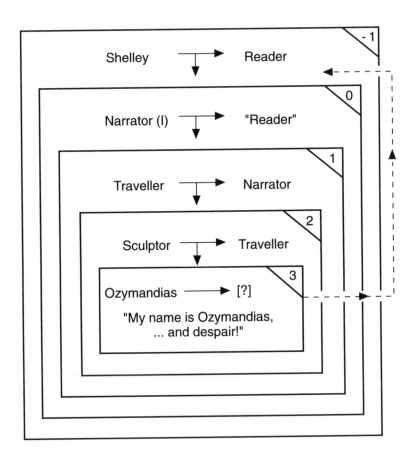

poem's real reader at Level − 1 direct and privileged access to the content of Ozymandias's discourse even though that discourse lies embedded a full four levels below it in the text.

If J. Gwyn Griffiths (1948:80) is correct, the editors of *Palgrave's Golden Treasury* were the first to hint at the fatal flaw in the preceding argument when they noted that "if the inscription was in hieroglyphics, it would have been unintelligible in Shelley's time, the key being only found by Champollion in 1822" (in the form, of course, of his decipherment of the Rosetta Stone inscriptions). Their observation does not mean that the carved legend reported by Shelley in "Ozymandias" is a fraud, the literary equivalent of the Piltdown Man, for Diodorus's and Hecataeus's Greek-language accounts represent perfectly logical intervening steps by which Ozymandias's words had been rendered fully "intelligible" to Shelley's contemporaries. But what should give us pause is the realization that the material "quoted" in lines 10 and 11 of Shelley's "Ozymandias" has been translated twice, once from hieroglyphics into Greek and then again from Greek into English.

A common linguistic convention is at work here whose effects may be discerned in many different kinds of discourse. In *Story and Discourse,* Chatman (1978:167) observes that in any "quoted dialogue, [a] necessary assumption is that someone has transcribed the speech of the characters." But more recent theorists have suggested that narratives that invoke two or more mutually unintelligible languages may require of the reader considerably more sophisticated "assumptions."

Applying the work of Voloshinov and Bakhtin to everyday conversational narratives, for example, Tannen (1989:99) shows how "even seemingly 'direct' quotation is really 'constructed dialogue,' that is, primarily the creation of the speaker rather than the party quoted" (see also Triki 1991:78–79). She chooses as one of her key examples a narrative in which one can assert with absolute confidence that the narrator's "report" of words that he attributes to his mother have been "constructed" in this way, since he frames the entire narrative in English even though his mother is exclusively Spanish-speaking (112). "Silent" translation is also common, as Michael Flynn (personal communication) has reminded me, in journalistic practice. Clark and Gerrig (1990:792n) cite a particularly amusing instance in which the *Oakland Tribune* claimed to be reporting " '*exactly* what his holiness, Pius X, said . . . to a delegation of the Union of Italian Catholic Ladies' " (my italics) but then proceeded to offer only an English rendition of what must in fact have been a speech in Italian.

It is equally simple, of course, to find appropriate examples in literary discourse. In discussing how we read the first line of Robert Browning's "Andrea del Sarto" ("But do not let us quarrel any more"), Eric Griffiths (1989:24) notes that we inevitably do so "within the fiction that Andrea del Sarto . . . is speaking not the English verse we read but Italian prose" (see also Clark and Gerrig 1990:798–799). Repeatedly, therefore, and in many different circumstances, we accept the tacit intrusion of (presumably reliable) translators as links in the chain of narrative transmission.

Shelley's use of quotation marks in this particular passage seduces the reader initially, then, both because it plays to our natural bias to "assume that when quotations are attributed to others, the words thus reported represent more or less what was said" (Tannen 1989:108) and because, even if we do notice the discrepancy in the languages involved, we will tend to accept that license as an inevitable and probably insignificant byproduct of describing informally the discoveries of classical archaeologists. His sleight of hand is all the more effective, furthermore, because of the various instabilities we have encountered in the preceding nine lines and our consequent yearning for some firm ground on which to plant our feet.

In the case of "Ozymandias," though, our trust in those general conventions is seriously misplaced, for the legend reported by Diodorus has *not* been faithfully translated into English; it has instead been quite significantly rephrased. Someone, in fact, has taken the decidedly cryptic words recorded by Diodorus ("if anyone wishes to know how mighty I am and where I lie, let him surpass any of my works" in Edwin Murphy's scholarly translation) and fashioned a far more morally tendentious and doom-laden text: "Look on my works, ye Mighty, and despair!" If we pause to listen, of course, the voice that we recognize here is that employed by Shelley himself in such rabble-rousing verses as "The Mask of Anarchy" or "Men of England" and not that of some musty history book.[18] While Shelley has borrowed from his sources both the fact that an inscription appeared at all on the base of the statue of Ramesses and the references in that inscription to the *mighty* and to their *works,* his use of quotation marks is dangerously misleading if viewed from a strictly "historical" standpoint. Where the external discourse markers most insistently assert historical accuracy, in fact, Shelley has inveigled his most unmistakably Shelleyan presence.[19]

The sense of disorientation that this discovery can produce results in part, I suggest, from the initially objective tone of the Level 0 narrative. In the opening line of the poem, after all, Shelley's Narrator insists on "reading into the record" the source for his narrative; the physical description he then repeats seems at first dry and factual; and he gives little evidence of evaluating the material he rehearses from any interested perspective. Taken together, such considerations naturally incline one toward reading this text not only as literature but also as a sample of "scholarly writing." And in that genre, as Clark and Gerrig (1990:800) observe, "the Western convention at least is to quote other written work verbatim." When the unbroken line of verbatim repetition that the quotation marks seem to imply can*not* be confirmed by consulting the sources available to us (as they were also to Shelley and to his contemporaries), it is our sense of genre that is undermined, for Shelley forces us at that point to recategorize his poem as wholly imaginative, rather than partially scholarly, writing.

Once our confidence in the accuracy of the inscription has been shaken, matters deteriorate rapidly. The famous opening words of that inscription, like the first line of the poem itself, are couched in the first person: *"My* name is Ozymandias." Who, we now ask, is this speaker who indulges in the fundamental discourse act of self-naming? We have mounting evidence that his authenticity as a historical figure—and thus the literal veracity of the words ascribed to him—rests on the shakiest of foundations. Nor is our incertitude in that regard much allayed when we pause to picture the entire scene that Shelley describes. The legend appears, after all, on a plinth that supports nothing even remotely resembling a human speaker. We see only "two vast . . . legs of stone"; the head, with its organs essential to both language and speech, lies some way off, "half sunk." The closer we look, in fact, the harder it becomes to discern who could possibly be "speaking" here.

A still more baffling challenge is posed by the second line of the reported inscription. "Look on my works, . . . and despair," the speaker commands. If the previous line's act of self-naming failed for lack of a well-defined speaker, the peremptory imperative in this one creates problems at least as great by referring to "works" that the reader (or, for that matter, the "Mighty") may find it hard to locate in any physical context that the poem depicts. A critic interpreting the poem along traditional lines would observe, of course, that Shelley's point lies precisely in the fact that "[nothing] beside remains"; Ozymandias's bombast collapses because, in the absence of any "works" to be "looked on," his command reveals itself as a fatally flawed speech act, an infelicitous directive that nobody can possibly fulfill. But such an approach neglects the fact that at least one "work" of Ozymandias does remain; the statue itself, ruined though it may be, is still available for inspection. Perhaps, then, Ozymandias's claim to a lasting legacy is not entirely groundless, even if what survives is a comparatively unimpressive and crumbling monument that hardly corresponds to our picture of a "King of Kings."

By what right, however, are we now counting the colossus as one of *Ozymandias's* "works"? I argued early in this chapter that Shelley's discourse and syntactic strategies in the octave of this poem all emphasize to the contrary that credit for the statue should instead accrue to the Sculptor who fashioned it. At first blush, it may seem preposterous now to extend that argument and to suggest that it is therefore the Sculptor who, as the first-person speaker of line 11, invites us to look on *his* works. Such a skeptical reaction to this proposal is perfectly natural and closely allied to our earlier, equally intuitive resistance to the suggestion that the Narrator of the entire sonnet might not in fact be Shelley himself. Yet we have already established that the Sculptor, in an important though nonobvious sense, did "utter" the words that appear here in quotation marks. And the more one considers this new possibility, the more grounds one finds for retaining it, at least as one of several possible readings of the line. For while each of the narrators featured in our hypothetical chain of transmission had some hand in shaping the words that we read today, the Sculptor, as first in line, wielded particularly significant power with regard to their content.

We can never know, in short, what Ozymandias actually said if and when he commissioned this statue; we read a copy of a copy of a copy of words he only may have spoken. For all we can tell, Ozymandias never authorized either the monument or the text beneath it; those words could just as easily represent an original contribution of the Sculptor's own devising, concocted either with or without the pharaoh's blessing and by no means necessarily reflective of the "true" character of the historical Ramesses II. Like every amanuensis from Moses on the mountaintop to Boswell, in effect, the Sculptor basks in the almost boundless trust of his readers that he will present them with an accurate transcription. Yet that trust is logically groundless; it ignores the fact that all texts are to some extent the creations of literary artists and thus subject to interpretation as literary discourses, a fact that Shelley allows his seemingly historical sonnet to expose.[20]

Let us take stock. I have argued that, in the octave of "Ozymandias," Shelley employs various techniques to throw into question the historicity of ostensibly historical narratives in general and the identities of the individual historians involved in relaying the story of Ozymandias in particular. In the sestet, he presents, as if it were a direct quotation, an utterance that, we subsequently realize, must at the very least have undergone translation on two separate occasions. This discovery then constitutes the first of a series of speculations about that "quotation" that depend on the recognition of significant slippage in several areas:

   i. If the inscription has indeed been translated, then might it not have been "shaded" in translation (our suspicions on this point being reinforced by the strikingly Shelleyan tenor of line 11)?

  ii. If the words set down in these lines are indeed quoted, then by whom were they "originally" spoken (the colossus itself being, after all, headless and inanimate)?

 iii. Even if they were once appropriately uttered, are they not now completely infelicitous (no significant "works" remaining to be "looked on" save the statue itself)?

 iv. If the speaker in line 11 is referring to the statue (whether ruined or intact) when he speaks of "my works," then is it not as reasonable to identify him with the Sculptor as it is to associate him with Ozymandias (a conclusion which, as we have seen, would jibe well with the emphasis in the octave on the Sculptor's role in fashioning the statue's final form)?

Collectively, this array of troubling questions effectively seals off the narrative "escape hatch" I had hypothesized in figure 18. We are forced to recognize that we have no privileged access to Ozymandias's words and are firmly reminded of the autonomous power of *each* level's narrator in recasting the story that he also transmits.[21]

We may rely on this radical reanalysis of "Ozymandias" to isolate a previously unnoticed nuance to the biting irony of its sestet, for in devastating Ozymandias's kingdom, time has added insult to injury. The pharaoh's imperial achievements, it now becomes clear, have been significantly outlasted by a sculptural creation ultimate credit for which rests not even with him but with one of his subjects. Whatever the erstwhile glories and accomplishments of this "King of Kings," we now know him by name alone, while it is the *un*named Sculptor's "works" (if any) that truly "survive" and his skill as a master of his craft that the Traveller appraises. In a very real sense, the Sculptor's "hand" has "mocked" the pharaoh, exploiting the extraordinary power that all acts of narration and quotation confer to hurl the tyrant's boastfulness (whether ever verbalized or not) back in his face.

Significantly, the carved inscription, hardly the aspect of a sculptor's work that we would isolate as displaying his greatest skill, has survived time's ravages better than the directly representational, purely sculptural parts of the work; the precious but precarious act of "telling" operates most effectively, we may infer, in the medium of language to which it bears a direct, rather than only a metaphorical, relation. For even if the letters of a verbal message stamped in stone become worn and chipped, as long as the abstract linguistic form that they represent can be discerned, their repetition (or effectively re-creation) by anyone who reads them will miraculously restore them to mint condition. "Trunkless legs" and "shattered visages," in contrast, can only very inadequately suggest the richness of detail that characterized the original.[22] Once again, in fact, we run up against the peculiar and magical power of quotation and of verbal narration to refresh and to refashion what it seems only to repeat.[23]

But we should not forget the apt characterization by the twentieth-century poet Robinson Jeffers of all sculptors as *"foredefeated /* Challengers of oblivion" ("To the Stone-Cutters," lines 1–2; my italics). A time had of course to come (in historical terms, indeed, has now come and gone) when *both* the ruined statue, as yet "half-sunk" in Shelley's poem, *and* the inscription would be completely submerged, the "lone and level sands" consuming them as they had already consumed whatever else once occupied the site. Only Shelley's poetic account of what they both once "told" will escape that process of physical decay. And this observation in turn brings us back one last time to the realization that the words we read in lines 10 and 11 of "Ozymandias" are still in the final analysis the nineteenth-century utterance of Percy Bysshe Shelley.

As before, this observation runs counter to our intuitions; we want to believe, with Halliday (1989:34) that quotation marks within a text serve to "ascribe some part of [that] text to someone *other than the writer*" (my italics; see also Toolan 1990:75). In fact, though, this is simply not so; to reiterate Tannen's point (1989:4), "language framed as dialogue is always constructed dialogue, a creation for which *the [current] speaker* bears full responsibility and credit" (see also Smith 1981:215). Or as Le Guin (1981:195) mischievously says of an old Plains Indian ghost story that she recounts: "It [is] told to you forty years later by the ten-year-old who heard it . . . by the campfire, on a dark and starry night in California; and . . . she heard it told in English by an anthropologist of German antecedents. But by remembering it he made the story his; and insofar as I have remembered it, it is mine; and now, if you like it, it's yours."[24]

This perspective still further complicates the many ways in which we can read Shelley's sonnet. I have no wish, certainly, to dispute that it greatly enriches our appreciation of this poem to hold in balance distinct readings of line 11 in which the first-person speakers are respectively Ozymandias and the Sculptor; the first supports Shelley's rendition of the familiar motif "sic transit gloria mundi," while the second, as we have seen, reapplies that moral more narrowly, stressing that the power of art (and particularly of verbal art) far exceeds that of empire. But the unavoidable fact of the matter is that Shelley himself also utters the words quoted in lines 10 and 11 (emending and versifying them as he does so); the lines that precede and follow them incontrovertibly represent *his* [Shelley's] "works"; and the reapplication of that boastful taunt in the immediate historical context surrounding Shelley's composition of the poem in 1817 yields its own insights. We realize, for example, that, at Level −1, Shelley has turned the material he inherited from various sources to his own ends, injecting into them his own vehemence and conviction. And in the resounding call to "Look on my works, ye Mighty, and despair," we detect a note that certainly rings true as the defiant and derisive gesture of the rebellious young poet in the face of the rebuffs he had experienced in 1817 at the hands of judicial authority, moral respectability, and conservatism.

In *English Romanticism: The Human Context*, Gaull devotes chapter 7 ("Inventing the Past") to examining the attitudes of romantic authors and poets toward history in general and more especially toward the physical evidence of ancient civilizations that was then coming to light. Like contemporary antiquarians, she notes, many literary figures of the period regarded "remnants" merely as convenient, suggestive bases for Platonic idealizing about Hellenic culture. No less a figure than Johann

Winckelmann, chief supervisor of antiquities to the Vatican, felt free to weave a mythology of "good, healthy, youthful gods . . . in rhapsodic essays based on paintings and statues he had never seen or, at best, had seen only in copies" (189). At the same time, however, many other "romantic writers and painters . . . recognized that they had power over the past, that they were responsible for the history they were creating" (176). Some of the best work of the period thus "turned history into art" rather than the reverse.

What sets "Ozymandias" in a class by itself, I suggest, is the skill with which Shelley manages to reflect both of these logically antithetical trends at the same time in a work of such limited scope as a sonnet. In an intellectual context where even the driest scholars regarded blatant speculation on scant physical evidence as perfectly proper, one can scarcely blame Shelley for having appropriated the story of Ozymandias and capitalized on its potential for promoting his own social and political beliefs. At the very same time that he is carrying off that task, however, he also exploits narrative framing and a highly developed sensitivity to the dynamics of direct quotation to draw our attention to the many pragmatic assumptions that make such appropriation possible in the first place.

By framing his account of the desert scene in a conversational context, to be precise; by underdefining that context in such a way as to invite (ultimately fruitless) speculation about its participants; by subtly redirecting readers' attention away from the statue's original and toward its creator; by placing at the poem's climax a "direct quotation" that thoughtful reflection inevitably reveals as less than word for word; and, finally, by twice employing first-person utterances in contexts that seem at first transparent yet ultimately develop troubling opacities—by all these means, Shelley injects into his poem a theme that both depends on and undercuts the political one. "Caveat lector," he warns; narratives, even those that ostensibly relate historical and autobiographical material, are still texts created by their authors in ways that fatally compromise their own historicity.[25]

Though we can—and, for Shelley's dual perspective to work its full effect, *must* —continue to read the political message off the sad plight of Ozymandias's fallen empire, in short, the contradictions, paradoxes, and elusiveness introduced by the multiple narrative frames prevent us from doing so without constant doubt and self-questioning. Like a skilled magician who can perform a trick, explain to his audience how he performed it, and then repeat the same feat in a way that still leaves them baffled, Shelley invites us to infer the "obvious" Level 3 moral while insistently pointing out the inherently abuse-prone technical contortions, even distortions, that make it possible.

This far-reaching reanalysis of "Ozymandias" fulfills, I submit, the text-specific objective that I set forth at its outset—that is, to establish the sonnet's claim to legitimacy as a complex and mature work in the Shelley canon. It also serves my broader goals for this essay as a whole, however, for in presenting it, I depended on several of the expanded strategies related to narrative framing that I had introduced in the opening pages of this chapter. It proved helpful, for instance, to take into consideration narrative levels more inclusive than those discernible strictly within the confines of the text, treating the poet himself as the Level -1 narrator very much on a par with the narrators at more deeply embedded levels. Much of the subsequent discussion revolved around the feasibility of co-indexing narrators at different levels; in this particular case, I concluded, such co-indexing was not only possible but could be accomplished in any number of ways on whose interpretive incompatibility Shelley capitalizes as one of several sources of textual uncertainty. And I made extensive use of the still wider historical context surrounding the poem in the form of the trail laid by Hecataeus and pursued by Diodorus and his translators.

Intriguingly, all of these added dimensions to the analysis in no sense narrowed my interpretive conclusions. Toolan (1990:143) cites Brown and Yule (1983:50) as alleging that "[the] more co-text there is, the more secure the interpretation is." He notes, however, that "one needs to add the proviso that new text can function to *un*ravel the sense woven by preceding text." "Ozymandias" would seem to be a case in point; the additional insights facilitated by discourse and narrative analysis do enrich our understanding of the poem, but they do so by adding to our awareness of its complexity and by resisting any absolute, deterministic reading. This is equally true, I now want to suggest, if we apply the same methods to "Resolution and Independence."

At the end of chapter 3, I suspended my analysis of that text having proposed one possible explanation for the Narrator's reiterated question "How is it that you live, and what is it you do?" The key to understanding that particular discourse anomaly, I suggested, lay in recognizing the function of the conversation *as a whole* in the framing narrative of the despondent Narrator's hike across the moors. The form of the dialogue that we encounter in that poem's closing stanzas, I argued, is not controlled exclusively by the conventions of natural everyday speech, for the entire exchange also forms part of an evolving narrative argument at Level 0 in which the Narrator interprets the Leech Gatherer's "lofty utterance" as proof that his own poetic powers will not necessarily atrophy with age as he had earlier feared and he asks the old man to speak again in part because he wants to reassure himself by hearing that proof reconfirmed.

As I noted at the end of that discussion, however, this account leaves unexplained the unruffled calm with which the Leech Gatherer accepts his unorthodox treatment at the hands of the Narrator and his willingness to repeat his reply. The poem does not slide into its abrupt conclusion, after all, immediately after the Narrator's second *inquiry;* considerable space is instead devoted to the old man's second *answer* even though we (unlike the hapless Narrator) presumably kept adequate track of his first response and thus do not need so close a paraphrase. Apparently Wordsworth himself regarded this last turn of talk as a significant part of his text, and Ann Rigney (1992:271) argues that readers will most probably do so too, since "[the] fact that [a given utterance by a character] is placed at the end of the narrative sequence defines it as the resolution of the complicating action . . . and the telos of the narrative." An adequate interpretation of the poem should therefore provide some account of it.

Such an account, incidentally, is no less necessary if one adopts an analysis of the Narrator's motivation in repeating his question that differs completely from my own. Toolan (personal communication) suggests, for example, that the Narrator's duplication of his request stems from his perception of a "[discourse] context change" triggered by the Leech Gatherer's "lofty" first reply, the *"more*-than-foreseen adequacy" of which startles him into revising his estimation of the kind of discourse he is involved in. The Narrator now sees the old man as a figure of "wisdom, [as] a guide," Toolan argues, rather than as a mere stranger met with by chance, and he therefore elects to start the conversation over again on that basis.

This justification for the Narrator's unorthodox decision to ask a second discourse-initiating question seems to me every bit as promising as my own, but it furnishes no explanation of why the Narrator should go about that task in the odd way that he does. Surprised by the need to follow the old man's lead from a more phatic type of discourse to a more substantive one, could not the Narrator have found a less exceptionable way to proceed than by bluntly rephrasing his previous query? Plenty of other less gauche opening gambits were available to him.

My own explanation, of course, would be that the prior context (the context provided by Level 0) has already established speech types, and specifically "lofty speech," as a matter preying on the Narrator's mind. When the Leech Gatherer's discourse suddenly challenges the conclusions that the Narrator had provisionally reached about speech types and about those individuals able to control them, that challenge cannot simply be passed over by introducing some new and unconnected topic. And it is precisely the banality of the old man's occupation over so many years that the Narrator must hear restated, for it alone can confirm the heartening if unexpected *dis*junction between youth and eloquence that the Leech Gatherer represents.

But it matters very little for our present purposes—the assessment of the Leech Gatherer's second reply—whether one prefers Toolan's hypothetical account of the Narrator's actions or my own. For at least on its surface, the poem offers no evidence that the Leech Gatherer receives a single clue from which he might reasonably infer the existence of either complex conversational agenda on the part of Narrator. *From the old man's point of view*, the Narrator's repetition of his earlier question will always constitute an unmitigated and, to all appearances, unmotivated call for replay. We still need to explain therefore why it is that his reaction does not reflect more annoyance than it does.

We may begin this stage of our investigation by reexamining the narrative structure of "Resolution and Independence" as a whole. Our last representation of that structure (figure 9, p. 90) took into account only two narrative levels; I propose now to include one additional level, evidence for which derives from both biographical and textual evidence.

"Resolution and Independence" was not originally composed as a public utterance designed by its author for wide dissemination in printed form. Rather, it constituted one contribution to a remarkable decade-long exchange of poems between Wordsworth and Coleridge, a literary debate that took them from the extraordinarily productive period of virtual collaboration between 1797 and 1800 through to the beginnings of the estrangement that would ultimately part them in 1810.[26]

One may dispute where exactly to fix both the first and the last contributions to what Stephen Prickett (1970:152–167) repeatedly and, as we shall see, insightfully calls this "poetic dialogue" (see also Magnuson 1988:308 and Ruoff 1989:17). It may begin as early as July 1798 with Wordsworth's composition of "Tintern Abbey," and its echoes may still be detected in Coleridge's lines to Wordsworth after he read the so-called 1805 *Prelude* in 1806–1807. But the core of the sequence is undoubtedly three justly famous poetic statements about the nature of artistic inspiration: Wordsworth's "Ode: Intimations of Immortality," Coleridge's "Dejection: An Ode," and "Resolution and Independence" itself.

The dating of these three poems is complicated by the fact that all three underwent considerable revision. The "Immortality Ode," for example, consists of two sections known to have been written at different times, and most of what we commonly read as the published poem "Dejection: An Ode" originated (though not in print) as "A Letter to ———," a work with a quite different addressee and a substantially different purpose. Gene Ruoff (1989) presents a fascinating case for regarding these complex textual histories as central, rather than peripheral, to an adequate understanding of the works, both severally and as a sequence. But the more limited stylistic goals of this study excuse, I believe, a less fine-grained approach. What matters for our immediate concerns is that, thematically, various parts of these three compositions, even in the forms in which they were finally published, do represent coherent, ordered contributions to the debate between these two men over the evanescence of poetic genius.

This assertion rests in part on rich textual evidence. A mere sampling of that evidence (again see Ruoff 1989) would range from verbal echoes such as the shared (and pivotal) reliance of both the "Immortality Ode" and "Dejection: An Ode" on rhyming *grief* with *relief* on the one hand to those same two poems' virtually complementary descriptions of the moon and stars as vessels in the night sky on the other. The "Immortality Ode" praises the "Child of joy, / . . . thou happy Shepherd boy"; an early version of "Dejection" presents a contrasting view of one "cloister'd in a city School / At the barr'd window"; finally, the Narrator in "Resolution and Independence" talks once again of a time, albeit a time now passed, when he was "as happy as a boy" (18). Chatterton, as we saw in chapter 3, incarnates in that poem the bleaker vision of boyhood, dying as a result of his refusal to accept what Wordsworth would come to call (in a section of the "Immortality Ode" that he wrote *after* reading "Dejection") the "prison-house" bars.

Still more transparently, the opening line of the "Immortality Ode" ("There was a time when meadow, grove, and stream") is echoed, but is then turned to a more somber end, by Coleridge in "Dejection": "There was a time when, though my path was rough . . ." And while Coleridge begins "Dejection" just before the outbreak of a fearsome storm that is howling about the house by its close, the opening lines of "Resolution and Independence" describe a storm's aftermath—one might almost say, as Ruoff (1989:118) notes, the aftermath of the *same* storm:

> There was a roaring in the wind all night;
> The rain came heavily and fell in floods;
> But now the sun is rising calm and bright.
>   [1–3][27]

This constant interlacing of phrases from one poem in this series into the language of the next represents, I suggest, the literary counterpart of a process described for natural discourses by Schiffrin (1987:17): "by repeating key phrases from prior conversation . . . [as] a cohesive device . . . [speakers] show that understanding the interactional meaning of the story requires reference to prior conversation."[28] If this is so, it entails that we should stipulate a narrative structure for "Resolution and Independence" rather more complex than that we have worked with thus far, a structure that takes into account the "poetic dialogue" from which it emerged, a structure such as that shown in figure 19.[29]

At the lower levels in this narrative structure—as also, for example, at the lower levels in "The Ruined Cottage"—one narrative fits into another as a function of standard conversational practice; at Level 1, for instance, the Leech Gatherer is asked a question to which the only appropriate response is an autobiographical narrative. But we now need also to establish what purpose the Level 0 story in "Resolution and Indepen-

Figure 19

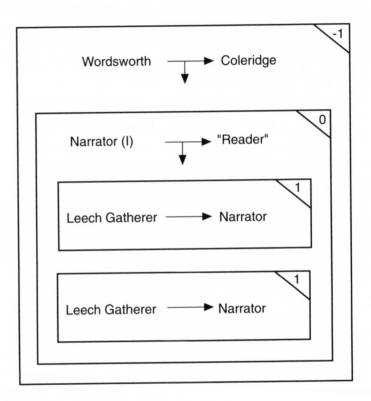

dence" serves in the Level -1 context of the Wordsworth-Coleridge debate.

One clue to the nature of that role lies, I suggest, in Oswald Doughty's observation (1981:205) that "a portrait of Coleridge at this time, a slightly critical one, appears in . . . 'Resolution and Independence.'" Doughty points to the many biographical parallels that link the description of the Narrator early in this poem as one who somewhat self-pityingly questions why

> others should
> Build for him, sow for him, and at his call

Love him, who for himself will take no heed at all,
　[40–42]

with Coleridge's own cloying dependency on William and Dorothy dur-
ing the period when these poems were being written. Coleridge, a hypo-
chondriac, unhappily married and already addicted to opium, leaned
heavily on his friends in the opening years of the new century while
simultaneously suffering frequent pangs of guilt over his lack of produc-
tivity as a writer.

It is surely Coleridge's voice, I want to suggest therefore, *and not
Wordsworth's,* that we hear echoing the strains of the "Dejection Ode"
near the beginning of "Resolution and Independence." Wordsworth has
daringly picked up the story of Coleridge's stormy night exactly where
Coleridge himself had left off, extending that narrative into the following
morning without ever shifting from the first-person narration of the
original into the second-person framework that we would naturally ex-
pect. The ostensibly first-person "I" in "Resolution and Independence,"
therefore, is categorically not the poet himself—another justification, if
we needed one, for the concept of narrative layering.[30]

But if it is Coleridge (or at least Wordsworth's representation of his
friend) who acts as the Level 0 Narrator in this poem, then where if
anywhere does Wordsworth figure in the text? Wordsworth, I propose,
realizes his own point of view, not at Level 0 but at Level 1, in the person
of the Leech Gatherer. The doctrine of stoic endurance, after all, of
pursuing "dwindling" opportunities for whatever they are worth, is ex-
actly that espoused in the "Immortality Ode":

We will grieve not, rather find
Strength in what remains behind; . . .
In the soothing thoughts that spring
Out of human suffering.
　[181–182, 185–186]

And the *"flash* of mild surprise" (my italics) that the Narrator glimpses in
the Leech Gatherer's eyes picks up tellingly on Wordsworth's recurrent
use of that metaphor throughout this poetic debate to describe his own
evanescent "gleams" of poetic insight (the original "fountain light"),
glimmerings that represented the last, best hope of the maturing poet.

I am proposing, in short, that we modify our visual representation of narrative structure in this text once again, substituting for figure 19 the revised figure 20, in which the subscripts co-index the participants according to the general principles outlined earlier in this chapter.

As always, we must take care not to "overinterpret" figure 20. Despite their identical indexes, the Narrator at Levels 0 and 1 is not *in fact* the historical Coleridge who appears at Level − 1. When Wordsworth has his Level 0 Narrator experience a change of heart upon hearing the Leech Gatherer's story, he is not reporting anything that Coleridge actually thought, let alone said aloud. Instead, he is attempting to employ nar-

Figure 20

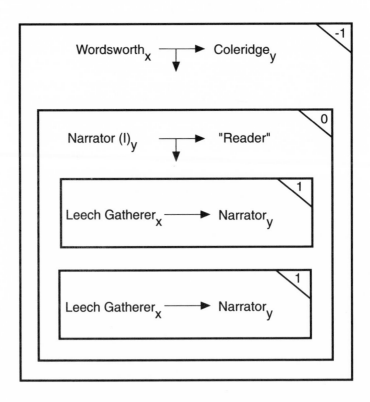

rative as a means to effect an audacious argumentative coup. Somewhat as in role-playing, he is trying to seduce Coleridge (his intended primary reader) into perceiving the reasonableness of a less gloomy outlook; "if my fictional Narrator can cheer up despite having initially expressed doubts every bit as black as your own," his implicit argument runs, "then why should not your spirits also revive after hearing this tale?"[31] Despite the power of this appeal, however, Wordsworth cannot be sure of success in creating in the real world the effect that he intended, because in *Coleridge's* reading of the poem's concluding stanza, the desired conflation of the y-indexed roles on which that interpretation depends may never occur.[32]

We may seem to have wandered rather far from our goal of explicating the Leech Gatherer's behavior in the closing stanzas of "Resolution and Independence," and it is indeed time to retrace our steps. I began my outline of the history of the composition of this poem because I hoped to discover the "point" that Wordsworth intended his poem to make as a contribution to the Level -1 discourse. Carter (1983:380) points out that "[however] direct and naturalistic the exchanges [within a given text] may be, it should not be forgotten that this forms only a part of the total message [the poet] communicates to his reader. The competent reader overhears [the] conversation [between characters within the poem], but he must be at the same time alert to the speech acts transmitted indirectly by the author himself." And "what is intended and understood as the point [of any such speech act] is," in Schiffrin's words, "strongly dependent on social, cultural, conversational, *and personal* contexts" (1987:16; my italics). Since "Resolution and Independence" was first written as part of a literary dialogue, our appreciation of its point cannot be altogether divorced from our knowledge about the contributions that preceded it and about the individual contributors themselves (see also Magnuson 1988:306).

In the context of that dialogue, each of Wordsworth's "turns" preceding "Resolution and Independence" (most notably, of course, the "Immortality Ode") had consisted of a mildly regretful exploration of the thesis that all poets' powers fade with time; each in turn had evoked in Coleridge only the blackest despair. Casting Coleridge as the Narrator in this poem, therefore, Wordsworth now encourages him to contrast his deep despondency with the Leech Gatherer's amazing spirit of endurance (a spirit that is, as we have seen, a dramatization of Wordsworth's own).

When the Narrator, standing in for Coleridge, initially balks at accepting what that confrontation ought to teach him, Wordsworth seizes on the opportunity that this offers him to display through the imperturbability of *his* chosen persona both his own good-humored tolerance of Coleridge's recurrent worries (hence, of course, the old man's "smile") and also, surely, his conviction that he has already articulated the only response to them that he can conceive. However earnestly or eagerly Coleridge "renews the question," Wordsworth implicitly points out, his misgivings will meet only with a restatement of the doctrine of calm endurance—not because Wordsworth has lost patience with his friend but simply because that is all that he has in him to offer. In a sense, therefore, this poem may be read as Wordsworth's good-natured attempt to terminate a dialogue that, as he sees it, is going nowhere.

If this reading of the Leech Gatherer's behavior seems oversubtle, it may be useful to set beside it a very similar argument about a very different literary work presented by Hurst (1987:350). Hurst analyzes a fascinating conversation between two family members in Ivy Compton-Burnett's novel *A Family and a Fortune*. As she shows, the weak older brother in the family (Edgar) allows himself to be browbeaten mercilessly by his manipulative younger sibling (Dudley). In particular, "Edgar remains unflustered even though Dudley violates all maxims of the cooperative principle. . . . The communication process would probably be halted with any listener other than Edgar." Edgar's tolerance for conversational bad manners on the part of an individual to whom he is particularly close offers an apt parallel to the attitude I have diagnosed as Wordsworth's in "Resolution and Independence." If we were to treat the Narrator and the Leech Gatherer as purely fictional characters and to disregard their relationship to Wordsworth and Coleridge, the Narrator's demeanor toward an old man whom he has only just met would appear intolerably condescending, and the old man's acceptance of it would brand him as either stupid or completely cowed—neither of them characteristics that would otherwise seem appropriate.[33] But reinterpreted in the context of an impassioned discussion between two close personal friends, exactly the same behavior captures on the one hand Coleridge's heartfelt cry for reassurance and on the other Wordsworth's equally earnest efforts to offer whatever consolation he can.

Don Bialostosky (1984) coins an interesting term for the group of Wordsworthian poems of which "Resolution and Independence" is, in his view, one prominent example: he calls them "dialogic personal anecdotes." The triple perspective that this phrase implies fits well with my own view of the poem.

I began my analysis of this text in chapter 2, after all, by observing two apparent violations of the conventions that, conversational analysts have proposed, govern "turns of talk" in a *dialogue*. No amount of contextualization, I argued, could explain those violations naturally—that is, explain them as having occurred in some realistic, though perhaps specialized, discourse setting. Instead, as I argued in chapter 3, they require an approach that acknowledges the preemptive importance of a series of embedded narrative frames (or *anecdotes*) surrounding the dialogue in which the violations occur, an approach that incorporates the entire dialogue as part of a larger story. Within such a structure, I suggested, narrative points may be made with the same material at each of several different levels. At least one crucial aspect of the dialogue's surface form (the Narrator's repeated question) may thus be satisfactorily accounted for by appealing not to its local realism but to its function in that broader narrative context. In this chapter, I have further extended my argument to include narrative frames outside the strict limits of the text itself, arguing that the inter*personal* debate of which this poem forms one element provides the motivation for the remaining conversational anomaly at its core (the Leech Gatherer's air of calm acceptance).

In chapter 5, I shall return one last time to explore how this provisional (but initially quite counterintuitive) realignment of narrative identities in "Resolution and Independence" can be corroborated using both stylistic and nonstylistic evidence. That discussion, however, will depend explicitly (as discussion in this chapter has depended implicitly) on arguments that cross the boundary separating intratextual from extratextual domains. One final digression may help to establish in principle the propriety (and even the desirability) of formulating such arguments at all.

FIVE

"Merely Corroborative Detail"?
Analyzing Texts from Multiple
Stylistic Perspectives

Because the interpretation is presented as an interpretation, *its claim to validity rests on the cogency of the supporting arguments, not on the authorization of the text.*

Patrocinio Schweickart, "Reading Ourselves"

Life is the art of drawing sufficient conclusions from insufficient premises.

Samuel Butler, *Note Books: Life*

In his otherwise restrained essay "Studying Literature as Language," Fowler castigates linguists for their intradisciplinary territorialism. Scholars who have not read extensively in linguistic theory (and that includes many literary critics) may be excused, he concedes, when they assume it to be a unified and homogeneous specialty. But linguists themselves should be fully aware of the field's true heterogeneity and should not stubbornly insist, as they too often do, on the absolute superiority of whatever theory they happen to espouse for the analysis of some specific language sample: "Such is the competitiveness of the schools of linguistics that a devotee of one theory will not acknowledge that a rival might have some advantages for the task in hand" (1984:172–173).

As my remarks in chapter 1 should have made clear, I enthusiastically endorse Fowler's view that stylists in particular should freely adopt whatever linguistic methods afford them interesting insights into the particular text they have chosen to consider (other, of course, than those that have been definitively discredited; see Austin 1984:20–21). His remarks do, however, sidestep one troubling drawback to such a "theoretically unaligned" stylistics: the opening that it creates for the emergence of two or more blatantly conflicting interpretations of the same text, each individually supported by sound stylistic arguments built upon the foundation of incompatible (but bona fide) linguistic theories.

Stylists' linguistic descriptions of literary passages do not of course dictate particular interpretations; in no sense should any stylistic theory be viewed as an "automatic analyzing device which, fed a text, will output a description without human intervention" (Fowler 1984:173). Nevertheless, stylists do rely heavily in constructing their interpretations on clues furnished by linguistic analysis, and it is surely quite conceivable therefore that, either by selecting differently from among the many linguistic clues available to them in the language of a given text or by describing those features from within disparate theoretical frameworks, two or more analysts might reach altogether distinct interpretive conclusions.

More typical in practice—at least since the heyday of Jakobsonian structuralism—have been cases in which multiple analyses from varying linguistic perspectives have turned out to support a single interpretation. To the skeptic, of course, such compatibility appears inherently suspect. Is the desired interpretation literally a *foregone* conclusion, as Fish might argue? Does that interpretational outcome surreptitiously *drive* the linguistic analyses themselves by predisposing the stylist in her or his role as a linguistic expert to look only for certain structures, certain correlations (see Smith 1978)? In this chapter, I argue instead that a judicious stylistic reading benefits from the added conviction that corroboratory evidence based on different theoretical premises can carry.[1] Particularly where one stylistic analysis can be demonstrated to "explain" another (in a sense that I shall shortly make clear), such parallelism constitutes a significant source of strength.

To illustrate this concept, I shall revisit three texts discussed in earlier chapters ("The Ruined Cottage," "Ozymandias," and *Ulysses*) and add some remarks on Coleridge's "This Lime-Tree Bower, My Prison." For each of these texts, I shall suggest, discourse-based stylistic analysis yields interesting insights—but so too do approaches from one or more other linguistic perspectives. And in each case, those parallel interpretive claims interlock in ways that significantly enhance our understanding of how language as a whole functions in the creation of literary meaning.

In earlier studies of "The Ruined Cottage" (see Austin 1977, 1979), I noted that Wordsworth relied more heavily on passive verbs in the original, unpublished text of that work than in his subsequent revisions of the material for incorporation into *The Excursion*. I argued that their appearance in the early version of the story enabled the poet to imply the agency of a superhuman, indeed supernatural, power as an active force in human affairs without at the same time compelling him to name that power or even to define it within the framework of any particular philosophical or theological beliefs.

In 1797–1798, for example, the opening lines describe how "the sun *was mounted* high" (1) and the "surfaces" of the far-off hills "with shadows [*were*] *dappled* o'er" (5). Later in the poem Armytage says of the increasingly shabby cottage garden that "It *was changed*" (313), and Margaret echoes Armytage's assessment of her appearance ("Her face was pale and thin, her figure too / *Was changed*" [338–339]) by herself volunteering: "I *am changed*" (352). Since passive constructions in English need not (and in these particular instances do not) involve overt specification of the agent presupposed by many transitive verbs, Wordsworth's repeated use of passives in this text allows the reader to speculate about who or what may have been the cause of the processes that the Narrator and the peddler describe as having occurred: who "mounted" the sun (like a picture on a wall)? who or what "changed" both the garden and its owner?[2] But the poem itself offers no clear answers.

As he grew older, I maintained in my earlier study, Wordsworth came to sense that this openness to speculative interpretation represented something of a liability. As an increasingly orthodox Anglican, he was no longer comfortable with the possible inference of an implacable, even cruel Nature, let alone the still more radically unconventional, "pantheistic" theology that would impute ultimate blame for the ills experienced by Margaret to the Creator himself acting indirectly through natural forces. As a result, I contended, he replaced some of the risky agentless passives with active past-tense forms. The garden, Armytage now reports, "*appeared / To lag* behind the season" (720–721), while the descriptive detail previously expressed in the lines "The earth *was . . . / With weeds defaced* and knots of withered grass" (414–415) is emended to read: *"weeds defaced /* The . . . soil." Agency is now straightfor-wardly and unambiguously attributed to the garden and to the weeds (and elsewhere indeed to Margaret herself), so that the syntactic form of the poem no longer permits the reader to associate the Almighty directly with Margaret's unhappy end.[3]

In my opinion, this argument remains substantially sound. Several colleagues have persuaded me to revise my emphasis on the passive-ness of constructions like "it was changed," arguing that they involve instead the use of past-participial forms as predicate adjectives. Such formal reanalysis, however, leaves intact the morphological link between each of those forms and a corresponding active construction and in no sense undermines the significance of my observation that each is later replaced by the appropriate active verb.

From the new perspective suggested by our discussions in chapter 3, we may now note a second important consequence of Armytage's re-liance on what I will hereafter refer to as "pseudopassive" constructions in the early draft of this poem. Such sentences, just like true passives, typically predicate something of a "patient" that has been affected by change rather than of the agent that brought change about (Halliday 1970:152; Clark and Clark 1977:93).[4] Hence, of course, the option of omitting all mention of the agent in true passives; hence too, though, the fact that hearers tend to associate these constructions with states rather than with events. Notice that *Barry burst the basketball,* an active sentence that undeniably denotes a past-time *event,* contrasts with *The basketball was burst,* which places the spotlight squarely on the burst *state* of the ball.

This observation dovetails neatly with what we noted in chapter 3 about the unusual way in which Armytage learns the details of Mar-garet's life story and about the unique effect that his perspective has on the way in which he mediates that narrative in "The Ruined Cottage." For his syntactic style with its emphasis on pseudopassive constructions accords precisely with his narrative standpoint. Armytage's report that the garden "was changed," for example, is holistic and static, lacking the explicit focus on the preceding process of change that appears as soon as Wordsworth emends the description to read: "It . . . had lost / Its pride of neatness." To "lose . . . neatness" occurs over time; it is an evolutionary process. To *"be* changed" (quite a different thing from *"having* changed") represents instead a blunt fact that takes no account of intervening steps, concentrating instead on a categorical opposition of "before" and "after."

In "The Ruined Cottage," then, the peddler's narrative perspective—crucially, a function of his "biographical" identity as a narrator at Level 1 (see figure 10)—turns out to be effectively inseparable from the sentential syntax of his account. If the unusual rhythm imposed by Armytage's unorthodox lifestyle explains *why* we learn of Margaret's history in the way that we do, then the pseudopassive sentences he employs constitute a local instance of *how* that effect is achieved.[5]

This analysis, incidentally, accords perfectly with the conclusions that I presented in the late 1970s. For, conveyed in this atypical way as a mere sequence of static images, the peddler's narrative in the original text elides the steps by which each individual image evolved from the one preceding it in time; as a result, nobody—not Robert, not Margaret, not Armytage, not some government bureaucrat, not even some metaphysical power—is explicitly indicted for having caused what transpires.[6] Readers, however, always retain the option of inferring for themselves whatever causal connections narrators may leave unspecified (see chapter 2, note 11). Presented by Armytage with two dissimilar pictures of the cottage or the garden, therefore, readers may connect them in almost any fashion—including those that the more mature Wordsworth later attempted to discourage by means of his syntactic emendations.

In a sense, then, the parallel approaches to "The Ruined Cottage" summarized here both address a single aspect of that poem's form, describing two sides of the same stylistic coin. Both the idiosyncrasies of Armytage's character and the technical details of how he tells his story alike are extrapolated from the text of the poem by its readers; neither exists—neither ever existed—in the "real world." My next example focuses on a similar situation but one in which only one of the narrative levels brought into play is intratextual, the other lying outside the text altogether.

Between 1977 and 1983, I made several passes at explicating a short excerpt from Coleridge's "This Lime-Tree Bower, My Prison" (see Aus-

tin 1977, 1984). The passage in question was first transcribed by the poet
as follows (Griggs, vol. I, 334–336):

> My friends . . .
> Wander delighted, and look down, perchance,
> On that same rifted Dell, where many an Ash
> Twists it's [*sic*] wild limbs beside the ferny rock.

In preparing these lines for publication in 1800, Coleridge shifted the
burden of expressing the visual impression of twistedness from the verb
itself onto a refashioned syntax that severely distorts the usual subject-
verb-object word order:

> Friends, whom I never more may meet again, . . .
> Wander in gladness, and wind down, perchance,
> To that still roaring dell . . .
> Where   *its slim trunk*   *the ash*   *from rock to rock*
> *Flings*   arching like a bridge.
>   [9, 12–13]

This emendation, I argued (1984:114–115), exploits syntactic form as
a channel for conveying meaning entirely independent of the language's
usual semantic resources. Employing a stylistic technique that I defined
as "iconic," the revised text wrenches the standard word order more
awkwardly than the language would tolerate in everyday contexts. Cole-
ridge's

> Its slim trunk the ash from rock to rock flings . . . like
>   a bridge

is structurally identical to

> ?*   Their finest performance the orchestra on the final night
>   provided with Beethoven's *Requiem.*

But the latter sentence would simply never appear in the newspaper
review of a real concert, let alone be uttered spontaneously by a con-
certgoer on her way from the hall. In struggling to wrap their minds
around the form of Coleridge's rewritten sentence, therefore, readers

instinctively recreate for themselves the tortuous profile of the ash tree he describes.[7]

None of my work since 1984 would lead me to retract what I wrote at that time. The more often I return to the poem, in fact, the more evidence I find of the rich texture that Coleridge achieved for this short passage by importing the expressive potential of iconic syntax. Notice, for example, that in the earlier text the vital concept of ungoverned energy is expressed twice (and thus redundantly) in the verb phrase: *"twists* it's *wild limbs."* Since, in his revision, Coleridge transferred this entire facet of the description to the syntax, as we saw above, one might anticipate that he would consign the surplus lexical material to the editorial scrap heap en bloc. Remarkably, though, he contrives to salvage the word *limbs*—if only in the form of phonological "spare parts"—deftly rearranging them to derive *slim* (see figure 21), an epithet that then enhances his overall description of the scene by drawing our attention to the uncluttered, almost architectural line of the ash's trunk rather than to its branches.

Figure 21

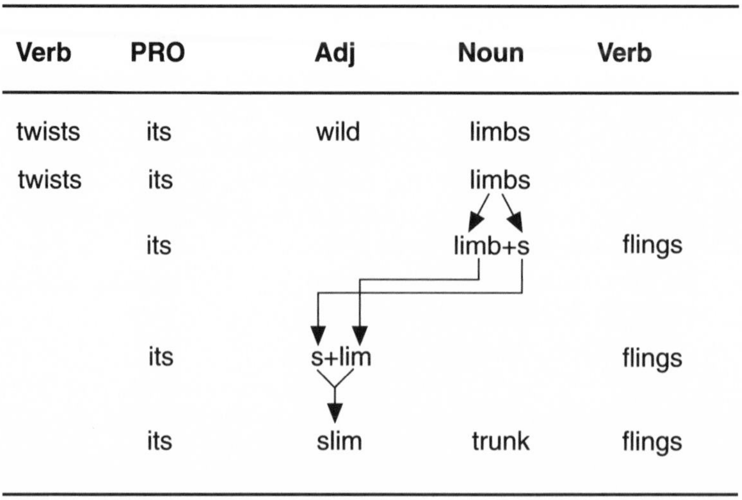

Verb	PRO	Adj	Noun	Verb
twists	its	wild	limbs	
twists	its		limbs	
	its		limb+s	flings
	its	s+lim		flings
	its	slim	trunk	flings

Just a few words later in the reshaped text, he then picks up on that lead, referring to

> . . . —that *branchless* ash,
> Unsunn'd and damp, whose few poor yellow leaves
> Ne'er tremble in the gale, yet tremble still
> Fann'd by the water-fall!
>   [13–16; my italics]

I have found no reason, then, to withdraw or modify any of my prior claims about the syntactic form of this passage. I originally advanced those claims, however, in isolation and without regard to the broader contexts within which Coleridge composed the two versions of his description of the "still roaring dell," contexts that deserve closer scrutiny.

The 1797 text was at most a few days old when Coleridge copied it into a letter to his close friend Robert Southey. By all means, it already constituted "poetry" and was as such literary. Nevertheless, it may have come close to representing what Coleridge himself claimed that a number of his works from this period were intended to be: a "conversation poem." Several features suggest that the text he published in 1800 was, by contrast, less personally candid, more consciously literary. Coleridge omits from the printed version, for example, the ultimately irrelevant detail of the reason for his having been left behind while his friends took their afternoon walk. His wife, Sara, had accidentally spilled scalding milk on his foot, and when writing to Southey, as so often when he was corresponding with his friends (see Ruoff 1989:180), the poet had been unable to resist an implicit appeal for sympathy. But in 1800 he apparently recognized (for once) that the broader public would care little about his aches and pains. He also expanded in the published poem his description of the moment when the walkers climb back up from the dell and survey the surrounding countryside, an addition that adds valuable thematic balance to the poem but apparently did not form part of his original, more spontaneous musings in the bower.

In general terms, discourse analysts and post–New Critical literary critics agree in acknowledging the influence of audience and genre (loosely defined as the type of discourse adopted) on the stylistic form of any utterance, whether spoken or written. Among linguistic theoreticians who have addressed this issue, Tannen (1989) considers the ways in which context and genre influence speakers' and writers' choices among the many discourse strategies available to them (see also Fabb and Durant 1987:7). And with regard to narratives in particular, Walter Fisher (1987:125) quotes Chaim Perelman ("the audience 'has the major role in determining the quality of argument and the behavior of *orators*'" [my italics]) before going on to argue that, since the ultimate aim of *narrators* is likewise to win their respective audiences' "adherence" to their narratives, they too need to take into account their hearers' (or readers') biases when selecting and arranging their material.

Among literary scholars, William Madden (1986:363–364), in a study particularly closely allied to our analysis here of "This Lime-Tree Bower, My Prison," examines Lewis Carroll's Alice stories, focusing in particular on the narrative material with which Carroll framed those stories when presenting them to different audiences. Though they were at first part of an "essentially . . . private communication," Madden argues, Carroll showed early evidence of an "impulse . . . to go beyond the mere transcription of the original tales that Alice Liddell had requested." That impulse then intensified as the texts were prepared for publication, the changes that Carroll introduced reflecting his sensitivity to the kinds of audience considerations described by Tannen, Fisher, and others. In a similar way, chapter 5 of Ruoff's *Wordsworth and Coleridge: The Making of the Major Lyrics, 1802–1804* offers spectacular evidence of how Coleridge devised one version of "Dejection" after another, each in turn "almost wholly shaped to fit the self he [was] creating for his newly found audience, or at least his construction of that audience" (175). I am hardly breaking new ground, therefore, when I assert that literary artists' conceptions of the probable audiences for their works help to shape the works themselves.

If we examine Coleridge's "This Lime-Tree Bower, My Prison" from this perspective, we can clearly discern the role played by audience expectation in motivating the syntactic emendations that I noted in my earlier, syntactic analysis. For the greater stylistic richness and subtlety of the 1800 text, manifested in the poet's reliance on iconic syntax not evident in the 1797 letter to Southey, is undoubtedly licensed by the expanded possibilities that accompany the act of "publishing poetry" as compared with that of "writing letters." As Coleridge moved his text a little higher on the scale of discourse formality—a scale that extends from the most casual chitchat at one extreme to the literature of high seriousness at the other—he reached a point where he could anticipate closer, more thoughtful readers, readers with greater tolerance, in particular, for the linguistic demands that iconic syntax imposes.[8]

Unfortunately, while such an explanation accords quite well with common sense, it seems at first to run counter to the findings of some discourse theoreticians. In one of Tannen's carefully selected examples of how speakers and writers adapt their own discourses for delivery under varying circumstances (1989:81–82), she compares the verbatim transcript of a scholarly address ("extemporaneously composed but nonetheless polished and fluent") with the speaker's own edited text of those same remarks as submitted later for the volume of proceedings of the conference at which they were delivered. She notes that one particular rhetorical effect that had, in the oral version, been achieved by capitalizing on the iconic power of syntax became "lexicalized in the written version (i.e. conveyed by external evaluation)." The passage from "This Lime-Tree Bower, My Prison" that we have just examined seems to exemplify exactly the reverse process: the heavily lexicalized, "external" technique of Coleridge's almost impromptu description in his letter gives way to a *more* integrated approach as he shifts into the *less* conversational genre.

One explanation for the unexpected direction of this technical shift undoubtedly lies in the disparate stylistic expectations that attend literary writing as opposed to expository prose. Iconic strategies (particularly that of repetition, as Tannen [1989:53–54] notes) are heavily disfavored in certain forms of written discourse; twentieth-century English expository prose is certainly one such form. The academic writer whose work Tannen discusses would thus have been heavily influenced by his conscious or subconscious recognition of this bias against iconicity as he prepared his material for publication. In romantic and postromantic British and American literary texts, in contrast, as E. L. Epstein (1975) argues, iconicity (which he calls "objective mimesis") has been accorded a rather high rating on our aesthetic scale of values. Coleridge's changes to the text of his work thus reflect his alertness (whether conscious or not) to the biases associated with this type of writing.

But there is, I think, another still more intriguing factor contributing to the scenario that we have been exploring. In the 1800 revision of "This Lime-Tree Bower, My Prison," as I noted above, a single ash (not "many an Ash" as in 1797) leads the reader's eye "from rock to rock." Just a few lines later in the text, a "slip of smooth clear blue [ocean]" stretches "betwixt two Isles / Of purple shadow" (25–26); and at the very end of the published text, a rook flies across the face of the setting sun, its path across "the mighty Orb's dilated glory" forming a third image of connectedness, this time between Charles Lamb (to whom, as the principal member of that walking party, the poem is addressed) and Coleridge himself. That justly famous conclusion, I suggest, would not achieve the major impact that it does, were it not for the fact that it is foreshadowed by both of its closely congruent companion images, the arching ashtree and the strip of blue ocean.[9]

In forgoing at least some of the conversational realism of his language when revising his description of the dell in 1800, therefore, Coleridge not only eliminated semantic redundancy in the earlier text but also laid the groundwork for an attractive parallelism between three important images (a parallelism, incidentally, that is as valuable in the published context as it might have been overly elaborate in the epistolary one). For the ash can function in this rather sophisticated way only because Coleridge has redrawn it, expressing the notion of contortion *implicitly* through syntactic inversion at the same time that he depicts the tree *explicitly* as a clean, curving form whose horizonlike, orblike shape matches the line he will later ask his readers to revisualize in the rook's flight. This goal of highlighting the iteration of a central image schema constitutes a second important motivation for Coleridge's choice of linguistic form in this instance, the choice that favors syntactic iconicity over lexicalization in description.[10]

Here as in "The Ruined Cottage," therefore, we discern an intimate connection between syntactic structure in a section of text and the nature of its discourse context. Once again, the interpretive conclusions to be drawn from linguistic analyses that adopt these radically different perspectives are fully compatible with one another. And also exactly as in the prior instance, the whole exceeds the sum of its two parts, for, by combining the insights afforded by both studies, we may offer a far more convincing stylistic description of the poem as a whole; apparently minor syntactic details in a particular discourse now emerge as the well-motivated consequences of seemingly equally trivial adjustments in the circumstances under which that discourse was conceived and uttered.[11]

Clearly, the two studies do not resemble one another in *all* respects, for my commentary on "This Lime-Tree Bower, My Prison" depends critically upon factual information about the record of that poem's composition. In discussing "The Ruined Cottage," I could rely exclusively on intratextual evidence, characterizing judgments that all readers make simply as a result of reading the poem at all. Here, in contrast, extratextual entities (the historical poet and his presumed audience) figure as elements important to the success of my attempt to cross-reference parallel stylistic analyses. Readers unaware of the relevant historical background could not make the connections that I have identified; indeed, inasmuch as my conclusions hinge on comparisons between different versions of the same material, they could not by definition be reached independently by a reader faced only with a single text.

But this observation in no way weakens the case I am attempting to build in this chapter, though it does raise an important issue that I shall need to address shortly: that of defining more precisely the "readers" whose experience I claim to capture in my analyses. For now, it is enough to observe the striking similarities between the purely intratextual corroboration of stylistic accounts that emerged from our investigation of "The Ruined Cottage" and the mixed (that is, intra- and extratextual) correlation that we uncovered in examining "This Lime-Tree Bower, My Prison."

In returning to *Ulysses,* I will again illustrate briefly both the strong bond between a text's genre and its linguistic form and the implications of that bond for stylistic criticism. This time, however, I shall be using the term *genre* in its narrower, traditional sense rather than as a broad synonym for "discourse type."

In chapter 2, I argued that two stylistic factors could be seen as jointly creating Ulysses' distinctive narrative voice in Tennyson's poem, the voice of an individual beset by self-doubt. On the one hand, Tennyson's sentential syntax tends to disguise first-person statements as universal dicta by either delaying or deleting outright underlying first-person pronouns; in many cases, as a result, readers can detect that a given sentence is uttered in the first person only inferentially. On the other hand, deictic markers, instead of informing readers accurately of the speaker's orientation toward events and characters that he describes, actually compound their disorientation by appearing to corroborate mistaken spatial and temporal relations that the syntax has created.

The confusion produced by these combined stylistic techniques, I concluded, contributes to the picture that we receive of Ulysses himself, one in which an air of self-importance lurks behind a facade of philosophical detachment. And our somewhat ambivalent appraisal of the speaking voice in the poem becomes still more significant once one takes into account Tennyson's probable state of mind when he wrote the poem. Profoundly disoriented by Hallam's death, Tennyson created in Ulysses a reflection of his own uncertainty about the future, the syntactic selections that mark Ulysses' discourse representing just one symptom of this apprehensiveness.

As I commented in chapter 2, the theoretical heterogeneity of the evidence that produced this reading of *Ulysses* itself demonstrates dramatically the value of a multifaceted approach to stylistic analysis; an examination of the role of deixis (a discourse-based phenomenon) works hand in hand with a study of sentential syntax to support a single interpretation. Let us now reconsider the general conclusions reached in that chapter, however, in the context of the literary genre of Tennyson's poem.

The dramatic monologue occupies an awkward position partway along a continuum that connects lyric poetry at one extreme with drama and the novel at the other. Bakhtin (1984:200–201) alleges that lyric poetry must always be at heart "monologic," whereas "for the prose artist the world is full of other people's words, among which he must orient himself and whose speech characteristics he must be able to perceive with a very keen ear." But David Lodge (1987:98), even while he accepts the broad outline of this formulation, argues that the contrast Bakhtin proposes is altogether too stark. Lodge asserts that "nineteenth and twentieth-century poetry, especially the popularity of the dramatic monologue in this period," gives "ample evidence of the novelisation of the lyric impulse," that is, of the importation of dialogic techniques into monologic texts (see also Mermin 1983:9–11).

As Cynthia Bernstein (1990:127) observes in an excellent study of the genre, the dramatic monologue certainly masquerades as realistic dialogue, as the objective transcription of (or at least, of one end of)

an overheard conversation. Yet at the same time its undeniable arti-
ficiality—the absence of overt collocutors, of stage directions, of gen-
uinely conversational features such as hesitations, speech errors, and
colloquialisms—marks it as something quite different. These properties
would seem to belong more naturally to lyric poetry, the personal utter-
ance of the poet him- or herself. Overall, the "half-veiled, half-open use
of autobiographical material . . . and the voices that mediate between
the poet and the protagonist" in this genre "combine to leave us in
considerable uncertainty about the poet's attitude and presence; these are
signs of . . . the poet's . . . conflicting impulses both to reveal and to
conceal his own experiences and feelings" (Mermin 1983:154).[12]

If one accepts this assessment of the dramatic monologue as a genre,
then one may infer that in choosing to write this particular poem as a
dramatic monologue, Tennyson was availing himself of a remarkable
opportunity both to express powerfully his fears, his aspirations, and his
reservations and, at the same time, to disguise the fact that he was doing
anything of the sort. Given the autobiographical background to this
poem, as we have seen, one may discern significant links between Ten-
nyson the poet and Ulysses the character, but as a dramatic monologue,
the text itself by no means insists on them. One may sympathize with
Ulysses, and by extension with all those enduring midlife crises, without
by any means assuming that it is Tennyson himself who is seeking conso-
lation and encouragement.

But this appropriation of the dramatic monologue form as a semi-
transparent blind from behind which to communicate painful emotions
without incurring vulnerability exactly parallels at the level of genre, of
course, what I earlier argued was the coordinated effect created by the
syntactic and deictic manipulations that permeate the poem. Appreciat-
ing the character of dramatic monologue as a genre demands consider-
able literary sophistication, of course, a fact that still further complicates
the task of defining "the reader," which lies ahead. But it would surely be
foolish to pass up the argumentative cohesion that results from adding
this third leg to what now becomes a stylistic tripod, resting solidly on
complementary analyses of sentential syntax, deictic semantics, and ge-
neric classification.

I am indebted to Michael Flynn (personal communication) for some
insights into the syntactic structure of "Ozymandias" that, set beside my

own discussion of that poem in chapter 4, prompted the fourth in this series of brief case histories.

Flynn observed a peculiar feature of the sentential syntax of lines 3–8 of this sonnet and especially of the construction italicized below:

> Near them, on the sand,
> Half sunk, a shattered visage lies, whose frown,
> And wrinkled lip, and sneer of cold command,
> Tell that its sculptor well those passions read
> Which yet *survive,* stamped on these lifeless things,
> *The hand that mocked them, and the heart that fed.*

As figure 22 shows, the direct object of *survive* in this sentence consists of two conjoined NPs, each of which contains a restrictive relative clause. The subject position in each of those clauses is (at least phonologically) empty, but syntactic rules require us to interpret each as identical with its corresponding head noun (*hand* and *heart,* respectively). *Them,* whose antecedent is "those passions," appears as the direct object of *mock* in the complement to NP_1, but no NP follows *fed* in the conjoined NP_2.

In any other context, this "gap" (indicated in figure 22 as the boxed node at the right-hand end of the tree diagram) might not concern us unduly; *feed* is not obligatorily transitive in English and could thus, at least in theory, function here intransitively. But the immediately obvious parallelism between the two conjuncts in line 8 strongly inclines us to entertain *them* as *fed*'s "understood" direct object, as too does the semantic improbability of a reading in which the heart simply "feeds" (on something unspecified).[13]

In attempting to read NP_2 as a truncated version of "the heart that fed *them,*" however, readers must stretch English syntax very considerably, for analogous constructions in everyday contexts are unacceptable. A process called Right Node Raising does account for sentences containing conjoined structures from which one of a pair of identical rightmost constituents has been omitted. In all such cases, however, it should be the occurrence in the right-hand conjunct that remains, the instance to the left being omitted. This convention accounts, for example, for the following pair of sentences:

> Mrs. Thatcher opposed a single European currency but Mr. Heseltine supported a single European currency.

Figure 22

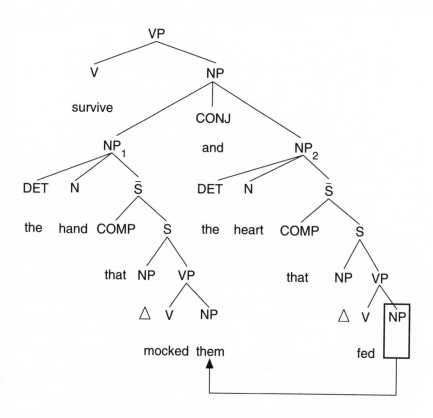

Mrs. Thatcher opposed ——, but Mr. Heseltine supported, a single European currency.

Standard usage simply does not tolerate the following variant:

* Mrs. Thatcher opposed a single European currency but Mr. Heseltine supported ——.

Yet line 8 of "Ozymandias" conforms precisely to this anomalous syntactic template, as a glance at figure 22 clearly shows.

Deviant syntactic constructions of this kind are certainly not unheard of in poetic contexts (see Austin 1984:53–55, 61; 1986), but readers who encounter them inevitably experience at least a moment's puzzlement. Even a critic as experienced as Van Maanen, it will be recalled, criticized "Ozymandias" in part because he found "the eighth line . . . clumsy and obscure." It is entirely appropriate for us, therefore, to ask what motive, if any, could justify such "clumsiness" and "obscurity."

In response to this challenge, we might point out first that, in the sentence that occupies lines 3–8 of the poem, a series of relative clauses and object complements succeed one another, each modifying a constituent at the right-hand end of the clause that dominates it. With some simplification, we might depict its syntactic structure as in figure 23.

This representation highlights quite dramatically several themes that I already addressed in chapter 4, albeit from other perspectives. The Sculptor, for example, yet again appears in a pivotal position, poised in S_3 midway between the ruined statue (in S_1) and the emotions that his skilled hands once mocked (in S_{5a} and S_{5b}). Similarly, at least at first glance, the balanced contribution of artist and subject to the creation of a work of art resurfaces in the congruence of S_{5a} and S_{5b}. And in a more global sense, the entire syntactic form might be seen as "mimetic" (see Austin 1984:111–112), the vertical axis in figure 23 representing the passage of time. In S_1, on the temporal "surface" so to speak, lie the fragments of the statue itself, available for immediate inspection. Somewhat further "down" comes the Sculptor, whose existence in S_3 can be discerned only after we have "excavated" two intervening levels of structure. The "historical" acts of both the Sculptor and Ozymandias lurk most deeply "buried" of all, a full four levels of syntactic embedding beneath the desert sands.

In several respects, then, this formal syntactic analysis supports the interpretive proposals I advanced in chapter 4. Its most striking contribution derives, however, from the additional observation that only after we have dug through layer upon layer of syntactic structure, after we have passed not only the physical evidence of the statue itself but also the mediating presence of the Sculptor, do we arrive, exhausted, at the apparently congruent clauses S_{5a} and S_{5b}. Once arrived, we discover to our surprise that while S_{5a} does indeed confirm the presence of the Sculptor

Figure 23

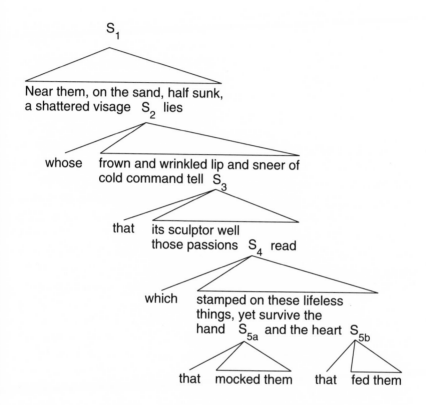

("the hand") at work representing passions ("them") at that remote level, S_{5b} mysteriously lacks an object. Syntactically incomplete, the only clause that could have expressed how Ozymandias's own heart actually contributed to the production of the monolith crumbles to syntactic dust before our very eyes. That the tyrant's heart *fed* (that is, *nurtured* or *supported*) *something* is clear; but that it fed the *same passions* that the Sculptor's hand mocked is a tenuous inference at best, based on an ad hoc interpretation of a syntactically irregular clause.

I am tempted to go still further and to observe that that same sentence, S_{5b}, crumbles because of a nonstandard "dominance" relationship between the conjoined clauses. Whereas S_{5b} should by rights have remained intact, Right Node Raising acting to truncate S_{5a}, in actual fact that order has been reversed. Since S_{5a} depicts the acts of the Sculptor and S_{5b} those of Ozymandias, we have here yet another linguistic reflex of the recurrent literary theme in "Ozymandias" that I outlined in chapter 4. Shelley reillustrates in this nonstandard coordinate structure his oft-repeated contention that the artist's work alone survives the erosion of time, while emperors and pharaohs are doomed to yield up their power to sculptors (and poets), who thus keep for themselves the final say as to how history will be read.

Structural analysis of the second conjunct of line 8 of this sonnet, to summarize, reveals at an altogether different linguistic level—that of sentential syntax—precisely the unconventional relationship between two of its protagonists that I earlier argued lay at the heart of its confusing narrative structure. Such corroboration surely strengthens the overall case for my reading of Shelley's poem (though still not at the expense of the conventional, purely political one), by providing a principled account for what would otherwise remain a frustratingly awkward line in the poem.

A potential challenge to this explication of "Ozymandias" takes as its point of departure the observation that many "real" readers, siding with Van Maanen, *do* find line 8 of that sonnet "awkward" and *are* "frustrated" by it, however effectively my analysis may demonstrate the line's thematic suitability. To Shelley himself, of course, it would hardly have been surprising to discover that language (even poetic language) had yet again proved inadequate in practice to express some subtle nuance of meaning that he had sought, whether deliberately or instinctively, to convey. To the Formalists, the text's complexity at this point would be evidence of the poet's intent to "foreground" that material (see Leech and Short 1981: chap. 2). To New Stylists, as I already hinted in the course of the analysis itself, those readers' sense of syntactic disorientation, of inadequate closure, would be viewed as mimetic, reflecting linguistically the inconclusiveness of historical and archaeological reconstruction.

But I propose to respond to the potential challenge on altogether more theoretically fundamental grounds by disputing the unstated premise that anchors the logic of the objection as a whole: namely, that stylistics concerns itself (or should concern itself) with the experience of "real" readers in the first place. Indeed, I made clear in chapter 1 my belief that stylistic arguments of the kind that I would be making in this study were in general not descriptive of the behavior or knowledge of real readers. My consistent goal has instead been to develop interpretive insights into the texts that I have addressed. It is certainly possible that, if the accounts I have offered carry sufficient conviction, my views may fundamentally affect the way in which a specific individual who reads them subsequently rereads the primary texts themselves. Alternatively, any new interpretive details I have suggested may simply supplement that individual's prior understanding of those texts. But the evaluation of stylistic analyses cannot in any case be reduced to an opinion poll of naive readers.

I am fully aware, of course, that the various stylistic analyses of individual works adduced in this chapter assume widely varying degrees of literary knowledge or interpretive skill. The effect of Shelley's omission of the direct object of *fed* in line 8 of "Ozymandias," though technically quite complex, will surely be experienced at some level of consciousness by every reader, because the structural deviance that results inevitably challenges his or her syntactic competence. The significance of Coleridge's revisions in "This Lime-Tree Bower, My Prison," in contrast, emerges only from a painstaking line-by-line comparison of the earlier and later texts. And it takes a quite different (though equally specialized and nonintuitive) kind of knowledge to appreciate the importance to *Ulysses* of Tennyson's employment of the dramatic monologue form. Appeals to such diverse kinds of capability would indeed cause problems for a stylistics that claimed to characterize real-world individuals' actual reading experience (surely a rather unattractive goal). But a stylistic model that emphasizes as its primary objective the overall enrichment of critical appreciation of the texts to which it is applied will not be vulnerable to attack on these grounds.

This theoretical premise is crucial to our ongoing analysis of "Resolution and Independence." For while the reading of that poem that I have developed in this essay does a far better job than any other I have read of accommodating the problems outlined at the beginning of chapter 2, it is certainly far from self-evident.

By the end of chapter 4, after all, I had argued (on the basis of the best stylistic evidence available) that Wordsworth casts his friend Coleridge as the first-person Narrator of the poem, the despondent poet who finds himself so bowled over by the Leech Gatherer's articulateness that he solicits a second demonstration of it. In the meanwhile, I proposed, Wordsworth puts his own sentiments in the mouth of the old man, repeating through him the advice that he had offered first in the "Immortality Ode." I have already conceded at several points that this interpretation will startle many who have always read the poem as straightforwardly autobiographical; it may be equally disquieting to others who come fresh to the text and read it autobiographically because that is the most "natural" thing to do.[14] But just as with the other poems discussed in this chapter, independent evidence (both stylistic and non-stylistic) can be found that lends ever-increasing strength and plausibility to my hypothesis.

We might begin by observing, for example, a problem that troubles H. M. Margoliouth (1953:108; see also Doughty's reservations, noted above). She expresses some surprise that "[there] is not a word about Coleridge [in "Resolution and Independence"] . . . in spite of their [William and Dorothy's] concern about him" during the period of its composition. In the analysis that I have just concluded, I respond directly, if unorthodoxly, to Margoliouth's apprehension. I move beyond Paul Magnuson's limited claim (1988:309) that Wordsworth "appropriated the Coleridge self-portrait for his own, and . . . made thoughts about Coleridge into thoughts about himself." And I go further even than Ruoff (1989:156), who does offer the shrewd suggestion that "[when] 'Resolution and Independence' proposes a model for the Coleridge of [the early version of 'Dejection'], it is not the leech-gatherer himself but the narrator of the poem" but does so only in the course of examining how the broader *themes* of the one poem respond to issues raised in the other. For it is my contention that Coleridge is indeed "mentioned" in this poem, if we are prepared to include under our definition of a "mention" the inscription of an individual into a text as its first-person narrator. Far from being absent from the poem, in fact, Coleridge occupies pride of place but in a way that would have been (and remains today) concealed from an innocent third party such as the naive reader.

Such an appeal to relatively obscure biographical facts as substantiation for a highly unusual interpretation of a canonical text would, of course, have been significantly harder to sustain at the end of chapter 4 than it is at this point in my book. For the striking effectiveness of precisely similar arguments in my discussions of "This Lime-Tree Bower, My Prison" and of *Ulysses* in this chapter has demonstrated the value to stylistic analysis of extrinsic evidence that helps to establish the communicative framework within which the poem was written.

A second means of arguing in support of the interpretation of "Resolution and Independence" that I have advanced here resembles more closely my discussions of "The Ruined Cottage" and of "Ozymandias." Several commentators have pondered a tense shift that occurs between Stanzas 2 and 3 of "Resolution and Independence" (see, for instance, Hartman 1964; Bialostosky 1984; Howard 1988; and Magnuson 1988). After only the briefest retrospective contextualization,

> There *was* a roaring in the wind all night;
> The rain *came* heavily and fell in floods;
>   [1–2]

(an introduction whose primary function, as we have seen, is to tie this poem in with Coleridge's "Dejection"), Stanza 1 embarks on an energetic, present-tense description of a morning walk:

> But now the sun *is* rising calm and bright;
> The birds *are* singing in the distant woods;
>   [3–4; italics here and in the other quotations in this paragraph are my own]

Indeed, the abrupt opening of line 3 ("But now") insistently draws the reader's attention to the primary present-tense orientation. Yet at the end of Stanza 2, Wordsworth equally abruptly abandons the present tense, reverting to the past without any apparent explanation:

> The hare *is* running races in her mirth;
> And with her feet she from the plashy earth
> *Raises* a mist; that, glittering in the sun,
> *Runs* with her all the way, wherever she *doth* run.
>
>   III
> I *was* a Traveller then upon the moor;
> I *saw* the hare that *raced* about with joy;
> I *heard* the woods and distant waters. . . .
>   [11–17]

This in itself would be striking enough to demand explanation, but as Howard (1988:225) points out, the situation is actually still more involved, for Wordsworth seems to have been particularly intent on emphasizing the salience of tense perspective. The word "then" in line 15 of the published text ("I was a Traveller *then* upon the moor"), Howard explains, "was not present in the earlier, unpublished, version" and was evidently "interjected" during the process of revision. We therefore cannot simply regard the adjustment from present- to past-tense narration as a casual or careless midcourse correction.

My suggestion, in line with all that we have already discovered about this poem, is that its first two stanzas should *after all* be read as belonging to Level −1 (see figure 20). The speaker who observes the sunrise in line 3 (but who significantly never actually refers to himself as "I") is indeed Wordsworth, speaking to the Coleridge of "Dejection" in an upbeat mood apparently reflective of his own emotional state of mind at the time (see Ruoff 1989:115) and reaffirming in particular that even "stormy" nights eventually give birth to "pleasant" mornings. Only when we reach Stanza 3 does the poet introduce the first framed narrative (Level 0), and only at *that* point is the voice that we hear linking first-person pronouns with past-tense verbs at the beginning of lines 15, 16, and 17 what I have been calling the voice of the Narrator (of "Coleridge"). It is as though one were to place one set of quotation marks around Stanzas 1 and 2, in which Wordsworth expresses his personal message of good hope, and then begin a new set of embedded quotation marks at the beginning of Stanza 3 as "Coleridge" embarks on his gloomy story.

Here again, therefore, one finds that purely syntactic analysis corroborates what had until now been, at its core, a discourse-based stylistic argument. And here too, as in the previous cases, one notices the extraordinary power of both types of investigation when harnessed in pursuit of a single interpretive goal.

Conclusion

While . . . we might accept that we cannot "do" critical interpreta-
tion and simultaneously reflect on its grounds, yet . . . we might
hold that a subsequent interrogation of the principles, rationales,
and strategies we appeared to be guided by in our critical practice
is . . . useful, in that we learn the logic of the lessons of our past
interpretative practice.

Michael Toolan, *The Stylistics of Fiction*

This essay has focused intensively on a mere handful of canonical poetic
texts. In conducting a stylistic review of each poem, I sought to correlate
an appropriate form of discourse analysis (broadly defined) with a read-
ing of the text that was both inherently plausible and consistent with the
reactions that readers might be expected to have to the linguistic phe-
nomena that I had uncovered. I continue to believe that such discrete and
self-contained analyses constitute the backbone of stylistic study; if the
persuasive power of those arguments fails to hold up, the whole enter-
prise collapses. In this respect, readers must weigh for themselves the
merits of my work.

Indeed, I view such vulnerability to critical evaluation and counter-
argument as one of the strengths of this kind of stylistic scholarship. I
owe to my early training in theoretical linguistics a healthy respect for
working hypotheses that display three characteristics: the capacity to
foster bold and original claims; the ability to explain more of (or more
about) the available data than those that preceded them; and suscep-
tibility to *falsification* as a necessary corollary to their prospects for
confirmation.[1] The interpretations of various poems that I proposed in
earlier chapters, though not hypotheses in the scientific sense, possess
precisely these qualities as significant strengths. Consider in this light my

lengthy discussion of "Resolution and Independence," in chapters 2 through 5.

Boldness and originality. Although Howard (1988) has recently advanced (on altogether different grounds) a reading of "Resolution and Independence" strikingly similar to my own, the view of that poem that we both espouse could scarcely be considered "accepted" among romanticists. Instead it confronts comfortable traditional assumptions about how that text should be read and proposes a radical shift of perspective. One could not, after all, simply absorb it into a more traditional reading without encountering some major conflicts of logic.

Comprehensiveness. If my convictions concerning the Leech Gatherer story break distinctly new ground, they also elucidate aspects of the text left unexplained by prior analysts. The off-kilter conversation in the later stanzas of the poem lends itself either to ridicule (as in Carroll's "White Knight's Song") or to outright censure unless, as in my account, one can find some way to defend it as a functional component of the text as a whole. Those who seek to supplant my reading in the future will therefore need to provide some other, equally satisfactory rationale for that dialogue unless they propose that we should revert to the view that Wordsworth simply handled that part of the poem ineptly.

Falsifiability. As for openness to falsification, my analysis of "Resolution and Independence" is at least as vulnerable as any other critical analysis currently on the books. One can easily conceive of new evidence, especially biographical and literary-historical evidence, capable of mounting a serious challenge by demonstrating that Wordsworth could not possibly have intended the old man's words to be read as his own. Nowhere have I argued (or even, I believe, implied) that my interpretation comes equipped with an unshakable guarantee of validity merely because it derives from linguistic analysis. And even where my notions with respect to some other text may be less radical than those I hold about "Resolution and Independence" (as in my treatments of "The Death of the Hired Man," for example, or of "The Ruined Cottage"), those notions both can and should be placed in active dialogue with interpretations furnished by other schools of critical theory.[2]

Whatever their *individual* strengths (as measured by these or by any other criteria), however, the various textual studies that occupied the preceding chapters also furnish support for some broader theoretical conclusions when taken *collectively*. One may infer from several of my analyses, for example, that only surprisingly short distances separate conversations that occur within certain poetic texts, "conversations" that take place between poets and their audiences through those texts and conversations of the kind that we witness and are frequently parties to every day of our lives. When we read, just as when we converse with our friends, we attempt to detect within the forms of the language that the author has used the personality of the human being who utters them, "to respond to a voice implicit in the text" (Eric Griffiths 1989:37). Instinctively, we seek linguistic clues that will allow us to flesh out the character of the speaker and to detect motivations behind the words that we read. And we postulate cause-and-effect relationships that bind the ongoing conversation into a coherent whole. Far from being an act of ventriloquism, a futile projection of the reader's own personality into the poet's words, this bid to discern a speaker in a literary work is a natural and probably essential aspect of the process of language comprehension.[3] And as our examination of "Ozymandias" clearly showed, the speaker *in* a text and the speaker *of* a text cannot be straightforwardly and uncontroversially distinguished, so that whatever implicit voice we hear will inevitably combine features of the poet's own with those of any characters he or she may introduce.

Let us briefly consider a case in point. One of the observations that I made about Frost's use of dialogue in "The Death of the Hired Man" concerned Mary's abrupt topic shift during her conversation with Warren. At one point, I suggested, Mary finds herself backed into a corner by Warren's rigid insistence that she tell him whether or not Silas's plea to return is based on the transparent pretext that he will do some work around the farm. Rather than surrender, though, Mary opts to change the subject by introducing her memories of a harvest time gone by. Ostensibly a conversational nonsequitur, her tactic turns out to have been well chosen, since her reminiscences draw Warren too into a rosy-spectacled glance back into the past and thus attenuate his antagonism toward Silas.

In constructing this argument I tacitly assumed *both* that literary conversations conform to what Leech (1987:82) calls "well-behaved discourse" (discourse in which we take for granted "that the goals of the addresser include reasonable adherence to [the Gricean] maxims" of polite interpersonal discourse) *and,* still more crucially, that readers know and expect this to be the case. Against this background, the reader, like the addressee in casual talk, "interprets infringements or floutings of [the maxims] by making certain inferences, drawing certain conclusions, about what the addresser intends to communicate."[4] Readers of Frost's poem, in particular, will interpret Mary's failure to stick to the topic not as a rude dereliction of her responsibility to keep discussion on an even keel, but merely as a temporary shift of direction with its own discourse-related purpose, which will emerge in due course—as, of course, it eventually does.

At a different level, the same assumption also informed my remarks about Wordsworth's own discourse strategy in "Resolution and Independence." One of the stranger features of the conversation between the Narrator and the Leech Gatherer in that poem is the way in which we witness the opening moves of both participants in almost painfully elaborate detail but are then hurried past later sections as if they contained nothing that could possibly be of interest. In chapter 2, I suggested two ways in which one might explain this ostensibly awkward imbalance. In the first place, I proposed, one might conclude that Wordsworth felt confident that whatever point he had had in mind when he included this conversation in his poem had already been made with sufficient force by the time that the old man reached the end of his second reply. But in the second, since what we have heard by that time, like the opening formalities of most casual encounters, is substantively quite unremarkable, one could also propose that Wordsworth must have been more interested in the dynamics controlling the turns of talk than in their actual content. We have seen how this proposal too pays off handsomely when vigorously pursued.

But I see no qualitative difference between the means by which I arrived at my assessment of Wordsworth's probable motives in cutting short his narrative account of the meeting with the Leech Gatherer on the one hand, and those by which I determined Mary's reasons for changing the subject when arguing with Warren on the other. Both Wordsworth and Mary flout Gricean conversational maxims (Mary violates the Maxim of Relevance, Wordsworth most obviously that of Quantity; see Grice 1975), and in both instances readers draw inferences about their motivation for doing so. Yet in one case we are considering how a poet "talks to" his audience, while in the other the focus is on two characters within the text as they converse with one another. It is in precisely this way that intra- and extratextual conversations seem repeatedly to share important characteristics.

But the very suggestion that conversations within poems, conversations between authors and their audiences and spontaneous everyday conversations are all, in some significant respects, on a par generates additional interesting observations—some of them immediately helpful, others more troubling.

This insight does provide a partial explanation, for example, for the variability inherent in all literary interpretation. Even if, in general terms, we agree with E. D. Hirsch and with others who assume a determinate and accessible meaning for each text, the discovery of which is the goal of critical analysis (see Hirsch 1967), the process of discovery will still under my analysis be subject to all the vagaries that inevitably attend on interpreting the utterances of others.

Everyday experience constantly furnishes illustrations of how two individuals who hear or overhear the same discussion may not at all agree about what was said; indeed, misunderstandings are so common that languages generate a whole array of linguistic procedures for negotiating them (see Wilson 1989:67–78 and sources cited there). This does not mean, however, that speakers do not intend to make their meaning clear when they speak or that hearers do not try their best to recover that meaning as they listen. It merely indicates that language does not act as a perfectly clear glass through which we may examine speakers' thoughts. Instead, the linguistic pane is clouded, to borrow a Shelleyan metaphor, and crucial features may be obscured, leading hearers to surmise those features for themselves—a process that they may not all carry out in exactly the same way. In a parallel fashion, readers too may sometimes mistake a poet's intention; indeed, since they lack a great many of the linguistic and nonlinguistic clues that would accompany a spoken utterance, it would be surprising if they did not. Readers also lack any straightforward means for establishing whether in fact a misunderstanding has occurred; since the poet is not there for them to interrogate, "there are no . . . safeguards against the appropriation of the text by the reader" (Schweickart 1986:53; see also Bex 1992:2). This risk does not, however, invalidate the whole enterprise of reading with the initial goal of discovering the author's meaning, nor does it rule out the thoughtful exchange of divergent interpretations in an effort to establish which one seems, after due consideration, to approximate more closely the poet's probable intention.

But if readers' strategies for approaching talk in literature, and more specifically in poetry, resemble in many respects those that they use in confronting everyday conversation, we must consider another issue of interest to the literary critic. For why, in that case, would poets select poetry over prose as the medium for narrative material, especially where the narrative in question involves conversation? To put the question another way, what difference between conversation in poetry and conversation in other genres would carry sufficient weight to attract writers such as Wordsworth, Coleridge, and Frost? Dramas, after all, offer authors the chance to concentrate far more directly on the natural dynamics of regular conversation; playwrights can count on audiences who surely anticipate as one of the most significant demands that any play will make on them the task of interpreting themes conveyed exclusively through dialogue. And even in novels, "the representation of speech through written language" is widely regarded as "a major part of the novelist's craft" (Chapman 1989:159). Why, then, did Wordsworth (whom Coleridge explicitly criticized for his "undue predilection for the dramatic form" [*Biographia Literaria*:258]), describe his meeting with the Leech Gatherer in a poem rather than as part of a play or in a short story? And what induced Tennyson to cast Ulysses as a dramatic monologue—that is, as a more poetic composition—rather than as a soliloquy that could then have led naturally into a dramatic speech of exhortation to Ulysses' subjects and to his fellow mariners who could appear beside him and respond to his call-to-adventure?

For the romantic and early Victorian poets, at least, it is tempting to evade the issue altogether by pointing to the low ebb to which serious dramatic writing generally had sunk in the early nineteenth century. In Gaull's characteristically trenchant summation (1988:81), "[according] to most writers, critics, and commentators, the theater during the Romantic period was a wasteland" (see also the numerous sources she cites on pages 384–385, note 1). With the drama essentially unavailable to them (smothered in large measure by the Licensing Act), that argument would run, writers had little option but to cast essentially dramatic material in other ways.

An altogether different historical response to the question at hand (and one to which I have already alluded briefly) sees works such as those we have discussed in this book as a consequence of the very vigorous growth of the novel, the interests and priorities of that genre spilling over, so to speak, into the poetry of the period (Mermin 1983).

And as a third option, one might, at least in certain specific cases, suggest purely local explanations for an individual writer's selection of the poetic medium. "Resolution and Independence," for instance, was written, as we saw in chapter 4, as part of a two-sided literary discourse. Since the other contributions to that exchange were clearly lyrical (indeed, were odes) and included no dialogue, one might argue that for Wordsworth to have shifted mode at this point in his debate with Coleridge would have radically disrupted the overall sequence and risked impairing its stimulating and productive give-and-take spirit.

Alongside these suggestions—abstract literary-historical speculations on the one hand and text-specific considerations on the other—we might, however, entertain one other reason why these authors should have chosen to cast conversations as poetry. In drama and to a slightly lesser extent in the novel, dialogue flirts constantly with a naive and mechanical realism. As Raymond Chapman (1989:171) remarks, "not all conversation is loaded with implicit meanings, either in a novel or in life," and even in the greatest, most "poetic" Shakespearian plays, the need to move the action along demands a steady stream of lines for "spear-carriers": "Why yes, my Lord!" "Go, see who knocks," and "Marry, do I." Readers and members of the audience recognize this talk as related to the business of the novel or the play and treat it much as they would the similarly functional small talk of everyday speech.

In poetry, I suggest, different expectations come into play. Each and every poetic line, whether part of a conversation or not, is expected to be substantial, freighted with significance of a kind not demanded of individual lines in the other major genres. We have, if you will, a genre-specific intensification of what Tannen (1982:13) calls "the charter of literary writing to pack maximum impact into minimal words." For all the apparent parallelisms between poetic and nonpoetic dialogue, therefore, poetry as a genre does offer authors a unique opportunity: a means by which they may imbue all of a conversation with particularly vivid significance and, again in an almost Shelleyan sense, raise speech to a plane above the humdrum banalities of everyday prattle.

One of many sources of this special substantiality in poetic dialogue is perceptively discussed by Eric Griffiths (1989:60–66), who illustrates how poets exploit the tonal and intonational inexplicitness of speech that has been committed to writing. Although a poet may sometimes lament his inability to "dictate his voice into print," Griffiths notes, "creative opportunities may also arise from the comparative absence of vocal qualities in print. . . . The intonational ambiguity of a written text may create a mute polyphony through which we see rather than hear alternatively possible voicings, and are led by such vision to reflect on the interresonance of those voicings." In a subsequent, almost Empsonian discussion of the ambiguity of a line from *In Memoriam,* Griffiths explains how its written form allows Tennyson to "compact" two readings "said by the same words"; in any actual vocalization of the line, in contrast, the speaker would be forced to choose between them intonationally (123–125; see also my own examples in Austin 1986:33).

But exactly the same point lay at the heart of my analysis in chapter 4 of Shelley's "Ozymandias." While the uncertainties that result from the multiple overlays of speaker/hearer pairs that we suggested for that text *could* also exist in another medium (and might even be expected in, say, a short story by Jorge Luis Borges), the tendency toward naturalism in prose genres would be more likely to disambiguate matters in favor of one reading or another. At least in the context of pre-twentieth-century literary convention, Shelley may have been effectively confined to poetry as the only genre in which ambivalence would count as a productive feature of style rather than as a destructive one.

If studies of the kind that I have undertaken in this book cast useful light on issues in literary and critical theory, they also carry implications for linguists' theories of discourse structure. I have assumed throughout this essay, for example, that techniques such as narrative framing manifest themselves not only in literary texts such as those studied in chapters 3 and 4 but also in the narratives that crop up constantly in everyday conversation. Certain concepts central to our (literarily motivated) discussion of framing in this study should therefore apply equally effectively in the analysis of "natural narratives" (for example, the proposal that the way in which framed narratives function depends in part on whether they are nested one within another, as in "The Ruined Cottage" and "Ozymandias," or are ranged in a series, as in "The Death of the Hired Man"). At the same time, notions introduced as premises for our analyses (for instance, the idea that readers expect the "point" of a literary narrative to be of greater salience than that of a story that forms part of casual interpersonal discourse) need to be tested against nonliterary data. But two specific areas of central importance to this book seem to me to offer particular promise for future work by theoretical linguists.

The first concerns what I referred to at the very beginning of chapter 1 as "readers' expectations" about narratives in the first person. In chapter 1, note 4, I drew attention to the considerable sophistication involved in claiming that it is somehow "natural" to read a first-person narrative as "literally autobiographical." We have no evidence, that is, that any such strategy is universal; speakers of other languages (and even English-speakers from certain cultural backgrounds) may make quite different assumptions. No obvious a priori considerations, for example, would rule out a convention dictating that a first-person narrative should instead be interpreted as the appropriation of the experiences of others unless the narrative itself contained explicit indications to the contrary. Alternatively, some culture might adopt the default strategy mentioned in chapter 4, note 24, and implement a discourse protocol whereby, in the act of reading, each individual initially casts her- or himself as narrator, ruling the author out of the picture altogether.

Even if there exists some articulable discourse principle that requires first-person narratives to be treated as the autobiographical statements of those who utter them, furthermore, it is far from clear how register-, age- and context-dependent that principle may be. A British rabbi, one of several regular contributors to the BBC radio program "Thought for the Day," routinely opens his remarks with wry personal anecdotes. It was recently remarked by one of his casual listeners (John Barlas [personal communication]) that, although this is certainly an effective way to present practical advice, "everyone knows that those things probably never really happened to him" (see also chapter 1, note 5). There is fertile soil here, in short, for developing a fuller theory of how and when hearers and readers in general interpret the word "I" as referring to the speaker or writer who utters it; one suspects that the situation is far from straightforward.

The second area in which linguists could provide particularly effective input concerns narrators' subordination of factual accuracy to narrative purpose. In chapters 4 and 5, I argued that in "Resolution and Independence" Wordsworth creates demonstrably unrealistic dialogue partly because, at a higher narrative level, its very unorthodoxy helps him to make a significant point. Mere objective historical precision also suffers severely, we saw, in Shelley's "Ozymandias." These observations raise questions whose scope ranges far beyond stylistic analysis: does the option of blatantly violating Grice's Maxim of Quality by ignoring factuality in order to make a point obtain in all narratives, or only in written, in literary, or perhaps even in poetic contexts?[5] Is this relationship asymmetrical, or could the usually compelling need to make a point ever be itself usurped by a requirement (like that imposed on the British policeman at the beginning of chapter 3 by his oath to "tell the whole truth") to maintain representational accuracy at all costs?

It lies beyond the scope of this study to follow up these leads in detail. But one highly suggestive example may indicate the potential for some exciting further work. Recordings of spontaneous speech collected by Deborah Schiffrin and William Labov include one story in which the narrator attempts to support his point that (to paraphrase) "it sometimes pays to talk to a friend or a neighbor rather than to a doctor when one is sick."[6] The narrative is told in the third person for the most part, the narrator relating events that happened to his friend, "Louie." The dismal story of Louie's medical misfortunes also involves at least three different doctors (all apparently male) and Louie's neighbor, the hero of the story, who finally diagnoses correctly the condition that all of the professionals had missed (a hernia). At the climax of his narrative, the narrator utters the following sentence: "He said it would've been a little bit more, he [Louie] could've strangled t' death."

One can adduce plausible arguments for interpreting the first *He* in this sentence in any of several distinct and determinate ways. Strict application of sentence-level rules of syntactic anaphora, for example, in the absence of any contrastive stress, would lead us simply to search back through the narrative for the most recently mentioned eligible antecedent noun phrase (in this case, one of the three doctors). Pragmatically, though, one has also to take into account the malapropism that occurs in the recorded indirect speech; Louie, one can be certain, risked dying of a *strangulated* hernia, not from being *strangled,* and the substitution of one term for the other thus points to an inexpert speaker, perhaps Louie himself, as the referent for *He.*[7] Then again, the fact that the narrator had chosen inclusive *they* in the immediately preceding clause to refer collectively to all the medical personnel who finally operated on Louie might be taken to rule out those individuals as candidates for the singular pronoun in the sentence excerpted above.

In the end, though, and particularly in the light of our discussion of "Resolution and Independence," one suspects that all of this searching may, quite literally, "miss *the point.*" The narrator here, after all, has somehow to work his way around to demonstrating to his audience that "*it . . . works* to talk to a friend." He has selected as his illustration of this conclusion a story that deals with "the danger of death or of physical injury," matters that, as Labov (1972a:370) notes, "occupy a high place on an unspoken permanent agenda" of discussible topics. But unless, in his story, the advice of some friend proves effectual where more traditional resources have failed, that narrative will not count as an appropriate illustration.

In this light, the evaluative comment "it would've been a little bit more, he could've strangled t' death," embedded as it is as a source of evaluation internal to the narrative and succinctly characterizing its crisis, seems structurally all but inescapable.[8] Determining the referent of *He,* then, and thus establishing to whom one should attribute the remark about Louie's close brush with death, may make sense as a goal for the theoretical syntactician. For the discourse theorist, however, it may well be moot, the "he said" tag serving merely to provide an ad hoc slot into which the triumphant narrator can then drop his clinching evidence of disaster narrowly averted (and thus also of the fact that talking to friends really does "work").

This case study supports Schiffrin's own repeated insistence on "the integrated nature of discourse" in which the sometimes competing demands of "different levels of analysis" have to be resolved by hearers who are intent, first and foremost, on "[making] *overall* sense out of a particular segment of talk" (1987:14, 22; my italics). But it surely shares this implication with several of the literary texts discussed in the preceding chapters, texts in which interpretive coherence could similarly be attained only by sacrificing strict adherence to one or more of the specific dictates of discourse theory.

Such parallelisms, I suggest, hint at the exciting possibilities for further work on similarities (and distinctions) between literary and nonliterary narratives, literary and nonliterary discourse. I hope in this essay to have demonstrated convincingly the usefulness to literary scholarship of linguists' work on discourse; but as yet we have surely only begun to describe the ways in which different types of discourse interact. By adding the narratives and discourses that occur in poetic works to the corpus of data that they seek to explain, linguists will admittedly complicate the task of achieving a comprehensive account; as I hope this discussion has illustrated, however, the long-term gains from such a move—whether in the realms of conversational, narrative, or literary theory—far outweigh the short-term frustrations that it will undoubtedly occasion.

Appendix

Resolution and Independence

I

THERE was a roaring in the wind all night;
The rain came heavily and fell in floods;
But now the sun is rising calm and bright;
The birds are singing in the distant woods;
Over his own sweet voice the Stock-dove broods;   5
The Jay makes answer as the Magpie chatters;
And all the air is filled with pleasant noise of waters.

II

All things that love the sun are out of doors;
The sky rejoices in the morning's birth;
The grass is bright with rain-drops;—on the moors   10
The hare is running races in her mirth;
And with her feet she from the plashy earth
Raises a mist; that, glittering in the sun,
Runs with her all the way, wherever she doth run.

III

I was a Traveller then upon the moor;   15
I saw the hare that raced about with joy;
I heard the woods and distant waters roar;
Or heard them not, as happy as a boy:

The pleasant season did my heart employ:
My old remembrances went from me wholly;   20
And all the ways of men, so vain and melancholy.

IV

But, as it sometimes chanceth, from the might
Of joy in minds that can no further go,
As high as we have mounted in delight
In our dejection do we sink as low;   25
To me that morning did it happen so;
And fears and fancies thick upon me came;
Dim sadness—and blind thoughts, I knew not, nor could name.

V

I heard the sky-lark warbling in the sky;
And I bethought me of the playful hare: 30
Even such a happy Child of earth am I;
Even as these blissful creatures do I fare;
Far from the world I walk, and from all care;
But there may come another day to me—
Solitude, pain of heart, distress, and poverty.   35

VI

My whole life I have lived in pleasant thought,
As if life's business were a summer mood;
As if all needful things would come unsought
To genial faith, still rich in genial good;
But how can He expect that others should   40
Build for him, sow for him, and at his call
Love him, who for himself will take no heed at all?

VII

I thought of Chatterton, the marvellous Boy,
The sleepless Soul that perished in his pride;
Of Him who walked in glory and in joy   45
Following his plough, along the mountain-side:
By our own spirits are we deified:
We Poets in our youth begin in gladness;
But thereof come in the end despondency and madness.

VIII

Now, whether it were by peculiar grace,   50
A leading from above, a something given,
Yet it befell that, in this lonely place,
When I with these untoward thoughts had striven,
Beside a pool bare to the eye of heaven
I saw a Man before me unawares: 55
The oldest man he seemed that ever wore grey hairs.

IX

As a huge stone is sometimes seen to lie
Couched on the bald top of an eminence;
Wonder to all who do the same espy,
By what means it could thither come, and whence;   60
So that it seems a thing endued with sense:
Like a sea-beast crawled forth, that on a shelf
Of rock or sand reposeth, there to sun itself;

X

Such seemed this Man, not all alive nor dead,
Nor all asleep—in his extreme old age: 65
His body was bent double, feet and head
Coming together in life's pilgrimage;
As if some dire constraint of pain, or rage
Of sickness felt by him in times long past,
A more than human weight upon his frame had cast.   70

XI

Himself he propped, limbs, body, and pale face,
Upon a long grey staff of shaven wood:
And, still as I drew near with gentle pace,
Upon the margin of that moorish flood
Motionless as a cloud the old Man stood,   75
That heareth not the loud winds when they call;
And moveth all together, if it move at all.

XII

At length, himself unsettling, he the pond
Stirred with his staff, and fixedly did look

Upon the muddy water, which he conned,   80
As if he had been reading in a book:
And now a stranger's privilege I took;
And, drawing to his side, to him did say,
"This morning gives us promise of a glorious day."

XIII

A gentle answer did the old Man make,   85
In courteous speech which forth he slowly drew:
And him with further words I thus bespake,
"What occupation do you there pursue?
This is a lonesome place for one like you."
Ere he replied, a flash of mild surprise   90
Broke from the sable orbs of his yet-vivid eyes.

XIV

His words came feebly, from a feeble chest,
But each in solemn order followed each,
With something of a lofty utterance drest—
Choice word and measured phrase, above the reach   95
Of ordinary men; a stately speech;
Such as grave Livers do in Scotland use,
Religious men, who give to God and man their dues.

XV

He told, that to these waters he had come
To gather leeches, being old and poor: 100
Employment hazardous and wearisome!
And he had many hardships to endure:
From pond to pond he roamed, from moor to moor;
Housing, with God's good help, by choice or chance;
And in this way he gained an honest maintenance.   105

XVI

The old Man still stood talking by my side;
But now his voice to me was like a stream
Scarce heard; nor word from word could I divide;
And the whole body of the Man did seem
Like one whom I had met with in a dream;   110

Or like a man from some far region sent,
To give me human strength, by apt admonishment.

XVII

My former thoughts returned: the fear that kills;
And hope that is unwilling to be fed;
Cold, pain, and labour, and all fleshly ills;   115
And mighty Poets in their misery dead.
—Perplexed, and longing to be comforted,
My question eagerly did I renew,
"How is it that you live, and what is it you do?"

XVIII

He with a smile did then his words repeat;   120
And said that, gathering leeches, far and wide
He travelled; stirring thus about his feet
The waters of the pools where they abide.
"Once I could meet with them on every side;
But they have dwindled long by slow decay;   125
Yet still I persevere, and find them where I may."

XIX

While he was talking thus, the lonely place,
The old Man's shape, and speech—all troubled me:
In my mind's eye I seemed to see him pace
About the weary moors continually,   130
Wandering about alone and silently.
While I these thoughts within myself pursued,
He, having made a pause, the same discourse renewed.

XX

And soon with this he other matter blended,
Cheerfully uttered, with demeanour kind,   135
But stately in the main; and when he ended,
I could have laughed myself to scorn to find
In that decrepit Man so firm a mind.
"God," said I, "be my help and stay secure;
I'll think of the Leech-gatherer on the lonely moor!"   140

Notes

1. Introduction: Raising Expectations

1. See also Fowler (1984:181), who rightly reminds us that our initial expectations may be "confirmed or disconfirmed or modified as the discourse proceeds"; Bialostosky (1994); and Miall (1990:326), who approaches a reader's anticipations from a more empirical standpoint.

2. The dramatic monologue, a first cousin to the first-person narrative, represents a somewhat special case in this respect and will be discussed in detail in chapter 2 and again in chapter 5.

3. The term *display text* was, as far as I can tell, introduced by Pratt (1977), whose influential work colors a number of my arguments in this chapter.

4. I am, of course, leaving aside (at least for the moment) the fact that even such a "straightforward" reading rests on a rather sophisticated set of a priori assumptions about how to interpret texts in general and first-person narratives in particular. The autobiographical reading is "straightforward" only in the sense that it seems to represent an instinctive, preferred, or default reading.

5. Rich as these resources are, of course, they still pale beside those available to a *speaker* (as opposed to *any writer*) for revealing or concealing her or his identity. I am thinking here not of major phenomena such as the conventional marking of certain genres of discourse as completely disjoint from the ongoing conversation (as, for example, when stand-up comics who open their acts with the cliché "A funny thing happened to me on my way to the club" are clearly understood not to be speaking autobiographically [see Wilson 1989:63–65]), but of a raised eyebrow, a shift in accent, a theatrical pose or a lowered pitch, each of which may alert hearers just as effectively to the speaker's adoption of a distanced narrative persona.

6. These are the first lines, respectively, of Wordsworth's famous poem discussed on the first page of this chapter (published in 1807); John Keats's sonnet "On First Looking into Chapman's Homer" (1816); George Herbert's "The Collar" (1633); and James Wright's "Autumn Begins in Martin's Ferry, Ohio" (1963).

7. It is Toolan (1990:61) who proposes 1976, the year when M. A. K. Halliday and R. Hasan published *Cohesion in English,* as a *terminus a quo* for the current linguistic interest in "contextual factors" and "contextual variation."

8. See my remarks in chapter 4, note 28.

9. I cannot resolve here the question of whether such discourse-based and/or functionalist approaches to stylistics can legitimately claim outright *superiority* over more traditional sentence-based or formalist methods. Toolan adopts the aggressive position that stylistic analyses that limit themselves to sentential structure are indeed fatally flawed (see, for example, his discussion of Ann Banfield's *Unspeakable Sentences* [1990:75–78]), a point of view that is echoed by Joyce Tolliver (1990:267). Eric Griffiths (1989:39) similarly alleges in support of a speech-act theoretic perspective that "an interest in . . . illocutionary potential . . . is not just an optional 'extra.'" And Nigel Fabb and Alan Durant (1987:10) argue that "a functionalist linguistics is more appropriate to [the] analysis of literary texts" (see also Leech 1987). For reasons that will emerge in the course of this essay, I myself favor a more eclectic and inclusive stylistics.

10. The quotation marks around the word *solution* here indicate its provisional status; it implies altogether too deterministic a critical technique. I return to this issue in the closing chapters.

2. Conversations in Poems / Poems as Conversations

1. This makes the relationship between "The Leech Gatherer" and "Resolution and Independence" *as texts* sound more straightforward than in fact it is. Gene Ruoff (1989: chaps. 4 and 5) argues that they should in fact be read as completely separate works.

2. His single most blatant revision was, of course, to omit any mention whatsoever of his sister's presence on the scene.

3. The twelve stanzas that contain the story of the meeting with the Leech Gatherer occur at the end of what is, in all, a twenty-stanza poem; I discuss the opening eight stanzas in chapter 3.

4. For a description of my method of citation and a full list of the editions of primary texts relied on throughout this book, see References.

5. "English orthography normally makes little attempt to indicate in detail the manner in which a written text is to be voiced" (Griffiths 1989:16–17, who also cites such earlier authorities as I. J. Gelb and Henry Sweet; see also Halliday 1989:30–33 and Clark and Gerrig 1990:782–785). As Griffiths subsequently observes, this failure to indicate "junctural features" is equally a problem for the reader who seeks to characterize the author's own voice—a point to which we shall have to return later. But see Chapman 1989, Halliday (1989:30–33) and Clark and Gerrig (1990:782–785) for discussion of certain extrinsic means that authors *can* employ to reintroduce at least *some* of the texture of oral delivery.

6. Tannen (1989:12–13) provides an excellent survey of such studies; see also Selting 1989 and many excellent contributions in McGregor 1986.

7. It makes matters considerably worse that the precise wording of the Narrator's second question varies only minimally from that of his first. As Labov and Fanshel (1977:95) explain: "Because repeated requests are an aggravated form of criticism, . . . it is a common practice for speakers to mitigate [such] repetitions by varying their form. Though a challenge to competence is always present when a request is repeated, the more the surface structure is varied, the less strongly is this challenge felt."

8. John Wilson (1989:57) discusses a sample of spontaneous discourse in which a precisely reduplicated sequence of question plus answer does indeed lead to what he terms "communicative breakdown," a sample strikingly parallel to what we find in Wordsworth's poem. A literary case in point from E. M. Forster's *Maurice* is discussed in R. A. Buck's (1993) dissertation. For other treatments of similar phenomena, see Gibbs 1986; Gumperz 1982:132; and Tannen 1984.

9. For a discussion of the relationship between direct speech and the strength of a narrator's claim to faithful reporting, see Leech and Short 1981:318–334. I shall myself have a great deal more to say on this topic in chapter 4.

10. I am myself adding this purpose to those that Levinson notes in his discussion.

11. This possibility illustrates an intriguing *non*literary extension of what Toolan (1990:236–237) calls the capacity of narratives that lack *"explicit* causal connections" (my italics) to "transfer the onus on to the reader [in the context of the courtroom, to the hearer or jury member] to adduce a causal interpretation" of his or her own making. Indeed, the defendant who treats the questions of a skillful cross-examining attorney *merely* as requests for information to be answered truthfully one at a time may find him- or herself convicted on the basis of an implicit argument whose very existence she or he never detected! See also Rigney 1992:274, esp. note 12.

12. I am grateful to a number of colleagues and to an anonymous reader of an

earlier version of this chapter for their insistence that I give serious consideration to this possibility.

13. In an excellent discussion of speech acts in Ivy Compton-Burnett's novel *A Family and a Fortune,* Mary Jane Hurst already foreshadowed Toolan's point, advancing the carefully qualified hypothesis that speech acts in that work "can be identified and *likened* to conversations that take place between living persons" (1987:356; my italics). But the position that both Toolan and Hurst espouse in fact constitutes a special case of a broader claim made by M. A. K. Halliday in *Spoken and Written Language.* "Written language," he insists, "never was, and never has been, conversation written down"; nevertheless, we must recognize that "both are manifestations of the same system" (1989:41, 79). Thus, while literary critics sometimes object to stylistic arguments on the grounds of the (undeniable) differences between discourse types (spoken versus written; literary versus functional; verse versus prose; fictional versus nonfictional), it pays to remember their common basis in a single system of linguistic communication (see Bialostosky 1994).

14. Herbert Clark and Richard Gerrig (1990) argue persuasively that both spoken and written quotations may most usefully be viewed as "demonstrations" (rather than transcriptions) of speech. Though the point is not germane to their thesis, their analysis certainly assumes that, although "selective," such "depictions" take as their starting point actual utterances. It is also interesting to note that, ironically, "written dialog in fiction and drama often strikes readers as more real than actual transcripts of spoken conversation" (Tannen 1982:13).

15. This is not to exclude the possibility that we may impose *additional* expectations upon *poetic* narrators; I return to this topic in chapter 3.

16. For additional discussion of what has sometimes been termed "the Ohmann Hypothesis," see Ohmann 1962:22; Freeman 1970:13–16; and Austin 1979.

17. A second consequence of the extraposed structure at the surface is that the overall semantic impact of the immediately following main clause predicate, *little profits,* is also attenuated because readers must now read on to the very end of the sentence before they will be in a position to apply the subordinate-clause material in its entirety as the main-clause subject.

18. This passage thus represents one instance of the tendency noted by David Shaw (1976:34) for Tennyson's sentences to be "so elaborately self-embedded" that the reader completely loses track of where their respective subjects are. Interestingly, Shaw himself illustrates his point by citing a second passage from *Ulysses,* lines 45–49.

19. Tolliver (1990:269) echoes Toolan in stressing that the study of deixis (for which she offers an excellent bibliography) is "of prime importance" for a

linguistic stylistics that employs discourse analysis. In a phrase that will be of particular usefulness in the discussion that follows, she describes how deictic markers "illuminate what entity is responsible for a given utterance and so throw some light on *narrative distance*" (my italics). See also Triki 1991:79–81.

20. This intersection of theoretical perspectives is not unusual. As Toolan notes (1990:275): "While [current] theorists represent different perspectives, their views are often compatible and can be made to converge on the data, so as to provide mutual support for a particular assessment of a particular dialogue" (see also Carter 1983:383–384). Naturally, such parallelism enhances the plausibility of the analysis in which it occurs, a point to which I return in chapter 5.

21. Dwight Culler (1977:85) explains that all three are more accurately designated examples of a *prosopopeia* or even a *monodrama,* since no "missing speech" from a second or third participant in the ongoing dialogue need be supplied by Tennyson's readers (see also Bernstein 1990). For convenience, I shall continue to use the more familiar term *dramatic monologue* throughout this essay.

Mermin (1983) adds *St. Simeon Stylites* to the list of Tennyson's 1833 compositions in this genre and, on pages 12–13, cites a number of valuable sources during her own thorough discussion of the most appropriate way of classifying *Ulysses.*

22. Emrys Jones (1964:xviii) suggests that Tennyson's syntax here may be explained as echoing that of a line from Book 2 of the *Aeneid,* "sed me magna deum genetrix his detinet oris." I am not altogether persuaded. And even if one accepts that source, the effect of Tennyson's line on today's reader remains pretty much as I have described it.

23. The term is William Fredeman's (1981:181). Fredeman also points out (183) that it was only in the 1875 edition of his collected works that Tennyson established this section of the poem as a freestanding verse paragraph distinct from lines 6–32. I find it very suggestive that he should have decided to set those lines apart from the ineluctably autobiographical "I cannot rest from travel; I will drink / Life to the lees" (6–7).

24. The second of these citations is made all the more interesting by the observation that, in yet another of his revisions to the first draft of this poem, Tennyson introduced the pronoun *it* as a replacement for the semantically somewhat less empty *this* ("and this were vile" [563n]).

25. Indeed, precisely such a wish to convey generic truths through infinitival constructions has been identified by F. E. L. Priestley (1973:54) as the motivation for Tennyson's revisions to the 1842 text of *Mariana in the South:* "the shift from 'I am all alone' to 'to be all alone,' " Priestley observes, "generalizes Mariana's condition to the universal." See also Shaw (1976:48–49, 79), who refers to the

"untensed eternity" of "the infinitives of the refrain" of that work. What we see in *Ulysses,* therefore, is an attempt by the speaker to *abuse* a technique that Tennyson himself *used* to good effect elsewhere.

26. Eric Griffiths (1989:118) considers a strikingly similar phenomenon when analyzing a passage from Tennyson's "De Profundis." He notes an inherent ambiguity between adjectival and adverbial readings of *still* in line 25 of that text ("To that last deep where we and thou are still") and remarks that if we once "allow . . . a contrariety of desire, . . . the accent of Tennyson's doubts about survival and inexistence begins to sound throughout the passage."

27. The phrase, which comes from Tennyson's own retrospective summary of the poem's content, is cited by Ricks in the notes to his edition (560).

28. Both descriptions are cited by Ricks (560); the italics are my own.

29. I note in passing that this abdication of regal responsibility scarcely accords well with the picture that Marilyn Gaull draws of Tennyson's Ulysses as "a Victorian imperialist, . . . the energetic, morally disciplined embodiment of the work ethic" (1988:207). Victoria and Gladstone, one feels, would have paled at Ulysses' selfishness and his scorn for the routine tasks of monarchy.

30. For the text of that letter, see Lang and Shannon I:109–110.

31. Among discourse linguists, Livia Polanyi (1985:185) seems to have been the first to use the term *storyworld.*

32. Such a procedure thus responds to the "need" noted by Fowler (1984:176) for a "linguistic criticism" that will "mend the neglect of the interactional facets of 'literary' texts: the rhetorical relationships between addressor and addressee, *the dynamics of construction of fictional characters,* and the sociolinguistic relationships between the producers and consumers of literature" (my italics; see also Chatman 1978:118).

33. See also Toolan (1990:141): "[understanding] and evaluating utterances cannot be divorced from a knowledge of who is doing the uttering and to whom, when and where."

3. Framing Poetic Narratives

1. See also the somewhat less formal treatments in Pratt 1977: chap. 6 and De Looze 1984:149 and the work of Henry Widdowson presented in, and discussed by, Carter (1983:380).

2. Marie-Laure Ryan (1990) summarizes the roles played by the concept of frames in various theories of narrative. Though the problems that she detects in their uncritical employment differ from those that I discuss in this chapter, we

both agree that, in her words, "[the] concepts of the frame family have become so deeply ingrained in our thinking about narrative that we tend to forget their metaphorical nature" (873).

3. In her discussion of the parallels between pictorial and narrative frames in the Middle Ages, Sylvia Tomasch (1985) specifically considers examples of *interrupted* frames in both media.

4. Indeed, framing has been discussed in connection with works as early as *Beowulf* (De Looze 1984). Chaucerian studies include Winstead 1988 (especially pp. 228–229), Holley 1986, and Donnelly 1987. For treatments of medieval authors other than Chaucer, see Fajardo 1984 and Tomasch 1985.

5. See especially Chatman 1978. Roger Sharrock (1987) notes the use of framing in analyses of prose fiction as early as John Bunyan's *The Life and Death of Mr. Badman*. Later authors subjected to analysis from this perspective include Emily Brontë (whose *Wuthering Heights* furnished fertile soil for such traditional literary analysts as Van Ghent 1953, Allen 1954, Kettle 1960, and Eastman 1965 and has more recently returned to favor with narratologists such as Pratt 1977, Matthews 1985, and Macovski 1987), Joseph Conrad (Sharrock 1987) and Rudyard Kipling (Draudt 1984).

6. Though Wordsworth completed the first draft of "The Ruined Cottage" in 1797–1798, its central events are narrated in the form of a flashback of "some ten years" (133). By the time the material appeared as part of *The Excursion* in 1814, the alleged gap had expanded but only to "[not] twenty years" (535). For the full textual history, see Jonathan Wordsworth 1969.

7. This axiom reflects a more general truth about the broader context of purposeful interaction within which all conversation proceeds. In Leo Hickey's words (1989b:71), "devices or strategies [are] used by interlocutors to organize, structure and develop their discoursal relationship *so as to achieve the ends they have in mind*" (my italics). See also Adams 1991:68.

8. As Chatman (1978:45) notes, E. M. Forster (1927:82-83) similarly employs the term *chronicle* for chronologically accurate descriptions of sequences of events that do not achieve the structured status of narratives. Forster, however, sees "causation" as the vital factor that, when added to a chronicle, will make a narrative of it (compare with his conclusion Toolan's assertion [1990:236] that "an implicit clause of reason underlies, and should give shape to, the entirety of any storytelling"). For this essentially discourse-internal criterion I am substituting the more contextually oriented notion of "purposefulness" or "point." It may be that some measure of both elements is required in any *"felicitous* narrative," but I do not have space here to pursue that line of thought.

9. The metaphor is Tannen's (1989:108).

10. In defining that reading context broadly, we shall, of course, need to make

allowance for such derivative narratives as Carroll's parody of "Resolution and Independence" in *Through the Looking Glass,* discussed in chapter 2, works whose "point" is precisely to comment on how effectively (or ineffectively) some other story made *its* point.

11. In this regard both Miall and I take issue with Pratt (1977:140–141), who argues that the standards that hearers/readers apply when assessing effectiveness do *not* vary from one kind of narrative to another.

12. That a narrator's personal background may indeed color the narrative he or she tells is demonstrated by Manfred Draudt (1984:317), who discusses the relevance to Kipling's *The Man Who Would Be King* of the fact that its first-person narrator is a journalist by profession, hence skeptical and interested primarily in factual history.

13. As his primary historical resource, Foster cites McKendrick, Brewer, and Plumb 1982:88.

14. The abrasive critic Francis Jeffrey, writing in an 1814 issue of the *Edinburgh Review,* complained that not "one word" uttered by Armytage had "the most remote reference to [his] occupation," and even the more sympathetic Coleridge complained in *Biographia Literaria,* "Is there one word . . . attributed to [Armytage], characteristic of a *pedlar?*" (both are cited by Jonathan Wordsworth [1969:92]). What escaped them both, I am suggesting, is that Armytage's *narrative perspective* is genuinely and unmistakably that imposed by the peddler's lifestyle.

15. As Evan Radcliffe (1984:112) rightly notes, Armytage himself recognizes a disparity between their viewpoints, telling the Narrator "I see around me here / Things which you cannot see" (67–68). But the lines that immediately follow in the text suggest that Armytage is here criticizing the Narrator's lack of *insight* rather than contrasting what each has *physically* seen; what the Narrator cannot "see," he says, is that

> We die, my Friend,
> Nor we alone, but that which each man loved. . . .
> Even of the good is no memorial left.
> [68–69, 72]

16. I particularly stress here that, as Matthews (1985:56) notes, an analysis such as the one presented here should not be assumed "to displace one center of [the text in question] in order to substitute another." I am absolutely not arguing with respect to "The Ruined Cottage" that "the frame narrative is 'actually' the more important part" of the poem. Rather, I seek to augment what has already been explicated and thus to build an enriched, more comprehensive interpreta-

tion that can take into account all of the text's various features at all of its narrative levels.

17. Wordsworth's repeated readaptations of the ruined cottage story actually raise a whole host of interesting considerations most of which I cannot address here. Let me briefly outline one that is particularly important. Jonathan Wordsworth (1969:23) characterizes the later history of the material that originally constituted "The Ruined Cottage" as "one of odd local improvements and general deterioration"—a view that, as William Galperin (1984) notes in his thorough survey of the literature, belongs to a critical tradition extending back at least as far as F. R. Leavis. This is not to say that the verdict is unanimous; Galperin himself follows Hartman (1964:139) in detecting major virtues in the version that eventually appeared in Book 1 of Wordsworth's epic *The Excursion*. But even he cannot dispute that the special integrity lent to this poem by Armytage's unorthodox narrative viewpoint inevitably evaporates as a direct result of the revisions that the poet made as he prepared later drafts. In the later adaptations of his material, Wordsworth greatly expanded his introductory description of Armytage, adding numerous details about the man's childhood, education, religious convictions, and political views. This shift in the way that Armytage was characterized may, as Galperin suggests, have been necessitated by the radically different context within which Wordsworth was embedding what had until then been an essentially self-contained narrative poem. At the same time, though, those very emendations clearly destroyed the coherence between the narrative levels of the text that, I have argued, represents one of the primary strengths of the earlier work. For despite the poet's ironic insistence on referring to Armytage less often by name and more often as "the Pedlar" (with a capital *P*) or "the Wanderer" (with a capital *W*) the reader of *The Excursion* virtually loses sight of his trade, a feature of his portrayal in the early text that is, I have argued, central to the way in which "The Ruined Cottage" as a whole works its magic.

18. More generally, it occurs to me that this characteristic of their discourse may follow to some extent from the fact that Warren and Mary are husband and wife. I suggest (on the grounds of nothing but intuition and personal experience) that arguments within families or between good friends—and their eventual resolution—may depend on implicit discourse cues of this kind more often than do arguments between comparative strangers.

19. The terms I use throughout this paragraph to describe the major structural components of a narrative derive from Labov's discussion in *Language in the Inner City*, but they may be readily translated to fit alternative systems. Labov's "orientation," for example, perfectly matches the more traditional "exposition" (see Chatman 1978:67 and sources cited there).

20. Late in chapter 5, I shall radically revise my analysis of these opening

stanzas. The outline provided in this paragraph is, however, the most plausible prima facie and, I suspect, that accepted unquestioningly by most readers.

21. Kneale's concerns in his essay do not coincide with mine. Nevertheless, I warmly applaud his contention (1986:358) that the Leech Gatherer's story in "Resolution and Independence" is not in itself "as impressive as the physical presence [or, I would add, the speaking style] of its narrator."

22. Indeed, it may have been the only theme in the earliest version of the poem, which, as I have noted, did not include the repetition of the question-answer pair that is so crucial to my reading of the "received text."

4. "So whose story is this anyway?" The Elusive First-Person Narrator

1. Co-indexing functions merely as a means for indicating narrative correlation. Under different circumstances, such correlation may reflect strikingly divergent surface phenomena: a narrator like Armytage in "The Ruined Cottage" may himself have played a role in the story he tells; elsewhere though, as we shall shortly see, the same formalism may instead capture the fact that a narrator has exploited a wholly fictional participant at a lower level as a spokesperson for his or her own opinions. In the long run, a means for discriminating between such options may prove desirable.

2. See Freedman 1986:63. My own work on "Ozymandias" was already far advanced when I first encountered this elegant and perceptive essay. While my own approach to Shelley's sonnet, as presented in this chapter and the next, adopts a markedly different theoretical point of departure from Freedman's and extends his analysis or diverges from it in a number of details, these distinctions are far outweighed by major areas of agreement, most of which I have tried to acknowledge explicitly.

3. As Steven Jones (1988) makes clear, Shelley was actually quite uncomfortable with the more "anarchic" aspects of the conventional satiric mode; it is nonetheless perceived to be a distinctive feature of his work.

4. In chapter 2 of my earlier study, *Language Crafted,* I examined in detail some of the stylistic contortions typical of much of Shelley's poetry, citing several critics who had characterized his style as complex. In chapter 5 of this essay, I place in question even the alleged syntactic straightforwardness of "Ozymandias" itself.

5. The individual contributions to this critical quest are excellently described and documented by Mary A. Quinn (1984:49, note 1); see also Janowitz 1984 and Freedman 1986.

6. Von Rainer Lengeler (1969:538), in an excellent discussion of this sonnet, makes precisely this point: "Diese Bruchstücke aber künden nicht von dem historischen Ozymandias, sondern von der Kunst des unbekannten Bildhauers" [These fragments, though, reveal not the historical Ozymandias but the skill of the unknown sculptor (my own translation)]. See also Freedman 1986.

7. In referring here to "present" and "past," I am, of course, using those terms in an entirely relative sense; the contrasted worlds to which I refer are, precisely, *story*worlds. We shall return in due course to a discussion of whether in fact the concepts of *present* and *past* that are expressed in this poem can be held to have any absolute reference within the framework of "real" time.

8. I am grateful to Sherry Brennan for encouraging me to reframe the material in this paragraph. Michael Toolan (personal communication) points out that the binary tense alternation throughout the poem (*tell* versus *read* [here a past tense form]; *survive* versus *mocked*) also assists in fostering a strong sense of contrastive temporal deixis.

9. Shelley's interest in both the purely representative and the original or creative aspects of the Sculptor's work may also manifest itself in an Empsonian ambiguity between the archaic sense of the verb *mocked* (in which it means merely "copied") and its modern, more assertive sense, "made fun of."

10. I must in fairness exempt from this generalization both Lengeler's short but insightful analysis of "Ozymandias" as a narrative creation (see note 6 above) and Freedman 1986.

11. In figure 16, it will be noted, I have substituted the Sculptor for Lengeler's Ozymandias as narrator at Level 2; my reasons for doing so should be evident from the preceding discussion. The usefulness of the formalism derived from Bruce's work is particularly evident in the case of "Ozymandias," where Lengeler is not the only scholar to have confused crucial narrator / auditor alignments in the text. The usually reliable Spanos (1968:15) asserts, for example, that "the sculptor is to Ozymandias what the traveller is to the speaker in the framework." But while the "speaker" (whom I am calling the Narrator) is the audience for the Traveller's story at Level 1, Ozymandias does not figure as a recipient at any level in this poem, let alone as the Sculptor's audience.

12. In the case of "Ozymandias," indeed, the brevity of the conventional sonnet makes it particularly unlikely that Shelley would have devoted twelve valuable syllables to creating a framing discourse without some substantial motivation. We may, in fact, apply to Shelley's Traveller a variation on Manfred Draudt's comment about the seemingly "peripheral first-person narrator" in Kipling's *The Man Who Would Be King* (1984:317, citing work by Thomas A. Shippey and Michael Short). Draudt relies on evidence regarding Kipling's artistic priorities (he preferred "perfection of structure in little space") to justify focusing

on the "surprisingly great detail" with which the figure of the narrator is developed in that story. In our case too, the enforced concision of the sonnet form seems highly inconsistent with the notion that the poet would have included a superfluous or transparent narrator.

13. We may, I believe, credit J. Gwyn Griffiths (1948) with having been the first to highlight Shelley's indebtedness to Diodorus, an observation that is now rather uncritically enshrined in notes appended to "Ozymandias" by such frequently consulted authorities as Neville Rogers (1968:468–469) and the editors of the *Norton Anthology of English Literature*. A number of challenges have been mounted to the claim that Diodorus was Shelley's *direct* source. Several critics have shown that the relevant passage from Diodorus's history had already been translated into English repeatedly by Shelley's day; possible intermediaries range, in fact, from Sir Walter Raleigh to the fourth (1810) edition of *The Encyclopedia Britannica* (see Notopoulos 1953:442–443; Parr 1957:34–35). Unfortunately no hard evidence supports any one of these pretenders conclusively, so that James Notopoulos's confident assertion that "it is unlikely that Shelley read Diodorus in 1817" (1953:442) actually rests on little more than the widely approved but probatively irrelevant judgment that Diodorus's opus magnum makes for "dull and anything but attractive reading" in the original (Van Maanen 1949:124).

14. It is typical of the way in which discussion of the complexities of this poem tends to proceed that I was able to discuss Diodorus's significance to its interpretation quite effectively without ever committing myself explicitly to his having seen the statue himself. Until one looks further, it never occurs to one to question whether he did or not.

15. Even figure 17 omits, after all, any representation of the possibilities addressed in note 13 above.

16. Much the same point might be made regarding another form of deixis within this poem. The second word in line 1, *met,* seems at first to set the stage for a conventional past-tense narrative (just as the third word in Tennyson's "Ulysses" defined either a present-time or a generic orientation). As Paul Ricoeur (1981:171) notes, "the art of storytelling places the narrative 'in' time." When a story begins, its audience is entitled to assume that, in the teller's mind, "everything is already spread out in time," a convention that, as Ricoeur also notes, is "usually overlooked" precisely because "the literary criticism of fictional narratives [takes] for granted that every narrative takes place . . . within a time that corresponds to the ordinary representation of time as a linear succession of instants" (165–166). In this poem, however, Shelley denies us this conventional refuge, since we can no more establish unambiguously the "exophoric" reference of the past tense in *met* than we can be certain of the identity of the speaker who utters it.

17. Again, I am anxious to be perfectly fair to Lengeler; although he is to my mind too quick to accept lines 10 and 11 of the sonnet as a faithful rendition of the pharaoh's own words, he does astutely perceive the paradox that it is precisely when we reach the most deeply embedded—and thus the least historically reliable—narrative level that the supposedly accurate quotation makes its appearance.

18. Intriguingly, this is not the only respect in which Shelley's artistic vision—rather than the impersonal testimony of history—finally controls the reader's experience of this poem. Earlier in our discussion, I dwelled at length on the issue of the facial features of Ozymandias's statue and on the probability that they would have been evident to witnesses in 300 or 100 B.C. but not to those in A.D. 1800. In a fascinating footnote, D. W. Thompson explains that such questions are in effect moot: "We now know that the Egyptians did not sculpture their kings in such fashion [that is, with a sneer, frown or wrinkled lip]. The face in the sonnet is not that of an Egyptian king, but that of Shelley's tyrant, a Godwinian monarch whose character has been ruined by court-life" (1937:63; see also Janowitz 1984:487). Indeed, as Thompson subsequently notes, the model for Shelley's Ozymandias lies not in Egypt, nor even in London, but in the descriptions of other, patently unhistorical kings that pepper the Shelley cannon (he cites *The Revolt of Islam*, Canto 5, Stanza 23, and *Prometheus Unbound*, Act 3). In image as in quotation, therefore, Shelley's apparent interest in matters historical cannot be relied on to ensure that he will report the details of his subject accurately. For Shelley, the only reliable truths of history are those perceived by the poet as he "creates anew the universe" in the interests of moral education (*A Defence of Poetry*, 137).

19. A more universal truth about the nature of direct quotation in framed narratives may lurk beneath the observation that I have made here in connection with "Ozymandias." In his excellent essay on *Wuthering Heights*, Matthews (1985:48) discusses the role of Nelly Dean as one of the novel's framing narrators. "Paradoxically," he remarks, "her remarkable recall of speeches, accounts, confessions, and letters actually testifies to a *freer* imaginative hand [at work in those passages]; the more letter perfect Nelly claims her memory to be, the more confident we can be that she has had to make up at least the surface of the narration."

20. I am grateful to Michael Toolan (personal communication) for clarifying the distinction I make in this paragraph.

21. It is interesting to compare the outcome of this analysis with Ursula Le Guin's analysis of a startlingly abbreviated narrative in her marvelously entertaining essay "It Was a Dark and Stormy Night; or, Why Are We Huddling About the Campfire?" Le Guin isolates what she calls an example of "reliable narration": "You will find it carved into a stone about three feet up from the

floor of the north transept of Carlisle Cathedral in the north of England . . . in runes, one line of runes. . . . Here is the whole story: *Tolfink carved these runes in this stone"* (193). The "reliability" that Le Guin claims to have discovered lies, she alleges, in the fact that "Tolfink bore witness at least to the existence of Tolfink." Our discussion of "Ozymandias," I submit, throws even this inference into doubt. Tolfink, it is true, unlike the Sculptor in "Ozymandias," apparently speaks of and for himself rather than ascribing words to someone else. But Le Guin's assurance may still be misplaced, resting primarily on the assumption that Tolfink had no motive for *mis*representing the authorship of those ancient graffiti. (How do we know, for example, that Tolfink did not die before work on the building had been completed, leaving his apprentice to carve the message as a posthumous tribute to the master's craftsmanship?) Of course it is our general expectation that, under certain circumstances like those surrounding the Tolfink runes, we shall be safe in discounting deliberate deceit on the part of an author. But we incur a certain degree of vulnerability when we allow such "general expectations" too wide a scope, vulnerability that a poet like Shelley may easily exploit.

22. This observation may slightly understate the creative power of individual readers' visual imaginations. Seva Johnson (personal communication) notes that, while the description in the text insists on the fragmentary state of the statue's "shattered visage," readers will still instinctively reunite the pieces when "envisaging" the disdainful expression that Shelley ascribes to it.

23. With Janowitz (1984:488), one inevitably recalls the triumphant promise of another great sonneteer to his lover: "you shall shine more bright in these contents [the sonnet itself] / Than unswept stone, besmeared with sluttish time" (Shakespeare, Sonnet 55, lines 3–4).

24. The final clause of Le Guin's comments suggests yet another complication (one also pointed out to me independently by Valerie Austin). Whenever she or he reads a text such as "Ozymandias," the individual reader necessarily "revoices" all of its first-person pronouns (both that in line 1 and those in lines 10 and 11), appropriating them in some measure as her or his own. This is by no means a trivial observation, but to investigate it fully in this essay would take us too far afield.

25. Intriguingly, Jones (1988:160) discovers a somewhat analogous process at work in Shelley's unpublished fragment of a "Satire upon Satire." Jones identifies as the fragment's "primary structural device" Shelley's restriction of his truly satirical material to a conditional clause that he then promptly disavows. As a result, Jones claims, the syntax of the passage effectively "dismantles its own satiric violence."

26. I have no space here to catalog the scores of monographs and journal

articles on this series of poems that have been furnished by what Gene Ruoff (1989:13) calls "a growing phenomenon in romantic studies, the Wordsworth/Coleridge industry." Ruoff's own introductory essay to *Wordsworth and Coleridge: The Making of the Major Lyrics, 1802–1804* offers a brief synopsis and rich bibliographical references.

27. One also notices here, of course, the second reprise of the opening "There was a ———" motif.

28. See also Hickey 1989a:53. In chapter 2 of *Talking Voices,* Tannen goes even further, arguing that repetition of this kind is central to all human discourse. She surveys various theorists' discussions of this topic and presents her own account of what she terms linguistic "prepatterning." Most germane to our present concerns, however, is her suggestion that "[repetitions] and variations make individual utterances into a unified discourse" (59). In the literary sphere, Carter (1983:381) hints at the insights that might result from applying such a generalization as a means of revealing "the 'negotiation' a text can have with its antecedents." The immediate context for his remark is an analysis of W. H. Auden's "Song V" (also known by its first line, "From Reader to Rider"), a text for which the potential importance of such antecedents "is particularly marked." For as Carter shows (citing Spears [1963:57 and 73, n.77]), Auden owed both the "first line [of 'Song V'] . . . and its rhetorical pattern" to "the folksong 'The Cutty Wren,'" an anonymous ballad that he would later reprint in his 1938 edition of *The Oxford Book of Light Verse.*

Carter's analysis is certainly stimulating; the texts of the folk ballad and of Auden's lyric do indeed share many striking features, including the use of ballad rhyme and meter and of the question-and-answer discourse format that often accompanies them. But far closer in detail to Auden's text is a poem Carter does *not* mention: Christina Rossetti's "Amor Mundi," a work that introduces precisely the "lack of referential clarity" and the sense of "a struggle between [two] speakers for dominance" that he rightly emphasizes as primary features in "Song V" (375). If one substitutes Rossetti's poem for "The Cutty Wren" as the more immediate antecedent for Auden's, however, one is led to redefine Auden's contribution to this interactively evolving poetic form. Intriguingly, Auden adds his own nuance precisely in the area of conversational dynamics. He reorders the question-and-answer "turns" in his text so that we hear all three questions first and only later encounter their corresponding "replies," and he reorients the dominance relationship between the speakers in favor of the second speaker, where the earlier tradition had given the questioner the whip hand. This conclusion, based on a richer literary context than Carter provides, does not weaken his argument; rather, indeed, it clarifies the extent to which Auden's poem exploits nonstandard conversational structure to vary an otherwise conventional literary form, thus itself contributing to a form of "conversation" between poets and between texts.

29. We may note in passing an independent consideration that confirms the necessity of positing a narrative Level − 1 for this poem. As we noted earlier, the Narrator claims as part of his Level 0 narration that he was so overwhelmed by the Leech Gatherer's manner of speech that he found himself unable to follow the details of the old man's reply to his first question ("nor word from word could I divide"); nevertheless, the text that we read still contains a fairly detailed report of its substance. For this to make any sense at all, readers must accept the tacit (and conventional) intrusion of a heretofore concealed narrator at Level − 1. This argument for the existence of a higher narrative level was first suggested to me by similar instances detected by Herbert Clark in transcriptions of spontaneous conversation and discussed by him in lectures delivered at the Linguistic Society of America Summer Institute at Stanford in 1987.

30. As I state them here, these claims are a little too sweeping. In chapter 6, I shall have reason to qualify them slightly.

31. One notes here, as in "The Ruined Cottage," Wordsworth's persistent belief that hearing about some event can have at least as great a therapeutic effect as experiencing that event for oneself and also his interest in casting himself as the "narrative therapist" (see chapter 2).

32. Indeed, despite what may have been an initially positive outcome (see Ruoff 1989:172–181), the longer-term failure of Wordsworth's strategy is evident in Coleridge's later poems such as "Work Without Hope."

33. The sociocultural context of the poem notwithstanding; see chapter 2.

5. "Merely Corroborative Detail"? Analyzing Texts from Multiple Stylistic Perspectives

1. As I argued in chapter 1, of course, this is equally true where the corroboration comes from an altogether nonlinguistic source such as the work's historical context.

2. This situation thus closely resembles the case of the omitted beneficiary in the opening lines of Tennyson's *Ulysses* discussed in chapter 2.

3. For a discussion of some of the other consequences of Wordsworth's attempts "to give the poem a Christian emphasis," see Jonathan Wordsworth 1969:26–28 and other sources cited in chapter 3, note 17. I am not, of course, asserting that Wordsworth undertook these stylistic emendations with the same degree of conscious care that certainly directed his insertion, for example, of the Pedlar's paternalistic and condescending "counsel" to Margaret "to have her trust / In God's good love, and seek his help by prayer."

4. Halliday applies the term "goal" to the subject of a passive sentence, a usage that I find less perspicuous than "patient."

5. In *The Stylistics of Fiction,* Toolan examines the central importance of the progressive aspect to William Faulkner's *Go Down, Moses.* He quite rightly insists that the effective interpretation of any such single syntactic feature should lean heavily upon a comprehensive grasp of the overall literary context and he criticizes one group of stylists for their "confident assertive style, where the agentless passive, for example, is *always* taken to be [that is, to correlate thematically with] culpable mystification" (307; my emphasis). My discussion of "The Ruined Cottage" confirms precisely the need for caution that Toolan pinpoints by suggesting an altogether different motive for the use of the passive voice in this poem, a motive derived instead from considerations of narrative perspective.

6. Indeed, given the nature of Armytage's narrative style (determined, as we have seen, by his occupation), one wonders whether the whole notion of causality may not be one that he finds very hard to grasp. His final consolatory remarks seem to depend upon just such a blindness to causes and effects:

My Friend, enough to sorrow have you given,
The purposes of wisdom ask no more.
    [508–509]

7. In the process, of course, they also assume a markedly more active role in "constructing" the meaning of this text than do readers of the poem's earlier draft. Tannen discusses such "involvement" strategies in chapter 2 of *Talking Voices.*

8. By the same token, he would also have been sensitive to those readers' *expectations* in picking up a poem deemed worthy of public circulation. These stylistic remarks thus complement my earlier discussion of readers' expectations about narrative "point."

9. We may note, incidentally, that in the earlier text the rook flew over the heads of the entire walking party, not over that of a single individual (Charles) capable of providing an appropriate anchor at the far end of the path to match the solo figure of the poet himself at its near end. Clearly *each* image (not just that of the ash) has been recast to satisfy the drive toward congruence.

10. Valerie Austin (personal communication) notes that, in yet another local improvement of this passage, Coleridge has his walkers *wind* down into the dell, rather than merely *look* down from above. Their serpentine path prefigures the twinings of the ash tree, another example of Coleridge's metaphorical extension of his physical description into the realm of interpersonal relationships.

11. An analogy to linguistic theory suggests itself here. Ever since the appearance of Noam Chomsky's early work, linguistic theorists have taken great

interest in the relative strength or "adequacy" of their working hypotheses. The several characteristics that are held to distinguish strong (or "explanatory") claims include their capacity to provide not merely an insightful description of the facts but a principled account of why those facts turn out in the particular way that they do (see Bach 1974: chap. 10, esp. 248). The stylistic analyses presented in this chapter could also be said to attain a modest degree of explanatory adequacy precisely because they move beyond isolated linguistic observations to reveal some of the complex ways in which language choices in certain works are linked both to one another and, outside the texts, to the demands of the communicative situations in which those poems were composed.

12. Mermin assumes here that the only possible linkage between the poet and the storyworld of his or her poem will be one that associates "the poet and the protagonist." This assumption, as we have seen, is not without its problems.

13. I have written elsewhere about the capacity of parallelism in poetic texts to "force" otherwise ungrammatical syntactic analyses: see Austin 1984:66–74, 119–124; 1986 and citations given there.

14. Interestingly, several scholars have previously pointed to the perils attendant on the "persistent confusion of Wordsworth with his [narrators]" in other texts. Discussing the narrative persona in *The Excursion*, Howard (1985:511–512) constructs for that work an analysis that in many respects parallels my own for "Resolution and Independence" and reminds his readers that the poet himself "frequently stressed the need to distinguish the biographical verity of a poet's life from the nuances of imagined personality that coalesce into his fictional characters." It pays, Howard suggests, to concentrate less on the formal fact of "Wordsworth's use of the first person" and to look closely instead at the "personality of the speaker." The added complication that is introduced whenever one studies poems from the period when Wordsworth was collaborating with Coleridge on a steady and intimate basis, furthermore, is well illustrated by comments H. M. Margoliouth (1953:112) makes about "Stanzas Written in My Pocket-Copy of Thompson's 'Castle of Indolence.'" That text, though written exclusively in the third person, depicts two figures, Margoliouth notes, clearly meant to correspond to those of the two young poets. Even a reader as careful as Matthew Arnold, however, found this confusing; he "thought the stanzas describing Wordsworth described Coleridge and *vice versa*."

6. Conclusion

1. See Scott 1974:92 for an elegant formulation of these desiderata, and Freeman 1978:15 for a discussion of how they apply in stylistic practice. Among

those who conducted my "early training" in these principles, I shall always be grateful to the late Adrian Akmajian and to Joan Bresnan, Dick Demers, and Jay Keyser.

2. For a concise statement of this view regarding the probative strength of stylists' conclusions, see Freeman 1980:168.

3. I do not mean to imply, of course, that considerations of (oral versus written) medium and of genre do not affect the ways in which we accomplish that task. But the ultimate goals of these activities are not, I believe, distinct, nor, since both processes depend at bottom on our language faculty, can the methods of proceeding be entirely unrelated to one another.

4. Pratt (1977:158–200) devotes a great deal of space to a fascinating discussion of literary texts in which Gricean maxims are *not* adhered to and of the effects that such violations produce. She too concludes that "deviant" turns of talk sometimes observable in such contexts do not differ materially from similar instances in "almost any realm of discourse"; as a result, "our ability to . . . interpret them must be viewed as part of our normal linguistic and cognitive competence, not as some special by-product of it."

5. Folklore suggests that "fishermen's tales" may figure among *non*literary forms where exaggeration, if not downright lying, are tolerated and even expected.

6. I am most grateful to Deborah Schiffrin for her permission to refer to this material, which she employed in teaching her course on "Sociolinguistic Approaches to Discourse" at Stanford University in the summer of 1987. Many of the competing analyses of those data that I present briefly in the following paragraphs were contributed by class participants on that occasion.

7. Of course, the malapropism could also have resulted when the narrator himself imperfectly repeated the word "strangulated" spoken to him either by the doctors or by Louie. We seem, it may be observed, to be uncovering complexities in this spontaneous narrative every bit as acute as those we found in "Ozymandias."

8. Indeed, as Schiffrin observed in her Stanford lectures, an exactly parallel sentence occurs in a story discussed by Labov in print (Labov 1972a:387), a story whose announced "point" is also almost precisely the same.

References

Editions

The following editions have been used for primary works examined at length in this book. For these authors, citations of *verse* passages, which appear in parentheses immediately following their respective quotations, give the title of the work (if it has not already been mentioned in the preceding discussion) and the relevant line number(s) only. Citations of *prose* passages give the work's title and page number(s) only.

Lewis Carroll (Charles Dodgson)
>*The Complete Works of Lewis Carroll, with an Introduction by Alexander Woollcott.* 1939. Rpt. London: Nonesuch Press, 1989.

Samuel Taylor Coleridge

>*Poetry*
>>Coleridge, Ernest Hartley, ed. *The Complete Poetical Works of Samuel Taylor Coleridge.* Oxford: Clarendon Press, 1912.

>*Letters*
>>Griggs, Earl Leslie, ed. *Collected Letters of Samuel Taylor Coleridge.* Oxford: Clarendon Press, 1956.

>*Prose*
>>Watson, George, ed. *Biographia Literaria.* Everyman's Library Edition. 1906. Rpt. London and New York: J. M. Dent, 1971.

Robert Frost
>Latham, Edward Connery, ed. *The Poetry of Robert Frost.* New York: Henry Holt, 1969.

Percy Bysshe Shelley

Works

Ingpen, Roger, and Walter E. Peck, eds. *The Complete Works of Percy Bysshe Shelley*. 1927. Rpt. New York: Gordian Press, 1965.

Alfred, Lord Tennyson

Poetry

Ricks, Christopher, ed. *The Poems of Tennyson*. London: Longmans, 1969.

Letters

Lang, Cecil Y., and Edgar F. Shannon, Jr., eds. *The Letters of Alfred Lord Tennyson*. Cambridge, Mass.: Belknap Press, 1981.

William and Dorothy Wordsworth

Poetry

For *The Ruined Cottage:* Wordsworth, Jonathan. *The Music of Humanity: A Critical Study of Wordsworth's* Ruined Cottage. New York and Evanston, Ill.: Harper & Row, 1969.

For *The Prelude* (all references are to the 1805 text): Wordsworth, Jonathan, M. H. Abrams, and Stephen Gill, eds. *The Prelude 1799, 1805, 1850.* New York: Norton, 1979.

For all other poems: De Selincourt, Ernest, and Helen Darbishire, eds. *Poetical Works of William Wordsworth*. 10 vols. Oxford: Oxford University Press, 1940–1949.

Letters

De Selincourt, Ernest, ed. *Letters of William and Dorothy Wordsworth: The Early Years*. 2d ed. rev. by Chester L. Shaver. Oxford: Oxford University Press, 1967.

Journals

Moorman, Mary, ed. *Journals of Dorothy Wordsworth*. London: Oxford University Press, 1971.

Prose

Owen, W. J. B., and Jane Worthington Smyser, eds. *The Prose Works of William Wordsworth*. 3 vols. Oxford: Clarendon Press, 1974.

Works Cited

Abrams, M. H., ed. *The Norton Anthology of English Literature*. Vol. 2. New York: W. W. Norton, 1979.

Adams, Jon-K. "Intention and Narrative." *Journal of Literary Semantics* 20:2 (1991), 63–77.

Agar, Michael. "Institutional Discourse." *Text* 5 (1985), 147–168.

Allan, Keith. "Hearers, Overhearers, and Clark and Carlson's Informative Analysis." *Language* 62:3 (1986), 509–517.

Allen, Walter. *The English Novel*. London: Penguin, 1954.

Attridge, Derek. "Closing Statement: Linguistics and Poetics in Retrospect." In Nigel Fabb, Derek Attridge, Alan Durant, and Colin MacCabe, eds., *The Linguistics of Writing: Arguments Between Language and Literature*. Manchester, England: Manchester University Press, 1987.

Austin, Timothy R. "A Linguistic Approach to the Style of the English Early Romantic Poets." Ph.D. diss., University of Massachusetts, 1977.

———. "Stylistic Evolution in Wordsworth's Poetry: Evidence from Emendations." *Language and Style* 12 (1979), 176–187.

———. *Language Crafted: A Linguistic Theory of Poetic Syntax*. Bloomington: Indiana University Press, 1984.

———. "(IN)Transitives: Some Thoughts on Ambiguity in Poetic Texts." *Journal of Literary Semantics* 15:1 (1986), 23–38.

———. "Narrative Discourses and Discoursing in Narratives: Analyzing a Poem from a Sociolinguistic Perspective." *Poetics Today* 10:4 (1989), 703–728.

Avni, Ora. "Narrative Subject, Historic Subject: *Shoah* and *La Place de l'Etoile*." *Poetics Today* 12:3 (1991), 495–516.

Bach, Emmon. *Syntactic Theory*. New York: Holt, Rinehart and Winston, 1974.

Bakhtin, Mikhail M. *Problems of Dostoevsky's Poetics*. Edited and translated by Caryl Emerson. Minneapolis: University of Minnesota Press, 1984.

Banfield, Ann. *Unspeakable Sentences*. New York: Routledge, 1982.

Barthes, Roland. "Introduction to the Structural Analysis of Narratives." In *Image—Music—Text*. London: Fontana, 1977.

Bartlett, Bertrice. "Negatives, Narrative, and the Reader." *Language and Style* 20:1 (1987), 41–62.

Bernstein, Cynthia Goldin. "'My Last Duchess': A Pragmatic Approach to the Dramatic Monologue." *SECOL Review* 14:2 (1990), 127–142.

Bex, A. R. "Genre as Context." *Journal of Literary Semantics* 21:1 (1992), 1–16.

Bialostosky, Don H. *Making Tales: The Poetics of Wordsworth's Narrative Experiments*. Chicago: University of Chicago Press, 1984.

———. "Dialogics of the Lyric: A Symposium on Wordsworth's 'Westminster Bridge' and 'Beauteous Evening.'" In Michael Macovski, ed., *Dialogue and Critical Discourse: Language, Culture, Critical Theory*. Oxford: Oxford University Press, 1994.

Blakemore, Diane. "Linguistic Form and Pragmatic Interpretation: the Explicit and the Implicit." In Leo Hickey, ed., *The Pragmatics of Style*. London: Routledge, 1989.

Bloom, Harold. "Tennyson: In the Shadow of Keats," in Harold Bloom, ed., *Modern Critical Views: Alfred Lord Tennyson* (New York: Chelsea House, 1985). (Originally published in *Poetry and Repression* [New Haven, Conn.: Yale University Press, 1976].)

Boer, S. E., and W. G. Lycan. "Knowing Who." *Philosophical Studies* 28 (1975), 299–344.

Booth, Wayne C. *The Rhetoric of Fiction.* Chicago: University of Chicago Press, 1961.

Bresnan, Joan W. "Theory of Complementation in English Syntax." Ph.D. diss., MIT, 1972.

———. *The Mental Representation of Grammatical Relations.* Cambridge, Mass.: MIT Press, 1982.

Brewer, William F., and Edward H. Lichtenstein. "Event Schemas, Story Schemas, and Story Grammars." In John Long, ed., *Attention and Performance IX.* Hillsdale, N.J.: Lawrence Erlbaum Associates, 1981.

Brombert, Victor. "Mediating the Work; or, The Legitimate Aims of Criticism." *PMLA* 105:3 (1990), 391–397. (MLA Presidential Address, 1989.)

Brown, G., and G. Yule. *Discourse Analysis.* Cambridge: Cambridge University Press, 1983.

Bruce, Bertram. "A Social Interaction Model of Reading." *Discourse Processes* 4 (1981), 273–311.

Buck, R. A. "Politeness, Invitations, and Discourse Structure: A Sociolinguistic Approach to the Novels of E. M. Forster." Ph.D. diss., Northwestern University, 1993.

Burton, Deirdre. *Dialogue and Discourse: A Sociolinguistic Approach to Modern Drama Dialogue and Naturally Occurring Conversation.* London: Routledge & Kegan Paul, 1980.

Carter, Ronald A. "Poetry and Conversation: An Essay in Discourse Analysis." *Language and Style* 16 (1983), 374–385.

Chafe, Wallace L. "The Deployment of Consciousness in the Production of a Narrative." In Wallace L. Chafe, ed., *The Pear Stories: Cognitive, Cultural, and Linguistic Aspects of Narrative Production.* Norwood, N.J.: Ablex, 1980.

Chandler, James K. "Wordsworth Rejuvenated." *Modern Philology* 84 (1986), 196–208.

Chapman, Raymond. "The Reader as Listener: Dialect and Relationships in *The Mayor of Casterbridge.*" In Leo Hickey, ed., *The Pragmatics of Style.* London: Routledge, 1989.

Chatman, Seymour. *Story and Discourse.* Ithaca, N.Y.: Cornell University Press, 1978.

———. "What Novels Can Do That Films Can't (and Vice Versa)." In W. J. T. Mitchell, ed., *On Narrative.* Chicago: University of Chicago Press, 1981.

Chomsky, Noam. *Aspects of the Theory of Syntax*. Cambridge, Mass.: MIT Press, 1965.

Clark, Herbert H., and Eve V. Clark. *Psychology and Language*. New York: Harcourt Brace, 1977.

Clark, Herbert H., and Richard J. Gerrig. "Quotations as Demonstrations." *Language* 66 (1990), 764–805.

Clark, Herbert H., and Catherine R. Marshall. "Definite Reference and Mutual Knowledge." In A. K. Joshi, B. L. Webber, and I. A. Sag, eds., *Elements of Discourse Understanding*. Cambridge: Cambridge University Press, 1981.

Clark, Herbert H., and Edward F. Schaefer. "Collaborating on Contributions to Conversations." *Language and Cognitive Processes* 2 (1987), 19–41.

Cohen, Phillip. "Narrative and Persuasion in *The Ruined Cottage*." *Journal of Narrative Technique* 8 (1978), 185–199.

Culicover, Peter W., and Wendy Wilkins. "Control, PRO, and the Projection Principle." *Language* 62 (1986), 120–152.

Culler, A. Dwight. *The Poetry of Tennyson*. New Haven, Conn.: Yale University Press, 1977.

De Looze, Laurence N. "Frame Narratives and Fictionalization: Beowulf as Narrator." *Texas Studies in Literature and Language* 26 (1984), 145–156.

Derrida, Jacques. "Signature Event Context." *Glyph* 1 (1977), 172–197.

———. "Limited Inc.: a b c . . ." *Glyph* 2 (1978), 162–254.

Donnelly, Colleen. "Challenging the Conventions of Dream Vision in *The Book of the Duchess*." *Philological Quarterly* 66 (1987), 421–435.

Doughty, Oswald. *Perturbed Spirit: The Life and Personality of Samuel Taylor Coleridge*. London: Associated University Presses, 1981.

Draudt, Manfred. "Reality or Delusion? Narrative Technique and Meaning in Kipling's *The Man Who Would Be King*." *English Studies* 65 (1984), 316–326.

Eastman, Richard M. *A Guide to the Novel*. San Francisco: Chandler, 1965.

Enkvist, Nils Erik, and Gun Leppiniemi. "Anticipation and Disappointment: An Experiment in Protocolled Reading of Auden's *Gare du Midi*." In Leo Hickey, ed., *The Pragmatics of Style*. London: Routledge, 1989.

Epstein, E. L. "The Self-Reflexive Artefact: The Function of Mimesis in an Approach to a Theory of Value for Literature." In Roger Fowler, ed., *Style and Structure in Literature: Essays in the New Stylistics*. Ithaca, N.Y.: Cornell University Press, 1975.

Fabb, Nigel, and Alan Durant. "Introduction: The Linguistics of Writing: Retrospect and Prospect after Twenty-five Years." In Nigel Fabb, Derek Attridge, Alan Durant, and Colin MacCabe, eds., *The Linguistics of Writing: Arguments Between Language and Literature*. Manchester, England: Manchester, University Press, 1987.

Fajardo, Salvador Jimenez. "The Frame as Formal Contrast: Boccaccio and Cervantes." *Comparative Literature* 36 (1984), 1–19.

Ferguson, Charles A. "Sports Announcer Talk: Syntactic Aspects of Register Variation." *Language in Society* 12 (1983), 153–172.

Fish, Stanley. *Is There a Text in This Class?* Cambridge, Mass.: Harvard University Press, 1980.

Fisher, Walter R. *Human Communication as Narration.* Columbia, S.C.: South Carolina University Press, 1987.

Fodor, Jerry A., Thomas G. Bever, and Merrill F. Garrett. *The Psychology of Language.* New York: McGraw-Hill, 1974.

Forster, E. M. *Aspects of the Novel.* London: Edward Arnold, 1927.

Foster, Mark Harrison. "Wordsworth and the Scene of Writing." Ph.D. diss., Boston University, 1987.

Fowler, Roger, ed. *Style and Structure in Literature: Essays in the New Stylistics.* Ithaca, N.Y.: Cornell University Press, 1975.

———. "Studying Literature as Language." *Dutch Quarterly Review of Anglo-American Letters* 14 (1984), 171–184.

Fredeman, William E. "One Word More—on Tennyson's Dramatic Monologues." In Hallam Tennyson, ed., *Studies in Tennyson.* Totowa, N.J.: Barnes & Noble, 1981.

Freedman, William. "Postponement and Perspectives in Shelley's 'Ozymandias.'" *Studies in Romanticism* 25:1 (1986), 63–73.

Freeman, Donald C., ed. *Linguistics and Literary Style.* New York: Holt, Rinehart & Winston, 1970.

———. "Keats's 'To Autumn': Poetry as Process and Pattern." *Language and Style* 11 (1978), 3–17. (Reprinted in Donald C. Freeman, ed., *Essays in Modern Stylistics* [London: Methuen, 1980].)

———. "Literature as Property: A Review Article." *Language and Style* 13:2 (1980), 156–173.

Galperin, William H. "'Then . . . the voice was silent': 'The Wanderer' versus *The Ruined Cottage.*" *English Literary History* 51 (1984), 343–363.

Gaull, Marilyn. *English Romanticism: The Human Context.* New York: W. W. Norton, 1988.

Gibbs, Raymond W., Jr. "What Makes Some Indirect Speech Acts Conventional?" *Journal of Memory and Language* 25 (1986), 181–196.

Gill, Stephen. "'Affinities Preserved': Poetic Self-Reference in Wordsworth." *Studies in Romanticism* 24 (1985), 531–549.

Goffman, Erving. *Interaction Ritual.* New York: Anchor Books, 1967.

———. *Frame Analysis.* New York: Harper & Row, 1974.

———. "Footing." *Semiotica* 25 (1979), 1–29.

Graesser, Arthur C., Richard M. Roberts, and Catherine Hackett-Renner. "Question Answering in the Context of Telephone Surveys, Business Interactions, and Interviews." *Discourse Processes* 13 (1990), 327–348.

Grice, H. Paul. "Logic and Conversation." In Peter Cole and Jerry L. Morgan, eds., *Syntax and Semantics III: Speech Acts.* New York: Academic Press, 1975.

Griffiths, Eric. *The Printed Voice of Victorian Poetry.* Oxford: Clarendon Press, 1989.

Griffiths, J. Gwyn. "Shelley's 'Ozymandias' and Diodorus Siculus." *Modern Language Review* 43 (1948), 80–84.

Gumperz, J. *Discourse Strategies.* Cambridge: Cambridge University Press, 1982.

Halliday, M. A. K. "Language Structure and Language Function." In John Lyons, ed., *New Horizons in Linguistics.* Harmondsworth, England: Penguin, 1970.

———. *Spoken and Written Language.* Oxford: Oxford University Press, 1989.

Halliday, M. A. K., and R. Hasan. *Cohesion in English.* London: Longman, 1976.

Hartman, Geoffrey. *Wordsworth's Poetry, 1787–1814.* New Haven, Conn.: Yale University Press, 1964.

Heath, Shirley Brice. "The Essay in English: Readers and Writers in Dialogue." In Michael Macovski, ed., *Dialogue and Critical Discourse: Language, Culture, Critical Theory.* Oxford: Oxford University Press, 1994.

Henkel, Jacqueline. "Linguistic Models and Recent Criticism: Transformational-Generative Grammar as Literary Metaphor." *PMLA* 105:3 (1990), 448–463.

Hickey, Leo, "The Style of Topicalization: How Formal Is It?" In Leo Hickey, ed., *The Pragmatics of Style.* London: Routledge, 1989a.

———, ed. *The Pragmatics of Style.* London: Routledge, 1989b.

Hirsch, E. D. *Validity in Interpretation.* New Haven, Conn.: Yale University Press, 1967.

Holley, Linda Tarte. "Medieval Optics and the Framed Narrative in Chaucer's *Troilus and Criseyde.*" *Chaucer Review* 21 (1986), 26–44.

Holmes, Richard. *Shelley: The Pursuit.* London: Weidenfeld & Nicolson, 1974.

Howard, William. "Narrative Irony in *The Excursion.*" *Studies in Romanticism* 24 (1985), 511–530.

———. "'Obstinate Questionings': The Reciprocity of Speaker and Auditor in Wordsworth's Poetry." *Philological Quarterly* 67 (1988), 219–239.

Hurst, Mary Jane. "Speech Acts in Ivy Compton-Burnett's *A Family and a Fortune.*" *Language and Style* 20:4 (1987), 342–358.

Jackendoff, Ray. "X-Bar Syntax: A Study of Phrase Structure." *Linguistic Inquiry,* Monograph 2. Cambridge, Mass.: MIT Press, 1977.

Janowitz, Anne. "Shelley's Monument to Ozymandias." *Philological Quarterly* 63:4 (1984), 477–491.

Jeffers, Robinson. *The Selected Poetry of Robinson Jeffers.* New York: Random House, 1924.

Jones, Emrys, ed. *Henry Howard, Earl of Surrey: Poems.* Oxford: Oxford University Press, 1964.

Jones, Steven E. "Shelley's Fragment of a 'Satire upon Satire': A Complete Transcription of the Text with Commentary." *Keats-Shelley Journal* 37 (1988), 136–163.

Jump, Harriet. " 'That Other Eye': Wordsworth's 1794 Revisions of *An Evening Walk.*" *Wordsworth Circle* 17:3 (1986), 156–163.

Kettle, Arnold. *An Introduction to the English Novel.* New York: Harper, 1960.

Klein-Andreu, Flora. "Speech Priorities." In Leo Hickey, ed., *The Pragmatics of Style.* London: Routledge, 1989.

Kneale, J. Douglas. "Wordsworth's Images of Language: Voice and Letter in *The Prelude.*" *PMLA* 101 (1986), 351–361.

Kroeber, Karl. *Romantic Narrative Art.* Madison: University of Wisconsin Press, 1960.

Labov, William. *Language in the Inner City.* Philadelphia: University of Pennsylvania Press, 1972a.

———. *Sociolinguistic Patterns.* Philadelphia: University of Pennsylvania Press, 1972b.

Labov, William, and David Fanshel. *Therapeutic Discourse.* New York: Academic Press, 1977.

Leech, Geoffrey N. "Stylistics and Functionalism." In Nigel Fabb, Derek Attridge, Alan Durant, and Colin MacCabe, eds., *The Linguistics of Writing: Arguments Between Language and Literature.* Manchester, England: Manchester University Press, 1987.

Leech, Geoffrey N., and Michael H. Short. *Style in Fiction: A Linguistic Introduction to English Fictional Prose.* London: Longman, 1981.

Le Guin, Ursula K. "It Was a Dark and Stormy Night; or, Why Are We Huddling About the Campfire?" In W. J. T. Mitchell, ed., *On Narrative.* Chicago: University of Chicago Press, 1981.

Lengeler, Von Rainer. "Shelleys Sonett Ozymandias." *Die neueren Sprachen* 68 (1969), 532–539.

Levinson, Stephen C. "Activity Types and Language." *Linguistics* 17 (1979), 365–399.

Lodge, David. "After Bakhtin." In Nigel Fabb, Derek Attridge, Alan Durant, and Colin MacCabe, eds., *The Linguistics of Writing: Arguments Between Language and Literature.* Manchester, England: Manchester University Press, 1987.

McGregor, Graham, ed. *Language for Hearers.* Oxford: Pergamon Press, 1986.

McKendrick, Neil, John Brewer, and J. H. Plumb, eds. *The Birth of a Consumer Society: The Commercialization of Eighteenth Century England.* Bloomington: Indiana University Press, 1982.

Macovski, Michael S. *"Wuthering Heights and the Rhetoric of Interpretation." English Literary History* 54 (1987), 363–384.

———, ed. *Dialogue and Critical Discourse: Language, Culture, Critical Theory.* Oxford: Oxford University Press, 1994.

Madden, William A. "Framing the Alices." *PMLA* 101 (1986), 362–373.

Magnuson, Paul. *Coleridge and Wordsworth: A Lyrical Dialogue.* Princeton, N.J.: Princeton University Press, 1988.

Margoliouth, H. M. *Wordsworth and Coleridge, 1795–1834.* Oxford: Oxford University Press, 1953.

Martin, Robert Bernard. *Tennyson: The Unquiet Heart.* Oxford: Clarendon Press, 1980.

Mason, Michael. *"The Timing of In Memoriam."* In Hallam Tennyson, ed., *Studies in Tennyson.* Totowa, N.J.: Barnes & Noble, 1981.

Matthews, John T. *"Framing in Wuthering Heights." Texas Studies in Literature and Language* 27 (1985), 25–61.

Mermin, Dorothy. *The Audience in the Poem: Five Victorian Poets.* New Brunswick, N.J.: Rutgers University Press, 1983.

Merritt, Marilyn. "On Questions Following Questions in Service Encounters." *Language in Society* 5 (1976), 315–357.

Miall, D. S. "Readers' Responses to Narrative: Evaluating, Relating, Anticipating." *Poetics* 19 (1990), 323–339.

Miller, George A. "Linguists, Psychologists, and the Cognitive Sciences." *Language* 66:2 (1990), 317–322.

Murphy, Edwin, trans. *Diodorus "On Egypt."* Jefferson, N.C.: McFarland, 1964.

Notopoulos, James A. "Shelley's 'Ozymandias' Once Again." *Modern Language Review* 48 (1953), 442–443.

Ohmann, Richard. *Shaw: The Style and the Man.* Middletown, Conn.: Wesleyan University Press, 1962.

Parr, Johnstone. "Shelley's *Ozymandias.*" *Keats-Shelley Journal* 6 (1957), 31–35.

Philips, Susan Urmston. "Some Sources of Cultural Variability in the Regulation of Talk." *Language in Society* 5 (1976), 81–95.

Polanyi, Livia. "Conversational Storytelling." In Teun van Dijk, ed., *Handbook of Discourse Analysis.* London: Academic Press, 1985.

Postal, Paul M. *Cross-Over Phenomena.* New York: Holt, Rinehart & Winston, 1971.

Pratt, Mary Louise. *Toward a Speech Act Theory of Literary Discourse*. Bloomington: Indiana University Press, 1977.

———. "Linguistic Utopias." In Nigel Fabb, Derek Attridge, Alan Durant, and Colin MacCabe, eds., *The Linguistics of Writing: Arguments Between Language and Literature*. Manchester, England: Manchester University Press, 1987.

Prickett, Stephen. *Coleridge and Wordsworth: The Poetry of Growth*. Cambridge: Cambridge University Press, 1970.

Priestley, F. E. L. *Language and Structure in Tennyson's Poetry*. London: Andre Deutsch, 1973.

Prince, Gerald. "Notes Toward a Categorization of Fictional 'Narratees.'" *Genre* 4 (1971), 100–105.

Quinn, Mary A. "'Ozymandias' as Shelley's Rejoinder to Peacock's 'Palmyra.'" *English Language Notes* 21:4 (1984), 48–56.

Radcliffe, Evan. "'In Dreams Begins Responsibility': Wordsworth's Ruined Cottage Story." *Studies in Romanticism* 23 (1984), 101–119.

Rader, Ralph W. "Literary Constructs: Experience and Explanation." *Poetics* 18:4–5 (1989), 337–354.

Richardson, James. *Vanishing Lives: Style and Self in Tennyson, D. G. Rosetti, Swinburne, and Yeats*. Charlottesville: University Press of Virginia, 1988.

Richmond, H. M. "Ozymandias and the Travellers." *Keats-Shelley Journal* 11 (1962), 65–71.

Ricks, Christopher. *Tennyson*. New York: Macmillan, 1972.

Ricoeur, Paul. "Narrative Time." In W. J. T. Mitchell, ed., *On Narrative*. Chicago: University of Chicago Press, 1981.

Rifaterre, Michael. "Describing Poetic Structures: Two approaches to Baudelaire's *Les Chats*." In Jacques Ehrmann, ed., *Structuralism*. Garden City, N.Y.: Doubleday, 1966.

Rigney, Ann. "The Point of Stories: On Narrative Communication and Its Cognitive Functions." *Poetics Today* 13:2 (1992), 263–284.

Rogers, Neville, ed. *Shelley: Selected Poetry*. Oxford: Oxford University Press, 1968.

Ross, John R. "Constraints on Variables in Syntax." Ph.D. diss., MIT, 1967.

Ruoff, Gene W. *Wordsworth and Coleridge: The Making of the Major Lyrics, 1802–1804*. New Brunswick, N.J.: Rutgers University Press, 1989.

Ryan, Marie-Laure. "Stacks, Frames, and Boundaries; or, Narrative as Computer Language." *Poetics Today* 11:4 (1990), 873–900.

Sacks, Harvey. "Notes on Methodology." In M. Atkinson and J. Heritage, eds., *Structure of Social Action: Studies in Conversation Analysis*. Cambridge: Cambridge University Press, 1984.

Sacks, Harvey, Emanuel A. Schegloff, and Gail Jefferson. "A Simplest Systematics for the Organization of Turn Taking for Conversation." *Language* 50 (1974), 696–735.

Schegloff, Emanuel A. "Some Sources of Misunderstanding in Talk-in-Interaction." *Linguistics* 25 (1987), 201–218.

Schegloff, Emanuel A., and Harvey Sacks. "Opening Up Closings." *Semiotica* 7 (1973), 289–327.

Schiffrin, Deborah. "Tense Variation in Narrative." *Language* 57 (1981), 45–62.

———. "How a Story Means What It Says and Does." *Text* 4 (1984a), 313–346.

———. "Jewish Argument as Sociability." *Language in Society* 13 (1984b), 311–335.

———. *Discourse Markers.* Cambridge: Cambridge University Press, 1987.

———. "Conversation Analysis." In Frederick J. Newmeyer, ed., *Language: The Socio-Cultural Context,* Cambridge Survey of Linguistics, vol. 4. Cambridge: Cambridge University Press, 1988.

Schweickart, Patrocinio P. "Reading Ourselves: Toward a Feminist Theory of Reading." In E. Flynn and P. Schweickart, eds., *Gender and Reading.* Baltimore, Md.: Johns Hopkins University Press, 1986.

Scott, Charles T. "Towards a Formal Poetics: Metrical Patterning in 'The Windhover.'" *Language and Style* 7 (1974), 91–101. (Reprinted in Donald C. Freeman, ed., *Essays in Modern Stylistics* [London: Methuen, 1980].)

Seamon, Roger. "Poetics against Itself: On the Self-Destruction of Modern Scientific Criticism." *PMLA* 104:3 (1989), 294–305.

Searle, John R. *Speech Acts.* Cambridge: Cambridge University Press, 1969.

Selting, Margret. "Speech Style in Conversation as an Interactive Achievement." In Leo Hickey, ed., *The Pragmatics of Style.* London: Routledge, 1989.

Shapiro, Marianne. "How Narrators Report Speech." *Language and Style* 17 (1984), 67–78.

Sharrock, Roger. *"The Life and Death of Mr. Badman:* Facts and Problems." *Modern Language Review* 82 (1987), 15–29.

Shaw, W. David. *Tennyson's Style.* Ithaca, N.Y.: Cornell University Press, 1976.

Smith, Barbara Herrnstein. *On the Margins of Discourse: The Relation of Literature to Language.* Chicago: University of Chicago Press, 1978.

———. "Narrative Versions, Narrative Theories." In W. J. T. Mitchell, ed., *On Narrative.* Chicago: University of Chicago Press, 1981.

Spanos, William V. "Shelley's 'Ozymandias' and the Problem of the Persona." *CEA Critic* 30 (1968), 14–15.

Spears, Monroe K. *The Poetry of W. H. Auden: The Disenchanted Island.* New York: Oxford University Press, 1963.

Stubbs, Michael. *Discourse Analysis: The Sociolinguistic Analysis of Natural Language.* Chicago: University of Chicago Press, 1983.

Super, R. H., ed. *The Complete Prose Works of Matthew Arnold.* 11 vols. Ann Arbor: University of Michigan Press, 1960.

Swann, Karen. "Suffering and Sensation in *The Ruined Cottage.*" *PMLA* 106 (1991), 83–95.

Tannen, Deborah. "Oral and Literate Strategies in Spoken and Written Discourse." *Language* 58:1 (1982), 1–21.

———. *Conversational Style: Analyzing Talk Among Friends.* Norwood, N.J.: Ablex, 1984.

———. *Talking Voices: Repetition, Dialogue, and Imagery in Conversational Discourse.* Cambridge: Cambridge University Press, 1989.

Thompson, D. W. "Ozymandias." *Philological Quarterly* 16 (1937), 59–64.

Thompson, E. P. "Disenchantment or Default? A Lay Sermon." In Conor Cruise O'Brien and William Dean Vanech, eds., *Power and Consciousness.* New York: New York University Press, 1969.

Tolliver, Joyce. "Discourse Analysis and the Interpretation of Literary Narrative." *Style* 24 (1990), 266–283.

Tomasch, Sylvia. "Breaking the Frame: Medieval Art and Drama." *Early Drama to 1600, Acta* 13 (1985), 81–93.

Toolan, Michael J. *Narrative: A Critical Linguistic Introduction.* London: Routledge, 1988.

———. *The Stylistics of Fiction.* London: Routledge, 1990.

Traugott, Elizabeth Closs. "Semantics-Pragmatics and Textual Analysis." *Language and Style* 22:1 (1989), 51–65.

Traugott, Elizabeth Closs, and Mary Louise Pratt. *Linguistics for Students of Literature.* New York: Harcourt Brace, 1980.

Triki, Mounir. "The Representation of Self in Narrative." *Journal of Literary Semantics* 20:2 (1991), 78–96.

Van Ghent, Dorothy. *The English Novel: Form and Function.* New York: Harper & Row, 1953.

Van Maanen, W. "A Note on Shelley's *Ozymandias.*" *Neophilologus* 33 (1949), 123–125.

Van Riemsdijk, Henk, and Edwin Williams. *Introduction to the Theory of Grammar.* Cambridge, Mass.: MIT Press, 1986.

Vipond, D., and R. A. Hunt. "Point-Driven Understanding: Pragmatic and Cognitive Dimensions of Literary Reading." *Poetics* 13 (1984), 261–277.

White, Hayden. "The Value of Narrativity in the Representation of Reality." In W. J. T. Mitchell, ed., *On Narrative.* Chicago: University of Chicago Press, 1981.

Wilson, John. *On the Boundaries of Conversation*. Oxford: Pergamon Press, 1989.

Wilson, W. Daniel. "Readers in Texts." *PMLA* 96 (1981), 848–863.

Winstead, Karen A. "The Beryn-Writer as a Reader of Chaucer." *Chaucer Review* 22 (1988), 225–233.

Wordsworth, Jonathan. *The Music of Humanity*. New York: Harper & Row, 1969.

———. "On Man, On Nature, and On Human Life." *Review of English Studies* 31 (1980), 17–29.

Author Index

Topic Index

About the Author

TIMOTHY R. AUSTIN was born in Tonbridge, England, the son of two secondary-school teachers of modern languages. Educated at Tonbridge School and at Lincoln College, Oxford, where he earned a "First" in English Language and Literature, he left Britain in 1973 to study linguistics at the University of Massachusetts.

Upon graduating with his doctorate in 1977, Austin accepted an appointment at Loyola University Chicago. He has taught full-time in the English Department at Loyola; directed an interdisciplinary Program in Linguistics Studies; and spent five years in research administration. He is currently Assistant Chairperson of the English Department.